TO THE BARNGROVES —

Rejoicing in Christ

❖

Steve Savoy

12/10/90

" REJOICING ON,
MY 50th / "

Rejoicing in Christ

The Biography of
Robert Carlton Savage

by

Stephen E. Savage

Shadow Rock Press
Reading, Vermont

*...a shelter from the wind and a refuge from the storm,
like streams of water in the desert and the shadow of a great rock in a thirsty land.*
—Isaiah 32:2

Published by Shadow Rock Press
101 Baileys Mills Road, Reading, Vermont 05062.

Library of Congress Catalog Card Number 90-062647

ISBN 0-9627848-0-X

This book is dedicated to my mother Wilda.
Dad rejoiced in all things
but especially
he rejoiced in you.

STATUTE MILES

0 10 20 30 40 50   100   200

Note: Boundary with Peru
in Southeast is disputed.

Contents

Maps

Acknowledgements

This story of Dad's life was a family project. The stories told by Uncle Jim (Dad's brother) and his wife June, and by Helen (Dad's sister) and her husband Dick were my best resource on Dad's youth.

My mother imparted eloquently the chronicles of the early days in Romeo, Pamplona, Chinácota, and Quito. Mom's splendid letters from the field were my richest source on their missionary years. (Dad and Mom wrote 1242 letters during their 26 years in South America.)

My brothers and sisters and their spouses, Jimbo and Nina, Carol and Jim, and Judi each offered me their own very personal memories of Dad.

My aunts, Frances, Nell, and Agnes, enriched my knowledge of the early years, especially of my grandparents.

I received beautiful letters and cassette tapes from my cousins: Paul, Rickie Lou, Tim, Peggy, Joy, and Jon.

My own five children, Allison, Bill, Cynthia, Lance, and Matt, each read various chapters and gave me intelligent advice.

The other grandchildren, Shari, Dan, Elenita, and Alexito each contributed their memories. And the one grandchild Dad never saw, Shawn Robert, was born about the same time this book was born—and grew to two years while it was being written.

Many missionaries and pastors who worked with Dad over the

years wrote me letters and sent me cassette tapes. I received 121 letters and 14 cassette tapes, full of funny and stirring memories.

Most of the quotes at the beginning of each chapter are from Dad's own books: the "pocket" series of "sentence sermons" he used throughout his lifetime of sermons.

Janet Grevstad typed and read through the manuscript several times, correcting errors, eliminating repetitions, and spotting unnecessary tangents.

Sally Sherman drew the maps, arranged the photos, did the typesetting, and designed the cover.

Gordon Baxter was my copy editor, who coached, coaxed, encouraged, scolded, applauded, and forced me to hold nothing back as I told my story of my life with Dad.

My most special thanks go to my wife Barrie, who listened attentively as I read each chapter aloud, sitting quietly while I choked and cried, giving me invaluable editorial help, encouraging me to write my heart out.

Foreword

A Christian should be a hallelujah from head to foot.

—Augustine

"Rejoicing in Christ!"

It was Dad's motto. It was his hearty reply whenever someone asked him how he was feeling. He signed every letter with that happy phrase. His book has earned that same title.

"¡Cantemos!" He would shout.

"Let's sing!"

With that robust command, thousands of people in North and South America sang. In Spanish and English they sang. Bob Savage stomped his foot on the platform, thrust his arm in the air and they sang—louder and lustier than they had ever sung before.

In South America he got them singing their own songs. Not translations from English, but hundreds of their own melodies, with a Latin beat, a minor sound. Dad discovered, published, and taught those songs via radio, television, church services, tent meetings, coliseum crusades, open air rallies, anywhere a crowd would gather. He revolutionized gospel singing in Latin America.

It was his legacy to missionary work.

"Let me shake your noble hand."

With that hearty greeting, he amused friends and strangers alike. But he meant it. He believed each person was noble and in his presence they felt exalted. Every person he touched walked away buoyed by the man who precisely practiced what he preached, who always rejoiced in Christ.

It was his legacy to the church.

"Three P's and an L."

With that curious abbreviation, Dad said farewell whenever we left his presence. It meant: "Proud of you, praying for you, praising God for you. And I love you."

When I wandered in my spiritual desert, he was an oasis. He was never a mirage. I was his oldest son.

This was his legacy to me.

1

Go gentle into that good night

The poet Dylan Thomas said to his father: "Do not go gentle into that good night."

For my father, it was quite the opposite.

Sunday morning, November 29, 1987

At 6:00 a.m. I kissed my wife Barrie goodbye as I left our home in Vermont, destination Michigan. Just as I was going out the door, I turned and said, "Wonder if I should take my dark suit. We might be having a funeral."

"Go on," she said softly. "I'll bring it if you need it."

I drove to the airport in Springfield, Vermont, and checked over my airplane. I planned to fly all the way to Muskegon, Michigan, a four-hour flight. The weather in Vermont and New York was fine, but snow showers and light freezing drizzle in the Great Lakes area made me reconsider. Icing was forecast in the area, and my airplane, a single-engine Cessna 210, was not equipped for ice. I decided to fly my plane to Hartford, Connecticut and take a commercial jet to Detroit, with connections to Muskegon.

The flight to Detroit was uneventful, but the commuter operation to Muskegon was in chaos. Commuter planes were delayed all over Michigan, and no ticket agent could tell us what was happening. My flight to Muskegon was delayed at least an hour, maybe more.

I called Mom and told her I was in Detroit, but that my flight to Muskegon was delayed. She said quietly, "Dad is not doing well at all. He's failing fast. Please come quickly." It was the first time she had sounded so grim, with such a note of finality. Then I said, "This commuter airline is very uncertain. I'll rent a car and drive to Muskegon. I can be there in about 3½ hours." I looked at my watch. It was 2:00 p.m.

The drive across Michigan felt like one of those dreams where you run as fast as you can, but can't get away from the monster bearing down. Your legs drag forward in agonizing slow motion and feel as though immense weights are strapped to them. I was driving 64 miles per hour, nine over the speed limit, yet it seemed I was creeping.

As I drove, I continued to practice the eulogy that I so very much wanted to give at Dad's funeral. I had been practicing it for several months, usually while driving, but every time I tried to say it I cried, and wondered if I would ever be able to maintain my composure before a crowd. Dad wanted a festive funeral and hoped we would rejoice with him as he entered the heavenly kingdom. I wanted to promise him that we would, indeed, give him his kind of funeral, but a few months earlier I had told him I would be too overcome to speak and hoped he'd understand.

As I crossed the Michigan peninsula, I thought of the hundreds of times my grandfather, Henry Savage, had journeyed this same route from his church in Pontiac to Maranatha Bible Conference in Muskegon. The route was well-traveled by my father, uncle, and aunt, all three of them missionaries who had each criss-crossed this state, sharing the story of their missionary work. Indeed, the road was familiar to all our family members, for this was a trek we had each taken often, past Lansing, Grand Rapids, Fruitport, and on into Muskegon.

Although time inched along as I drove, the trip to Muskegon took only 3 hours and 20 minutes. It was 5:20 p.m. I pulled in the driveway, jumped out of the car, ran up the steps, and flung open the kitchen door as I had done so many hundreds of times before. I called, "Hey, Mom! Hey, Dad! I'm here."

The house was silent. I paused in the kitchen, puzzled. Then my nephew Dan appeared, eyes red, and threw his arms around me. "Grandpa's in heaven," he sobbed. "Oh, Dan!" I whispered. The moment I had dreaded had come and quickly gone. My father was dead. I sighed and asked, "When did he die?" "About five minutes ago," replied Dan. He had died at 5:15 p.m.

I felt a flash of disappointment. Why five minutes ago? Why couldn't he have waited a few more minutes?

The hurt quickly vanished as a selfish relief took over. I had feared seeing him suffer, and his early departure had spared me that pain. Dad was whole again, and his titanic spirit could soar, uninhibited by a frail, cancer-ridden body.

Then the sadness set in. All these thoughts had taken but a few seconds, for Dan and I were already down the hall, entering the room where Dad's body lay. Standing around the bed were my mother, Wilda; my sister, Carol; my brother-in-law, Jim; and my niece, Shari. Always our greetings were boisterous and loud, with vigorous hugs and enthusiastic welcomes. Now I looked at them briefly through blurred eyes, but was immediately transfixed as my attention was riveted by the corpse of Robert Savage, the magnificent, energetic, bubbling, joyful creature who now lay utterly still.

His eyes were closed, lips slightly parted, face composed. His arms draped at his side, his legs sprawled, rested, loose. There was nothing grim or rigid about his appearance. He was wholly relaxed, his countenance peaceful. I had never seen him look so lovely and was surprised to hear myself say, "He's beautiful."

Then I put my arms around Mom and we sobbed into each other. She finally spoke: "We've called the nurse from Hospice to come and verify his death. I'm quite sure he's gone. We couldn't feel any pulse. Do you want to check?"

Then for the first time I touched him. I felt his wrists, still warm but altogether still. My palm touched his forehead, gently at first, then more firmly as I felt for some sign of life. I put my ear on his chest, listening for a heartbeat. I felt none, but liked the feeling of resting on his breast, and let my head sink into him for a moment. Finally, I looked into his face and kissed his cheek, saying, "You were the finest father any son could have."

I turned to Carol and hugged her tightly. The sorrow seemed to flow between us. Then Jim and Shari. Finally all six of us huddled together and held each other. Carol said, "We encouraged him to let go. He was struggling so hard at the end. We just told him to reach out into the arms of Jesus, and he did exactly that."

I looked again at that silent and handsome figure of my father and pondered it. I told Mother: "I guess that little body just couldn't hold his giant spirit anymore." She said, "He was a sweet man, a wonderful husband." A sweet man. I had never thought of my dad as sweet, but as I savored Mom's word, I agreed it fit.

Dad had prepared for his death in the same way he had worked out every event of his life: with meticulous detail and happy feelings. He had typed out a whole list: people to contact, things to do. It was a simple matter of following his instructions. The checklist was full of cheer, especially when he advised us how to organize his funeral service: "lots of singing with songs of praise and hope such as 'Wonderful Grace of Jesus' and 'How Great Thou Art.'"

Different family members took turns on the phone, calling our loved ones, each of whom Dad had been careful to include on his list. When I called Barrie, I could not get beyond the words, "He's gone." She gave me her love and sympathy, then took charge of the conversation, for I was unable to speak. She told me she'd fly to Muskegon the next day and reassured me she'd bring my dark blue suit.

Near the top of his checklist was the name of the funeral home we should contact and I made that phone call. They told me they'd be out shortly to take away his body. I told Mom the folks would soon be coming from the funeral home and she protested with anguish: "Don't you think it's rather sudden? Do we have to be in such a hurry?" I looked at her, sitting in the living room, dazed, plaintive, and wondered if I should call them back. It was sad enough to watch him die, but unbearably wrenching to have him snatched away. I did nothing, and the relentless process continued.

The men from the funeral home arrived, two polite men in their mid-30's, dressed in dark suits, sympathetic and businesslike. I looked over at Mom and could tell she was once again alarmed, almost panicked. The morticians were unfailingly courteous but I resented them and wanted them out of there. "I'm not sure if my mother is quite ready for this," I told them. They looked confused, for they had a job to do. They nodded their heads in understanding, telling me they knew how we felt, but that it would be best to go ahead and get it over with.

Most of the family stayed in the living room, but I wanted to watch. The undertakers were doing everything right, but what they did surprised and alarmed me. They brought in a big stretcher on rubber wheels, the kind they roll down hospital corridors. On the stretcher lay a big body bag, open, unzipped. As they began to lift Dad from bed to stretcher, his body slumped between them and I thought they were not ceremonious enough. Then they slung him on the stretcher. I grimaced; I wanted them to be more tender.

It was jarring to see him so very dead, yet it filled me with tenderness as I helped arrange him on the stretcher. I wanted my father to be handled with special care, not like any other dead person. Reluctantly, I had to admit there wasn't a more graceful way to do it. Then I thought of Christ being lowered from the cross, as his body slumped over the shoulders of his disciples. I watched my dad lying there, so altogether Christ-like in death as he had been in life. There was a solemnity and majesty about the scene despite his utter limpness. It helped me to gaze upon him, for I was beginning to absorb, minute after minute, the stark reality that Dad was really gone.

Then I asked what would happen to him when they carried

him down the stairs, for I was afraid his body would slip off the stretcher. The black-suited figures told me not to worry, they would strap him on. This shocked me, also, for no one had ever tied Bob Savage down.

I was barely adjusting to that idea when the men began to zip up the body bag. As they pulled the zipper over his face, I was startled. It had been too cold, too sudden. I leaned over, drew the zipper back down to his shoulders and said, "Let's leave his face uncovered until he's out of the house. I think it will be easier for my mother." The two men looked slightly astonished but agreed.

I patted the bag around the sides of his face so his head would show clearly as they wheeled him out of the house. They placed thick leather straps over the bag and pulled them tight. My chest constricted, taut, and I could hardly breathe as I watched. I considered Dad's dignity and loveliness even as he lay encumbered with those cold and mundane props for the dead: stretcher, straps, and bag.

Then, despite my sadness, I had to smile for a second, for I thought how Dad would have joked about his own burial preparations. "Soon all that'll remain is this old shell," he had grinned a few weeks earlier, "but the nut will be gone." He was right. This body over which I poised was merely the frame of the splendid Bob Savage. "Just an old bag of bones," he had bantered, "but soon my soul will rejoice at the feet of my Savior." Then he had added, "Well, Steve, I've tried to teach you how to live; now watch me, because I'm going to teach you how to die." These thoughts cheered me. Dad was dead, but there was nothing morbid about it. He was rejoicing in Christ.

They began to wheel the stretcher down the hall, skirting through a corner of the living room where the family was sitting. It was their last look at him. They were weeping, and I was glad his face was not covered.

I continued to hover over the stretcher as the undertakers wheeled him through the kitchen, then down the steps to the driveway. It was drizzling outside, the same drizzle that had threatened icing on aircraft wings, kept me from flying my own plane, prevented my being at my dad's side as he died. I said to him silently, "Dad, I tried to get here. I guess God did not mean it to be." I felt comforted.

As the stretcher emerged through the kitchen door, the drizzle began to wet Dad's face and I told the two attendants, "OK, you can cover his face now." They readily assented, finished zipping the bag, then quickly loaded him into the ambulance.

Without further ado, the quiet men flitted ethereally down the dark driveway, on either side of the ambulance, entered opposite doors, and drove slowly away. It was 9:00 p.m. on that November night, and the red lights of the ambulance sparkled against the mist. The cold moisture felt good on my head and drizzle cooled hot tears. My father was gone.

2

Death to the heretics

You can measure a man by the opposition it takes to discourage him. —Robert Savage, *Pocket Wisdom,* p.9

It was 1943 in Pamplona, Colombia. It was the first time Dad had faced death head-on. An angry mob of several hundred people surged up the narrow cobblestone street toward our house, screaming defiantly:

"Down with the Protestants!"

"Death to the heretics."

I was 4 years old, Dad 29, Mom 24. I stood at our second story window, watching the colorful religious procession with childish delight. Mom was kneeling by the bed, praying. Dad stood beside me, serene. Roman Catholic penitents with hoods and robes carried images of the Virgin. Boys with incense pots were scattered throughout the assemblage. Several tough-looking men spied us looking out our second-story window. They shook their clenched fists as they shouted with fury and hate:

"*Agentes del diablo!*" (Agents of the devil!)

"*Muerte a los infieles!*" (Death to the infidels!)

On and on went the screaming. Occasionally Mom would look up from her prayer and implore Dad and me to come away from the window. Finally she succumbed to an urge of curiosity and joined us at the window. Quickly she returned to pray.

Every newspaper in Colombia carried accounts of the procession. One described the scene like this:

THE MARVELOUS SERENITY OF A PROTESTANT PASTOR
(From *El Combate* of Cúcuta, August 4, 1943).

As the procession passed in front of the home of the evangelicals, we saw within the window of the second floor a young man with a small child in his arms, calmly witnessing the magnificent manifestation of the Catholics. Unruffled, he was smiling kindly. He felt no fear before the shouts of 'Down with the protestants.' The composure of this United States citizen caused the most intense sensation.

By morning, things had calmed down, but hostility was still in the air. As Dad walked down the street, kids ran by and screamed *"Virgen Santísima"* (Holiest Virgin). The words were normally used in a prayer, but now instead of praying to the Mother of Christ they used her name in a blasphemous way, turning the prayer into a shout of defiance.

Dad came home for lunch and told us his attitude was best expressed in the verse: "No ill can harm me, no foe alarm me, for we are safe in the hollow of His hand."

With some humor and no little courage, Mom quipped, "It was nice of them to go to the trouble of planning such a big celebration in honor of my birthday." At only 24, in a strange land, this classic posture is an indelible memory I have of my mother, able to stand by her God and stand by her man.

A week later there were still reverberations from the mass procession. The whole town talked about it. But the event took on a reverse coloration which worked against the purposes of those who instigated it all. Many people were disgusted, and the priests lost respect in their eyes. On the other hand, the priests accomplished their objectives: most of the townsfolk swallowed the propaganda and viewed all missionaries as evil people. None of our neighbors, including the children who had been my playmates, entered our house anymore. My parents did not let me out of their sight.

After all this turmoil, attendance was down at our Sunday services and prayer meetings. Three college students visited Dad, but no one appeared for the formal Bible class. He asked them point blank if they had been prohibited from entering our home or attending Saturday night Bible class.

"Absolutely," they answered, "but we enjoy our visits so much that we are going to come—privately."

Dad inquired, "What reasons do the priests give in claiming it is a sin to have any connection with the Protestants?"

"It is a rule without reasons."

"Is it a sin to search for the truth and learn what the Bible teaches?"

"Of course not."

They told Dad the Roman Church forbade its members under penalty of sin to attend religious services other than their own. The students liked the gospel but the opposition would be unbearable if they lined up with the Protestants. Although Dad's heart was heavy, he lightened and laughed when they bid farewell and kidded him, "*Don Roberto, muchos saludos a Padre Mendoza.*" (Give our greetings to Father Mendoza, the priest who had instigated the procession.)

A verse in Ephesians that Dad had often quoted in his sermons now took on a very present meaning, and he read it during our family devotions: "We wrestle not against flesh and blood, but against principalities, against powers, against the rulers of the darkness of this world, against spiritual wickedness in high places."

A few weeks after this frightening episode we moved from Pamplona to Chinácota to set up our new home and establish a mission station. We had been in Chinácota two months, and at the end of October, All Saints' Day marked the occasion for another gala affair. With great trepidation, my folks watched the crowds form, unable to shake the nervous knots that held their stomachs.

I was delighted with the festivities. My parents still had frightening memories of the angry procession that had swarmed past our house in Pamplona and kept windows and doors shut; they did not want to stand in plain view for fear of inciting the populace's antagonism. Dad allowed me to peek through a crack in the door, while Mom knelt by the bed and prayed.

Several of the men were drunk, and their eyes looked surly and mean. They climbed the hill toward our house near the top of a long and narrow street. The gang gathered outside our house, shouting obscenities against the "foreign Protestant devils." Suddenly a truck careened down the cobblestone street, horn blaring, headed right for the crush of revelers. The truck, loaded with vegetables, had lost its brakes and the swarm of angry people divided on either side. The huge vehicle careened down the hill and the mob of excited villagers forgot the Protestants as they rushed down the hill to see what would happen to the truck.

At the bottom of the hill, the truck stopped without incident and the burly driver leaped out and faced the crowd: "I'm Teófilo Mesa. I'm a conservative. These people have a right to live." He glowered at the crowd as they silently looked at the ground, then one by one shuffled slowly off. His brakes were fine; he had fooled the crowd. He called himself a "conservative" to identify himself as one of them, for the conservatives in Colombia were the ones who supported the Roman Catholic Church without question, exclusively. He was a pious man who could not stand what his church was doing to the Protestants. Later, he became a friend of Dad's, accepted Dad's invitation to follow Christ, and emerged as one of the pillars of the evangelical church. His voice always carried authority, and over the years of violence in Colombia, especially in the terrible decade from 1948 to 1958, he often stepped into similar situations and saved fellow evangelicals from mob violence.

We lived in the province of Norte de Santander. Although Dad's missionary work focused on his assigned mission post, the town of Chinácota, he also went out into the rural areas. Most mountain villages were remote and could not be reached by bus or truck. Dad conducted much of his ministry over the next two years mounted on a horse, Bible in saddlebag, exactly as frontier preachers in North America had done about 100 years ago when such dedicated men were known as "circuit riders." Often he took me with him, and my earliest memories are colorful ones—bouncing in the front of Dad's saddle through orchid-studded mountains in northeastern Colombia.

After his maiden horseback trip he wrote the first of his 1200 letters from the mission field:

December 15, 1942

The trip from Pamplona to La Donjuana took us through coffee, banana, and sugar cane plantations. Beautiful bright-colored flowers lavishly bedeck the roadside.

La Donjuana's total population is only 500, but boasts the largest Scandinavian Alliance Mission congregation in Colombia. There were 120 at our service—held in the afternoon because most have a long way to walk to get home.

I gave my first testimony in Spanish. It gave me such a thrill that it almost brought tears to my eyes when I sat down. The people were kind and attentive as they patiently allowed me to struggle through my first public words in their lovely language.

Sunday is market day, and every little trading post swarms with people bartering, hacking off meat from a hanging beef, getting haircuts, and chatting with each other.

On Monday, we hiked up a mountain, two and a half hours from La Donjuana. It was steep and hot, traversing rivers on swaying slender "hammock-bridges" and plugging away over unmarked trails. When we arrived at our destination—hot, dirty, tired, and happy—I discovered I was only the fifth North American to visit here.

The valley was beautiful, flat, and fertile. Seldom have I met folks who love the Lord so devoutly. Almost everyone in

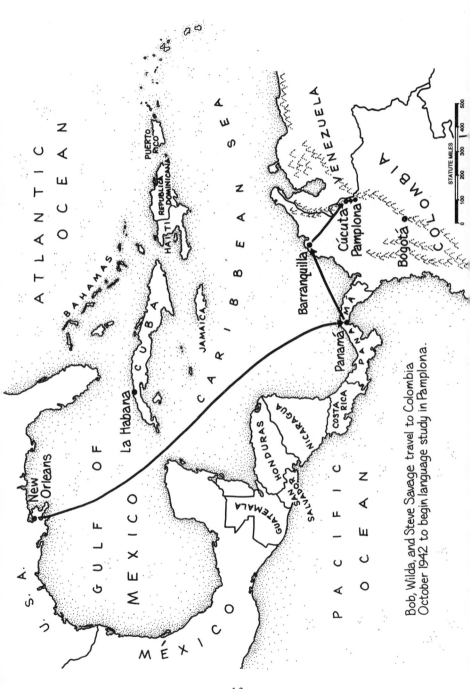

Bob, Wilda, and Steve Savage travel to Colombia October 1942 to begin language study in Pamplona.

this valley is a baptized believer and they seem to feel like missionaries are practically angels from heaven. I can't tell you how refreshing it is to be in a spot where they are longing, hungry, and deeply appreciative of the gospel. This is an unusual situation in Colombia.

That night we had a candlelight service in a humble little home—and I enjoyed one of the finest meetings of my life. No other homes were visible, and the nearest road was an hour's walk away—yet 80 people were present.

We had arrived in Colombia in November, 1942. Mom and Dad quickly plunged into language study. Within a few short weeks, Dad served his first communion service in Spanish. He didn't like the idea of reading the service, as he felt reading smacked of too much formality, but conceded, "I've been practicing the service in Spanish but haven't gotten it memorized so will have to read much of it." Several older missionaries told them their progress in the language was remarkable, and that most missionaries were not ready to speak in public until they had been studying the language for several months.

One language was universal from the beginning: music. Both were musicians, Mom on the piano, Dad on the trumpet, both in singing. They sang high-spirited duets and solos, and joined their voices with several Colombian Christians and other missionaries in an ebullient mixed quartet and a robust choir.

On Christmas Day, Dad left with fellow-missionary Elof Anderson for another "out-station," a small cluster of huts in the verdant mountains. He wrote enthusiastically about this rugged trip:

The roads were terrible. We had to ford swollen rivers, plow through muddy ruts, detour around broken-down bridges, and squeeze over against the edge of precipices to avoid land-slides that had blocked off two-thirds of an already narrow trail.

The marvelous Christmas service lasted three hours and

twenty minutes, the crowd packed tightly both inside and out. I sat on the platform marveling to realize that only seven years ago none of these people knew anything about the gospel. When these folks become Christians they produce a real "out and out" testimony. They do not tolerate inconsistent Christian living. For three hours, I mingled with over 100 men, and not once did I see anyone use tobacco.

Now that we have seen some of the other stations, we have a greater appreciation of our challenge here. Colombia is getting into our systems, and we are enjoying it more all the time.

Two weeks later, full of enthusiasm for rural work, Dad once again went out on horseback, this time accompanied by Wilf Watson, also of the Scandinavian Alliance Mission.

On January 10, 1943, Dad wrote his father, Henry Savage, pastor of the First Baptist Church in Pontiac, Michigan:

Wilf Watson, five Colombian believers, and I began a horse-back trip that turned out to be a humdinger. After riding two hours at night, we put up in a little country home, sleeping on our army cots in a straw-thatched, mud-floor hut. At 6 a.m. we rose to eat a native breakfast of agua miel (a hot drink made of Colombian brown sugar), soup, and plátanos (cooking bananas).

After an arduous 10 hours, we entered Raganvalia, a town of 7000 near the Venezuelan border. Missionaries had never been here; never had a North American seen the place. What a thrill to be both the first American and missionary to ever step into that city.

There were two gospel sympathizers, but alas!—both were out of town. How discouraging after such a long and laborious journey. Wilf thought we should postpone our attempt to begin work there, so with some sadness we started home the next morning.

All was not lost. We discovered three country districts

"ripe unto harvest." In San Pedro, we were received cordially in almost every home. Our next destination was Arozco, but we had to slosh through the most beautiful foliage on the most abominable trail. Mud came up to our horses' knees and overhanging branches frequently slapped us and almost knocked us off. Ascents and descents approached perpendicularity.

Mud holes sucked at our horses' hooves; we were relieved to cross an occasional river, for the rocks gave our poor animals a firm footing.

At last we arrived in Arozco—and what a warm welcome we received. We decided to hold a service that night. In less than two hours, the news got around and 30 people gathered for a glorious service. They urged us to return and promised that if they had advance notice the whole population would be present. One wealthy farmer told us he would donate land upon which to build a church.

Such a cordial reception of the gospel is a miracle in Colombia. The cities are cold, indifferent, and unresponsive. It is an oasis in the desert to find a warm place like Arozco.

Before coming to Colombia, I was convinced we should evangelize the cities first—and then have native Christians evangelize the countryside. Now I am considering a program of evangelizing the country places and surrounding the cities with the gospel. I think of military strategy: Just as the Russians are encircling German strongholds and the U.S. Army is girdling the Axis forces in North Africa, so we can envelop these cities that are strongholds of the devil—and gain the victories for which we pray.

Dad enjoyed eating Colombian food, and cheerfully ate all the food served him on his journeys. Many Americans refused to eat native food, worried about parasites and tropical diseases. Dad never worried—and never got sick. The only thing he was cautious about was water. He drank water only if it was boiled; otherwise he drank bottled water or soft drinks.

He did not complain about the accommodations at local hotels. In Raganvalia, his hotel cost 14 cents (U.S.) and the bed consisted of planks with a half-inch straw mat on top. After 10 hours on horseback, he slept soundly.

When Dad was first called to be a missionary, he envisioned preaching Christ to the "heathen." The "heathen" as described in the Apostle Paul's epistle to the Romans were those who had never heard the name of Christ. Now, in Colombia, where almost everyone professed to be a Christian, Dad saw evidence everywhere that Christ was not really "living in their hearts." He was horrified to see public drunkenness, and shocked that the Roman Catholic Church did not denounce drinking. He was appalled when he saw the citizens of Pamplona indulging casually in gambling, smoking, dancing, and wife-beating, which to him were all equally vile sins, and drew up in righteous indignation at the failure of the Church to take a stand against these practices. The more he saw, the more he became convinced that the so-called Christians of Colombia were just as lost as the "heathen" of the deepest Amazon who had never even heard the word "Christ."

More than anything else, Dad was aghast as he learned of courtship and marriage practices in Colombia. His first impression of Colombian attitudes towards marriage, from our guide in Barranquilla who thought nothing of living with a woman and having children without getting married, was strengthened daily as he heard stories of other couples living out of wedlock. He wrote his parents about how the issue distressed him: "The social set-up is filled with corruption and immorality. One of the most difficult problems missionaries face is determining for the converts what their marital arrangement should be. Nearly all have children with several women and it makes for a mixed-up mess."

Dad continued to fret about the courtship patterns: "I get the impression that no one around here can imagine a man and woman being alone without immorality resulting. If young people are to do any respectable courting, the girl must come to the window, the fellow stands outside, they talk but don't touch."

Dad was stunned but amused to hear that Elof Anderson had performed a marriage ceremony for a couple and dedicated their three children to the Lord at the same service. One young Christian man in La Donjuana told him he had 75 or 80 brothers and sisters. Another said, "I have been married twice—nine children by my first wife; eleven by my second."

Dad learned that Colombians classified children in three ways: legitimate, illegitimate, and natural. The "illegitimate" child did not know who his father was whereas the "natural" was recognized by the father as his own, but the parents remained unmarried.

Unfortunately, concluded Dad, legitimate children were few and far between. He decried the Roman Catholic Church because priests charged an impossibly high price for a marriage—way beyond the range of poor people. He condemned the Church: "They have been guilty of promoting and continuing this abominable marriage situation." It cemented his conviction that there existed a vast and irreparable fissure between the true faith in Christ and the teachings of the Catholic church.

Dad's ministry in the rural areas was colorful and exciting, but he was also working hard to help build the little churches in the towns of Pamplona and Chinácota. Compared to the enthusiastic reception he had gotten during his horseback trips to the remote rural areas, the response in the cities was stony. A few notes of discouragement crept into his usually chipper letters:

> We don't have the crowds, the enthusiasm, nor the encouragement we had in the U.S., but are more convinced than ever that this is God's highest calling for us. The work here is hard; people are indifferent and antagonistic. Yet, we are gloriously happy.
>
> We get very impatient because of our inability to speak the language fluently. Our hearts burn to be able to talk with these people heart to heart.

Despite their stated impatience, both Mom and Dad made remarkable progress in learning Spanish. One reason was their good sense of humor at their own mistakes and their willingness to speak Spanish constantly and at every opportunity. In their morning devotions, they prayed in Spanish with their servant girl, Teresa. After three months, Mom gave an 8-minute flannel-graph lesson in Sunday School. In that era, 10 years before slides and 40 years before video tapes, the most dramatic and colorful way to present a gospel story was with flannel-graph, in which figures cut out of flannel cloth could be adhered to a board of the same material. The flannel board held the flannel figures, and little children watched with rapt attention as they saw and heard the stories of Bible characters.

Within a year, their Spanish was fluent, and both Mom and Dad spoke with almost no trace of an American accent. I grew up speaking Spanish as a second language, and there were years when I spoke it better than English, especially in those early days in Colombia. Dad always looked back on his time in Colombia and concluded he never would have learned to speak such good Spanish if he hadn't been thrust into it in a small town where he had to speak it to survive.

They continued to delight the crowds with their music. Mom's delicate touch on the piano was a soft counterpoint to Dad's exuberant trumpet playing. They made the most of their musical skills, and found themselves "tooting, playing, and singing" at every service. But their first glimpse of hymn singing in Colombian churches was discouraging. On March 13, 1943 Dad wrote: "We had rosy illusions concerning our music before we arrived. We imagined people raving with delight upon hearing our piano playing, duet singing, and horn blowing. So far not an eyelash has flickered, nor have we had any expression of delight."

Within just a few months, both Mom and Dad began to sense the inadequacy of hymns translated from English. Mom wrote to her parents: "Our piano is sheer happiness. We love it. Many come to our home to hear it and we pray it will be used to His glory. Except for our few Christians, most Colombians do not care about hearing hymns. They don't know any hymns and it doesn't mean much to them. However, they certainly know their classical music and are crazy about Beethoven, Shubert, and all the other masters. They also have Colombian favorites that I am learning."

The young Savage couple had been in Colombia five months and had expected quick results—but were discouraged. Mom wrote to her parents on March 16, 1943:

> Sometimes we can't see that we will ever be able to do a thing for the gospel here. If we ever felt our complete nothingness it is here. We are absolutely powerless in ourselves to do a thing. Only as God does miracles will people be saved here. We were so optimistic at first, but now we see things without rose-colored glasses. People are nice to us—but not to our gospel.
>
> Please pray that we'll have patience. You know how we love to see things happen and you can imagine how this stone wall affects us. God has some purpose in having us here—but what is it? Sometimes it is hard to think that we are giving our lives where people don't care one iota about our faith. We have to keep praying that our eyes will be fixed upon Jesus rather than circumstances.

Dad was used to preaching to hundreds of people in the USA, but it would be many years before he would stand before crowds like that in South America. The early years were slow and discouraging. He echoed Wilda's discouraging letter in his own:

> I'll confess that my wife and I are downhearted. Our joy in the Lord is full but our happiness is below par. The devil gets us down by taunting us with the thought that we are ministering to handfuls here—whereas we had hundreds back home.
>
> Paul and Moses had prolonged desert experiences of

inactivity and in future years I will probably praise the Lord for these patience-trying periods.

The one bright spot continued to be rural work. Trips to places like La Donjuana gave both of them an uplift—one of the few places where gospel work was thriving. The concept of an "indigenous" or "native" or "national" work was beginning to form in Dad's mind as he wrote home, describing the phenomenon that had taken place in La Donjuana: "This work was started by a Colombian, not missionaries, proving that national workers are vital."

While Mom and Dad were in the depths of their discouragement over the slow progress of their work, a glimmer of light shone upon them from a little country to the south: Ecuador. In Quito, the capital city of that country whose name means "equator," an exciting gospel mission was vigorously announcing the message of Christ to the entire world by means of shortwave radio. It was called the World Radio Missionary Fellowship, and their radio station in Quito had the call sign HCJB. From that spot high in the Andes mountains, my parents now felt a magnetic force.

When Dad was a high school student, he heard HCJB's president, Clarence Jones, speak at First Baptist Church in Pontiac, and pledged the then large sum of 30 cents per month to support the work. He faithfully sent in his pledge for three months until he ran out of money. Later, during his college years, he often heard about HCJB during his summers at Maranatha, when Jones came to speak about the missionary radio station.

Clarence Jones and Reuben Larson, co-founders of HCJB, were corresponding with Dad and invited him to come and join them. His imagination leapt at the thought of ministering not just to 20 or 30 people, but to a radio audience of thousands. However, he felt God had put him with the Scandinavian Alliance Mission for a purpose, so he was not ready to sever his ties with the mission.

When Clarence Jones first suggested that he come to Quito, Dad thought of going there on a temporary basis—for a year. As Mom and Dad discussed the notion, they thought they might possibly serve the Lord more effectively in Quito while continuing to study Spanish. Furthermore, they could give Clarence Jones a chance to take a long overdue furlough in the United States.

While they pondered the possibilities in Ecuador they kept their minds on their tasks in Pamplona and continued to soak up the Spanish language and Colombian culture. Mom and Dad delighted in the oddities that made Colombia special. Most missionaries were able to keep a light-hearted smile about the quirks of day-to-day life in Colombia, and they resolved to keep themselves fascinated rather than annoyed with the Latin way of doing things. This loving acceptance was one of the secrets of their success.

Dad smiled and laughed whenever he saw things that made Colombians unique. Although he felt that smoking tobacco was a sin, he was amused to see some Colombian women smoking cigars. The cigar-smokers also wore men's hats. He reflected, "I don't see how a fellow could fall in love with a cigar-smoking gal wearing a man's hat!"

He was also entertained by Latin American inefficiencies, such as the constant closing of the post office for fiestas, and wrote good-naturedly: "The post office closes at the lightest excuse. Out of six days, it has been open only a day and a half, because after all, they had to observe the following fiestas: Corpus Christi day, St. Peter's day, and a day to get ready for St. Peter's day."

Another insight into Colombian nature was the relaxed view of time. Mom and Dad tried to blend into the Latin American culture and slow their own life style, and commented about the virtue of trying to become more like the relaxed Latins with whom they now lived. A friend from the United States wondered how a fast man like Bob Savage could get along in a slow society. He wrote: "One hears about fiery tempers of Latin Americans. Perhaps, but they don't get mad about the same things we do. Our fits of temper are caused by delays, interruptions, and things not going as planned. Such things never ruffle the temperament of most Latins. Whenever we have the inevitable transportation delays, I've never seen driver or passengers get the least bit upset or excited. What difference does it make whether we get to our destination today, tomorrow, or the next day?"

Many preconceptions were quickly dissolved. "Before coming to South America I was under the impression that Latins were very emotional, but it is quite opposite in these parts. People of Pamplona and Salazar are as inexpressive, unemotional, vacuous, and stolid as the proverbial wooden Indian. They rarely say a word of appreciation for music, message, or any part of the service." Dad was later to find out that the formal setting of Catholic services set the tone for a religious meeting, and that many of these people were only responding in the way they thought was right and proper.

Another factor Dad began to note: warm versus cold climate. He started to form the opinion that the warmer the climate, the more expressive the people. Over the years, as he traveled across the continent, this opinion became firmer as he compared the lively meetings he had in hot coastal cities with more reserved meetings in cold mountain towns.

In Chinácota my parents found a lovely place in which to live. It had a 100-foot veranda, giving me an excellent place to play. They paid 30 pesos a month, about twice the going rate in Chinácota, but it seemed like a great deal to the North American missionaries.

Our furniture was modest: two benches built in anticipation of a new congregation; a make-shift table out of shipping crates, army cots, and a "missionary closet"—a rope stretched from one wall to another from which hung our clothes. Mom had mastered the kerosene stove in Pamplona. Now she had a bigger challenge: a "carbon" stove. Carbón (coal) was used for cooking, and chunks of carbon were part of our necessary fuel supply. Mom did not have to struggle long, for we were fortunate to find a Colombian cook to work for us, a master at bringing the coals to just the right temperature to cook delicious and perfectly prepared meals.

Five orange trees in our back yard provided us with plenty of Vitamin C, and the invigorating climate allowed for shirt-sleeve dining on the veranda in the evenings. Chinácota, at 4,362 feet, was almost 3,000 feet lower than Pamplona and 15 degrees warmer.

Dad's own vision of his mission was to extend the gospel frontier, to establish a pioneer work instead of building on another's foundation. He longed to win Chinácota for Christ. But he also included the surrounding areas as part of his mission. He pastored the group of 30 believers in El Caney, and made a biweekly visit to Arozco, beginning regular services there for the first time.

All those country districts could be reached only by horseback or by walking. Dating back to the Spanish Conquistador period, mountain trails were rough, narrow, and steep. He enjoyed taking me on horseback rides to these villages, and in a letter home described my childish exuberance as we rode the trails:

November 14, 1943

"Steve jabbered all the way. 'Oh yook, Daddy, butterfly. There's a *vaca* (cow). There's Nuisance! (Wilf's colt.) Oh yook, the river's got foam in it (waterfall).' He wouldn't let me pass out any tracts—wanted to do it all himself. '*Hola! Tome. Usted quiere uno también?*' (Hello! Take. You want one also?) I guess the priest will soon publicize that we force our little boy to distribute the heretics' propaganda."

My childhood memories are full of accompanying Dad to many places, not only by horse but by car, bus, train, and plane, always with a meeting as the focus for the trip, but always with a great deal of jolly laughter and unbridled enthusiasm for the lands through which we traveled. He was as delighted with the sight of a lady cooking pork tripe over an outdoor coal stove as he was with the contemplation of a majestic feat of Twentieth Century engineering, like a Boeing 747 or the Golden Gate Bridge. His curiosity and passion for life were boundless; it was impossible to take a trip with Dad and be bored.

Dad loved Colombia and was intensely involved in his work and language study, but he was becoming increasingly restive over the slow pace of evangelism. Always eager to maintain cordial relationships with his fellow missionaries, he kept most of his feelings to himself. The one person he confided in was Mom. He also shared his thoughts freely with his father and wrote him about what he considered to be the stodgy ways of the Scandinavian Alliance Mission.

> The work is pokey and results few. Our church statistics are shocking. Many missionaries have few results—yet the missionaries are satisfied. Think of this: We have 54 missionaries and 38 Colombian pastors but only 46 baptisms in 18 months.
>
> Church memberships are disgraceful. If you count deaths and fallouts, there was only a gain of 13 members in 18 months.
>
> Something is terribly and radically wrong. One thing I don't accept is the Scandinavian Alliance Mission policy of forcing a new convert to prove his lasting qualities before baptism, and that usually means a year or two. That's not the New Testament practice.
>
> Also, they won't let a person take communion until he is baptized. That's not New Testament practice either.
>
> God help me if I ever view things in this spirit. I have but one life to live and if I slip into a rut of complacency being satisfied to win six or eight to Christ every four or five years, I ought to be ashamed of myself.

This powerful and positive faith energized him throughout his 54-year ministry. He always thought in bold visionary strokes. The only times he felt stifled were when he was in situations that held him back from accomplishing all that he felt he could do for God.

He felt his scope was limited. He dearly loved the people with whom he worked and felt no bitterness towards them. He often remarked in later years that many of his feelings were due to the impetuousness of his youth, and he felt that the gallant men and women of the Scandinavian Alliance Mission had accomplished a tremendous amount of work in their own way. But his style was different. He simply began to realize that he needed to surround himself with men and women of similar farsightedness and energy. The thought of Clarence Jones at HCJB often came into his mind, and he longed for the vibrant atmosphere of the worldwide scope of the missionary radio station. Then he told himself to try to be patient and to concentrate on the work at hand.

Living near the Venezuela/Colombia border my folks hoped they would be able to have frequent visits with my uncle and aunt, Jim and June Savage, missionaries in San Cristóbal, Venezuela, only 50 kilometers from Chinácota. However, the difficulties of crossing international borders during wartime made visits almost impossible. We saw them only once, for ten days in July, and we all celebrated with great joy. Jim preached several messages at the church. Having preceded his older brother to the field by a year, his mastery of Spanish was excellent, and Dad remarked, "He can use Spanish more effectively than many missionaries who have been here several years." The two brothers regaled us with jokes and stories, and our little home was filled with raucous Savage laughter for several days. Dad shared with Jim his feelings about the limited horizons of his present mission. They talked about missionary radio and its enormous possibilities. Dad was intrigued to find that Jim was also thinking of radio. For the coming year, Jim and June had two goals in mind: to start a radio ministry on a commercial broadcast station, and to found a Bible Institute. The days slipped by quickly, and then they were gone. The house seemed silent, but no house in which Bob Savage presided was quiet for long.

One day Dad came home with the mail and filled the house with his usual whooping greeting, but this time it was even louder than ever. He had in his hands a copy of his first English book in prose: *Lord, Send Me*, published by Zondervan of Grand Rapids, Michigan. The book was a collection of several of the missionary messages he had preached in the United States the last few months before leaving for Colombia. The book went through several printings over the next few years, and many young missionaries said it had a powerful influence on their decision to go out to the foreign missionary field.

Although Dad's interests were mainly religious, he had a keen curiosity about the world around him. From the day he left the United States, he never missed an issue of Time magazine and always read it cover to cover. When Time arrived in each week's mail, Dad rifled quickly through all the pages and tore out all the ads, so they wouldn't slow him down in his reading. Then he charged through the whole magazine, browsing through world and national news, glancing at medicine and science, skipping arts and theater, then settling down to his main interest: sports. His interest in sports never waned, and he was never too far back in the mountains to keep track of his favorite baseball team, the Detroit Tigers. He wrote home to his father: "I would appreciate more than I can tell if you would each day cut out the Tiger box score from the paper and once a week cut out the Major League standings and send them down here. I get hungry for sports news."

Although he was a preacher and always in the public eye, Dad never took much interest in his clothes. He almost always wore a suit and tie, but had almost no sense about colors, fabrics, or style. His mother's lifetime crusade to get him to wear good-quality, stylish clothes failed. He wore the nice suits his mother gave him, but preferred to buy his clothes cheaply. After he had been in Colombia for a year, he wrote and needled her good-naturedly about her doomed efforts to dress him up: "Mother, did I ever confess to you about those linen suits I purchased in Pontiac before leaving? If I had admitted to you that I picked them up at a pawn shop at $4 per suit I knew you would have insisted I trot right back down town and get a 'decent' suit—bless your heart, soul, and gizzard."

Mom, on the other hand, dressed stylishly, although with modest taste appropriate to her role as a missionary. The matter of dress was an issue that could cause raised eyebrows among the saints with whom we lived. Mom and Dad came from the conservative, fundamentalist wing of the Protestant churches in America, but there were missionaries even further right. Mom was amused to find herself considered "liberal" on the issue of dress. Many missionary women wore long dresses and refused to wear make up, whereas Mom wore dresses cut just below the knees, as that was the fashion in 1943. She was delighted when one of the single missionary ladies shortened her dress three inches. She wrote with merriment: "Thank goodness, some of the girls are beginning to become conscious of how they can keep themselves up. Since some of us new missionaries have arrived, they are realizing that 'times have changed' and they are no longer looking so antique."

Dad always had a simple taste in food. He got intense pleasure out of plain foods like an onion sandwich or a bowl of oatmeal. What he ate, though, he gulped down in huge quantities. "Wilda fixed me my favorite meal—baked meat pie. I meekly limited myself to three platefuls." During our first year in Colombia, Dad was 24 years old and could eat as much as he wanted without worrying about putting on pounds. He weighed about 150 pounds and never gained weight. He ate heartily and lived merrily. He never smoked a cigarette and never touched a drop of alcohol, but no gourmet ever enjoyed a glass of fine wine more than Dad enjoyed a glass of cold milk.

He had enjoyed perfect health for 15 consecutive years and was proud to tell people that he never got sick. However, in late 1943 he was embarrassed when he was stricken with jaundice. He didn't want anyone to know he was sick, and wouldn't let Mom fuss over him. He just wanted to get up and get back to work.

"Don't worry about me, honey, I'm OK. I'll get over this lousy good-for-nothing stuff in another hour. I'll just take another nap." Most North Americans stayed in bed at least two weeks when they got malaria, but Dad "abandoned the horizontal position" after only two days, still feeling weak, but refusing to let the disease get him down.

Mom and Dad had a secret, and no one knew except Uncle Jim and Aunt June. Mom was pregnant—and the baby was due to arrive in early 1944. They made plans to travel to the capital city, Bogotá, right after Christmas, to seek a good doctor and clinic, and to wait there until the baby arrived.

As they looked forward with eagerness to the birth of their second child, they looked back with despair on the rocky soil in which they were trying to sow their seed. At the end of 1943 Dad wrote: "I had thought we could prove to people that ours was the true, the better faith. But logic isn't enough. Most people don't care! What is true or false matters not. They were born Catholics and Catholicism is good enough for them—despite its errors and regardless of the gospel's truth."

What was it about those Catholics anyway? Weren't they Christians? Were they really lost? Why did Mom and Dad feel they needed to be saved?

3

Why convert the Catholics?

The test of tolerance comes when we are in a majority;
The test of courage comes when we are in a minority.

—*Pocket Wisdom*, p. 125

Mom and Dad came to Latin America convinced that their mission was to convert Roman Catholics to follow Christ. Colombia in 1942 was about 99 per cent Roman Catholic, so theirs was not a mission to pagan heathens who had never heard of Christ. Indeed, Christ was on the lips of all Colombians, and nearly everyone considered himself a Christian.

What, then, was their mission? The way Dad saw it, the Roman Catholic Church had strayed terribly off course from the true faith. For him, the Catholics were not only erroneous on a few minor points of doctrine, but had completely perverted the original teachings of Jesus. As far as he was concerned, a Roman Catholic was just as lost as a person who had never heard of Christ.

Most Roman Catholics in Colombia in 1943 attended mass in Latin, which they could not understand, and never read the Bible, so had little understanding of doctrine or theology. They did not use phrases such as "a personal relationship with Jesus Christ" as did the evangelicals, but rather emphasized loyalty to the Church and allegiance to Mary, the Mother of Christ.

This was a full generation before the reforms of Vatican II were initiated by Pope John XXIII, and the Roman Catholic Church was far different from the one we know today. Furthermore, the Roman Catholic Church in Latin America was quite different from the one in the United States: much more intolerant of other faiths, deeply devoted to the Virgin Mary, and subtly adapted to ancient pagan religions of Latin America. Feasts which long ago were dedicated to pagan gods were now saints' days, but many Protestants questioned whether the people knew the difference between the gods of antiquity and the saints they now worshipped. Furthermore, the Roman Church did not take a strong stand against behavior that my parents considered abhorrent—drinking, smoking, dancing, gambling, and sexual immorality. Indeed, many great feasts of the Church featured drunken festivities.

It was the mission of Bob and Wilda Savage to lift these people out of their devil-controlled lives and show them the path to Christ.

Their message to the Colombian Roman Catholics was simple: "You do not need a priest as your mediator, because you can go directly to Christ—the way, the truth, and the life. You do not need to have a priest interpret the Bible for you, but you can read it yourself. You do not have to go through a whole lot of ceremonies and have your prayers intoned by a priest, for you can enjoy a personal relationship with Jesus Christ."

That was the essential message, but there were other important themes: "You do not need to worship Mary, or ask for her intercession; you can still love and respect her, but you can pray directly to Christ. You do not need to dwell on the dead Christ represented in your morbid crucifixes, but on the risen Christ and the empty tomb. You do not need to perform so-called "good works" and pay money to earn forgiveness of sin; you simply need to repent and ask Christ to come into your heart."

Getting people's beliefs straight was essential, but it was not all, for faith in Christ demanded a total change of direction. "When you accept Christ, He will demand that you change your life. You must get married to the woman with whom you live. You must quit drinking and smoking. You must not curse or gamble.

You must be a good husband and father. You must be a good citizen, honest in your dealings, fearless in your faith."

The Roman Catholics were the obvious target of evangelism, and the Catholic hierarchy responded to the Protestant missionaries mostly with suspicion and fear. But not all Catholics were hostile. The brothers in the local Catholic college treated my parents warmly. Mom was surprised and puzzled as she wrote her parents:

January 14, 1943

The Catholics have been super grand to us. Brother Gonzalo, the president of this college, is perfectly lovely and goes out of his way to be nice to us, so decent that Bob wondered if he had our number wrong. He kept inviting Bob to the college to take lessons in Spanish, until finally Bob said, "You understand, don't you, that we are Protestants and we participate in the Protestant services here?"

Brother Gonzalo replied, "Certainly. It makes no difference. Come anyhow; we are your friends."

He was so grand to us that we hardly knew what to make of the situation. It makes it hard to actively work against their faith. Each day we pray that every contact we make will be for His glory, so we are sure He will lead us. The funny thing is, other missionaries say the priests are very cool to them. You know Bob—he can make friends with anyone, bless his heart.

Dad took language classes from Brother Alfredo, and they took turns, with Dad teaching English to the brother on alternate visits. Dad took every opportunity to witness and viewed his language classes as a chance to convert the priest. What a surprise when Dad discovered that the priest had the same goal in reverse: he hoped to convert Dad to Catholicism.

Dad wrote about his attempts to use his language classes as a means of evangelizing the priests: "Our language classes with the Catholic brothers are interesting. There is very little grammar study as we discuss our beliefs practically all the time we have together.

He hopes to convert me to Catholicism. This week I am writing an article in Spanish on 'How to Obtain Salvation' for him to correct and for us to discuss. We carry on most of these discussions in Spanish, so I am at a disadvantage, but it is vastly worthwhile."

Another feature of Roman Catholicism that both riveted and repelled the evangelical missionaries was the religious processions. When the Church celebrated one of the grand occasions of their religious calendar, such as the feast of the Ascension or the feast of All Saints' Day, the priests orchestrated a stately and splendid procession through the town. Parishioners marched behind the men who carried an image of a saint or the virgin. It was usually a massive procession, with thousands of people falling in train. Children joined, enjoying the high-flown affair. These colorful parades were festive events, but the mood of the multitude made missionaries nervous. It felt eerie, almost ominous, to watch the dazed crowds ooze by, mindlessly following an image. The image was usually carved from wood, painted in bright colors. For many people, the image itself, not God, was the object of worship, and Dad disparaged these little statues as a direct violation of the second of the Ten Commandments: "Thou shalt not make unto thee any graven image." After watching a Holy Week procession, Mom described her fascination and sadness:

March 29, 1943

Yesterday, I saw my first religious procession. Leading the parade out of the beautiful Cathedral were altar boys with incense, followed by priests, then Catholic students dressed in uniforms, and finally the main crowd.

John, the beloved disciple, was the first image—carried by men doing "penance" for sins, dressed in purple robes with masks, eyes peering out. Each image was mounted on a heavy platform, decorated with beautiful flowers and candles. Christ on the Cross was carried along, followed by Mary, in gorgeous black velvet, depicted in sadness as her Son was crucified.

The city band moved slowly to the most minor,

melancholy music I have ever heard. The effect on me was gloom, awe, and wonder. It was spooky. Hundreds of people responded to the priests' chantings. I remarked to some children how sad it was. "Yes," they replied, "but wait until the procession next week...then you'll really see something sad."

The saddest part of all was that their whole emphasis was on the Christ of the Cross—not the risen Christ.

The processions continued on through Holy Week, one every afternoon, and were the main topic of conversation among Colombians and missionaries alike. Dad watched with increasing disgust. He did not savor the beauty of the garments as did Mom. To him it was all ugly and sinful and he was appalled. He wrote:

April 25, 1943

It causes me great heartache to realize that all this pompous elaborateness and idol worship has nothing of the real gospel. I feel these activities produce little more than "lip worship" to Christ rather than "heart surrender." In Amos 5:21 the Lord says: "I hate, I despise your feast days, and I will not smell in your solemn assemblies."

There are 13 Catholic churches in this city of 20,000 and bells of all 13 ring simultaneously. Clouds arising from incense pots permeate the atmosphere with strong odors.

The images of Christ, the Virgin Mary, Peter, John, and others are a strange mixture of the elaborate, the beautiful, and the gruesome. These images have alleged miraculous powers and people pray to them in idolatrous faith. Each image is carried by a group of masked individuals wearing robe and headgear resembling a Ku Klux Klan uniform dyed purple. Multitudes follow chanting mechanical prayers from their rosaries.

Amid all this religious emphasis, the climax for the entire year is simultaneously reached in dancing, drinking, and carousing festivities. They see nothing inconsistent about solemnly marching down the street chanting their prayers in the afternoon and stumbling down the same street that night—dead drunk.

At 12:15 a.m. we were suddenly awakened by noise and commotion. Looking out the window we saw yet another procession depicting Christ carrying his cross. It was haunting with their weird singing, strong smell of incense, masked penitents carrying images, candles, and boys with noise boxes.

What Colombia needs is not Christ on their lips, but Christ in their hearts. If religion would save a soul there would be no need of missionaries here, but a religion that is based upon ceremony, images, mechanical worship, and superstition will never avail in bringing to the people of Colombia the peace, certainty, and transforming power that we have in the glorious salvation of our Redeemer, Jesus Christ.

The adoration of the Virgin Mary was a prominent theme of these processions, and my parents felt that this was a major deterrent in people's ability to focus on the person and work of Jesus Christ Himself. Mom wrote on April 26, 1943: "Mary always seems to be in on it. However, they had one procession we didn't expect. We had the impression they never emphasized the resurrection of Christ, but the Easter Sunday procession proved us wrong. They portrayed Christ resurrected and Mary in a joyful attitude meeting Him. The band played triumphant music versus the haunting minor melody of the previous days."

It was strange that two religions, both claiming to be the true followers of Christ, should each see the other as godless. One day, Teresa, who worked as our housekeeper, told Mom, "The people next door think you are agnostics."

Mom was shocked. "Us? Agnostics? Why?"

"Because you don't believe in the Virgin Mary's power to answer prayer," responded Teresa.

"But their girls play with Stevie," said Mom. "They must like us."

"Oh, yes," rejoined Teresa, "they like you very much—but they think your faith is very bad."

"Isn't it queer for us to be the ones thought of as the unbelievers?" mused Mom. "Naturally, I can see how they feel. They have been steeped in this business for so long that anything contrary must seem wrong to them."

Dad broke new ground by making friends with many local priests. His boisterous congeniality crashed through many frigid barriers that existed between Catholics and Protestants. Some older missionaries were troubled by his friendship with "the enemy"; they were stunned when he went even further—by attending mass. He wrote:

February 28, 1943

This is Sunday noon and I have already attended two church services: Catholic mass and Protestant Sunday school. Brother Alfredo asked me if my religion prohibited me from attending the Catholic church. I told him of course not, and he invited me to mass.

All 450 college students attend mass, including many of the fellows that I have been inviting to Bible class. I was quite a conspicuous item in the service as I did not cross myself or kneel.

I hope that by attending some Catholic services, I can tell the college young men that they should repay the compliment and attend our services.

A week later, Dad wrote an essay entitled *"Mis Impresiones de la Misa"* ("My Impressions of the Mass") and took it to have Brother Alfredo correct it during his Spanish class. The brother read Dad's observation that Catholics pray with such rapidity as to make thoughtfulness impossible. "Yes, Roberto, you are right—to my shame and chagrin."

But Brother Alfredo did not agree with Dad's point that prayer should be made only to the Father, Son, and Holy Spirit—and should not include Mary. They talked at length about the place of Mary in the Protestant faith.

Dad asked, "OK, tell me. Where in the Bible does it say that we should pray to Mary?"

Brother Alfredo smiled and shrugged, "That has been added by the Church."

Encouraged, Dad pressed on, "And where in the Bible does it say we should make the sign of the cross?"

Spreading his hands good-heartedly, Brother Alfredo said that, too, had been added by the Church.

Warming to his subject, but sensing his inadequacy in Spanish, Dad pushed on, "What about Revelation 22:18 and 19?" Dad thought this Bible verse would end all arguments about the authority of the Scriptures. Brother Alfredo reached for his Bible and read: "If any man shall add unto these things, God shall add unto him the plagues that are written in this book." Brother Alfredo immediately saw what Dad was trying to prove. Chuckling, he said, with a benign and all-knowing look on his face: "Oh, come now, Roberto, these verses refer only to making immoral additions to the Bible."

Brother Alfredo agreed that it was a horrible blot on Catholicism that some missionaries had been persecuted and stoned. He claimed that people who did such things were not good Catholics. Dad held his tongue and restrained himself from saying what Brother Alfredo already knew: that the priests themselves were invariably instigators of such persecution.

At the end of the class, Dad told Brother Alfredo what profound respect he had for Mary and that she was the best woman God was able to find when he chose a Mother for our Lord. Brother Alfredo leaped to his feet, took Dad by the hand, lifted him out of the chair, and gave him a big hug saying, "I thought you Protestants hated Mary—I'm so glad you feel that way."

The visit had been a tremendous success, and to top it off, Brother Alfredo asked Dad if he would like to visit the Bishop, whose "palace" was in Pamplona. The following Sunday, Dad became the first North American Protestant missionary to have an audience with the bishop, one of the highest officials in Colombia.

They talked of world events, and Dad asked the bishop what he thought the future of the Church would be in Germany and Europe.

Dad did not understand Spanish well enough to get a complete idea of what he was saying, but gamely pressed on with another question: "How do you feel about the Second Coming of Christ in connection with the war and other world events?" The bishop said the coming of Christ was a great event he was anticipating. Dad asked him for his interpretation of I Thessalonians 4:17: "Then we who are living at that time will all be gathered up along with them in the clouds to meet the Lord in the air." The bishop agreed that this would indeed happen someday.

At the end of the interview, Dad suggested they have a word of prayer. Brother Alfredo, not willing to let an impromptu Protestant prayer take place, quickly suggested they recite the Lord's prayer together. After the prayer, the bishop gave Dad a book on Catholic fundamentals and stressed that he hoped this would not be their only visit. Brother Alfredo knelt before him and kissed his ring. Dad shook his hand, and they bid adios.

Dad wrote home: "We hope fanaticism will break down as people realize that their leaders are treating us with exceeding courtesy and kindness. I dream of the time when the Lord will use me to lead these leaders into a knowledge of the truth of the grace of God. I suppose they also have hopes of converting me."

Although Dad had established a good relationship with the bishop and the brothers at the Seminary, several local Catholic priests were not as well-disposed towards the Protestants. Parish priests viewed evangelical Protestants as ominous threats to their own positions, and they were concerned that their own parishioners would abandon the Roman Church. During Easter week, the mood in Pamplona began to turn sullen. Mom walked into the *sala* (living room) and found several burning cigarette stubs that vandals had thrown in through the open window onto our rugs and furniture. A thud of fear swept through her. Then she reflected and said to herself that this was nothing compared to what some missionaries were experiencing daily. The thought braced her and gave her courage.

It was rumored there was going to be a stone-throwing campaign against the Protestants because a North American woman in Pamplona had made a few uncomplimentary remarks about the Virgin Mary. Nothing came of it, but the missionaries felt increasingly tense.

The tide of anger and hostility against Protestants was growing; some missionaries were victims of violence. The Lutheran missionaries in Duitama, 150 miles south of Pamplona, found themselves in the middle of an uproar. Dad wrote about their troubles: "During a big procession the priest got the people infuriated and they stormed the Lutheran headquarters. Behind the image of the Virgin Mary, they broke down eleven doors, tore up every Bible and hymnal, and destroyed the furniture with rocks. It is a disgrace to think that a religious leader led this mob. Their religion doesn't change hearts; it seems to make them worse."

Trouble also loomed close at hand, right in Pamplona. The Scandinavian Alliance Mission had its annual conference in Pamplona and created a visible presence with 25 North American Protestant missionaries. This caused an immediate reaction among the local priests. When someone stole the silver chalices from the altar of the Catholic church the priests used this as a pretext to instigate new harassment against the Protestants.

"The Protestant missionaries stole our altar equipment!" cried out the priest, as he stood in front of the church and excitedly tried to organize a mob to attack the Protestant meeting place. The crowd began to surge down the street towards the missionary meeting hall, but police quickly arrived on the scene and kept the crowds from rallying and attacking the missionaries.

When Dad saw the crowd disperse, he led the missionaries in a prayer of thanksgiving: "How gracious Thou art, Oh Lord, in seeing these things and preventing mischief. We thank Thee for sending the police just in time. We thank Thee for making the mayor and police chief sympathetic to our safety. However, we know that sometimes Thou dost allow trouble for Thy glory, and if we are called upon to suffer for Thy name, give us the courage to bear whatever the Devil may send our way."

The matter was not quickly ended. The priest insisted that the police search the house of the missionaries to look for the stolen silver chalices. They took careful pains to search the bedroom of missionary Cora Soderquist, whom the priests begrudged most because she had started the work in Pamplona. The idea that the saintly Cora would steal a chalice from the Catholic church was preposterous, and many of the town's citizens scoffed at the priest's presumption. But he persisted: they must go ahead with the shakedown.

As the search went on, the missionaries huddled nervously in the parlor, worried that someone had planted the stolen silver in Cora's room, but nothing turned up. The police were embarrassed and apologetic: "We have to fulfill the priest's demand," said an officer, shaking his head lamely.

A short service of praise followed the search, but the meeting was not free of worry. A gang outside broke the windows while the missionaries prayed, but wooden shutters inside the windows spared them from flying glass. (Shutters did not open out to protect the windows, but inward to protect the house.) Dad concluded in prayer, "Lord, the Devil is worried these days and things are beginning to happen. Give us courage and calm."

Despite the heavy fear that hung over them, Dad never lost a chance for a light touch, and a good meal. During a break in the missionary conference, he relaxed by going into the kitchen and preparing himself an onion sandwich. When he emerged, sandwich in left hand and glass of milk in right, Elof Anderson asked him, "What's that, Bob?"

"An onion sandwich," replied Dad.

"You mean, just onions and bread?"

"No, I've got butter on the bread," laughed Dad.

"I guess after eating all that Colombian food this past year, you can eat anything," bantered Elof.

"I think it's the other way around. I've eaten onion sandwiches since I was 15. Maybe that's why I've enjoyed Colombian food so much."

The missionary conference was over, and the missionaries returned to their stations in northern Colombia. The missionaries followed Latin American custom and hugged a hearty farewell to both Colombian men and women. But they merely shook hands with each other, for in those days missionaries did not hug one another.

As Dad settled in to his work in Chinácota, the local priests became alarmed, and began to publish periodicals explaining to their people what the Protestants were trying to do.

> The most scandalous and regrettable of all schisms is called "Protestantism" which in the 16th century pulled many nations away from the bosom of the Church to put them in captivity to all errors and vices.

> Protestantism abounds in ministers, well-fed and well-provided for by wealthy, Protestant governments. But what are they good for? They have no ministry to perform. They do not say mass, because this was blotted out by the hypocritical founders. They have abolished all Sacraments except Baptism. Preaching is useless, because they say each Protestant can interpret the Bible for himself.

> What then is left for the minister? Nothing. Protestant ministers are as necessary as a dog at mass.

So spoke the Holy Roman Catholic Church of its fellow Christians. The relationship between Catholics and Protestants remained tense, ranging from cool politeness to violence. The situation did not change until the mid-1960's, a fascinating story that will be told in a later chapter.

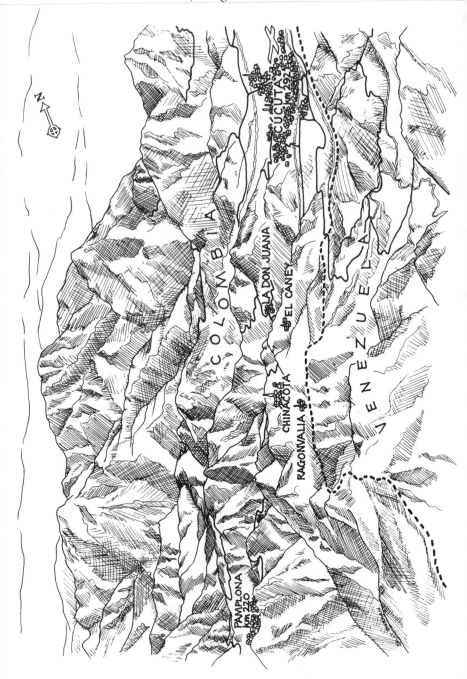

4

Chinácota

❖

Don't be discouraged—it may be the last key in the bunch that opens the door.   —*Pocket Wisdom*, p. 39

New Year's Day 1944 found us in Colombia's capital city, Bogotá, where we had traveled to await the arrival of my baby brother or sister. Mom and I flew from Cúcuta to Bucaramanga to Bogotá, while Dad went overland. He enjoyed a magnificent overland journey, taking a 13-hour bus junket from Pamplona to Duitama. Colombia lies in a series of three north-south mountain ranges, called *cordilleras*, so a trip from east to west involved a series of climbs and descents, with ancient trucks wheezing as they ascended into rarefied Andean air, then maneuvering and skidding down tortuous winding roads in low gear to keep the mass off already feeble brakes. It was not a trip for the faint-hearted, but the adventurous Bob Savage exulted in each hairpin turn. He wrote an enthusiastic description of his journey:

> At 7,000 feet, Pamplona is quite high, but we climbed much higher. We kept rising for three hours until we reached a high, barren, uninhabited mountain plateau. It was cold, cold, cold—and over in Venezuela's direction I saw a range of snow-capped peaks.

The standard equipment for highland men is a *ruana* (Colombian for "poncho") carelessly thrown over their shoulders. Millinery equipment for a woman is a man's straw hat.

Oxen as beasts of burden were more common than horses, mules, or burros, and I saw them plowing, hauling cargo, pulling carts, and even carrying people on their backs.

The bus stopped at many towns of 1000 to 2000 inhabitants. None has the gospel. I prayed the Lord would show us how they might be reached.

The last leg of Dad's trip was on a railroad from Duitama to Bogotá. The train was diesel-engined, streamlined, aluminum construction, only one car, ultra-modern with red leather, over-stuffed, reclining seats. The countryside, surprisingly, was almost identical to United States midwestern landscapes. The temperature was the same as Michigan in October. Even farms were similar, and Dad said: "Except for fences made of mud, and roofs made of straw or tile, there is little to remind me I am not back home in my native environs."

Meanwhile, Mom and I flew, covering Dad's two-day trip in an hour. But our trip was not nearly as pleasant. Our Avianca DC-3 flight from Cúcuta to Bucaramanga started out smoothly, but as we entered turbulence of mid-afternoon Andean swirls, the plane dipped and swayed, and Mom grabbed the paper sack from the seat pocket in front of her. As I watched in fascination, the same urge overtook me, and I stuck my little head into the same sack with Mom. Thinking I just wanted to see what was going on, she pushed my head back, then realized I was in the same plight.

In Bogotá our family took up residence in the home of a Dutch family on Avenida Caracas, a beautiful, two-lane, asphalt boulevard with a splendidly landscaped 30-foot parkway down the center. Many Dutch oil people from the island of Curaçao spent their vacations there, and we were dazzled during meals with conversations in three languages: Dutch, English, and Spanish. In addition we met other residents who spoke German, Italian, and

Czechoslovakian. In a day when war was raging throughout the northern hemisphere, this splendid city was a haven where the international community could gather and live in relative quiet.

My parents found Bogotá an exciting place, offering much of the same allure that had made them love Washington, D.C. Although they had adapted gracefully to the primitive life of rural Colombia, they relished the cosmopolitan city and savored its modern conveniences. Dad wrote about this place of splendor:

> Bogotá doesn't seem foreign. They have the latest stream-lined street cars, taxis, buses, and trucks. The shopping district surpasses that of Pontiac, Michigan, and when you enter one of the dime stores, it requires little imagination to picture yourself back in the U.S. Yesterday in our dime store visit we bought luxuries like candy-coated peanuts, Coca-Cola, playing blocks, and HOT DOGS.
>
> The people of Bogotá don't look like the rural Colombians. Half the time, I look at a person on the street and wonder, "Perhaps he is from the U.S. also."
>
> Bogotá appears more modern than most U.S. cities, and if you want to purchase a new refrigerator, washing machine, or radio, despite wartime rationing, they still have ample supplies of those U.S. scarcities. The architecture of Bogotá is ultramodern, and 90% of the buildings look like visions from Chicago's World Fair.

Mom and Dad may have been away from their post of duty in Chinácota but they missed no opportunities to witness for Christ. One Dutch family had a daughter, Berrietta, age 16. Her mother asked Dad if he would talk to her about church. Dad eagerly and earnestly told her how the Lord had died for her. Later he told us, "She became convicted of her sin, and accepted Christ as her Savior." He used the word "convicted" to describe the feeling a person got when he was overwhelmed with his sense of sin, a deep and heartfelt acknowledgement that he must repent and turn to God.

Dad guided Berietta through the simple prayer he had used with so many others. It was an unsophisticated but life-transforming prayer: "Jesus, I am a sinner. You died to save me. I repent. I accept you as my Savior. I will follow you." That was it. It was to help people say that prayer that Dad had dedicated his life, for it was his cherished goal that every creature on earth would pray as Berietta did that day, and turn to Jesus Christ. His heart rejoiced whenever he had the opportunity to lead someone to Christ, and on that particular day he focused his attention on her—and only on her—making sure her decision was not frivolous and her determination to follow Christ would stick. To assure this, he immediately set up an instruction class with Berrietta, after confiding with Mom, "The pity is there is nowhere she can get help in the Christian life. The Presbyterian Church is modernistic, and her dad is a big gun in a beer company, so there is no one to help her grow in grace."

"Her mother is lovely," said Mom.

"Yes," replied Dad, "but just like Berrietta she hasn't had much chance to know about things of the Lord."

Mom's time was drawing near. Preparations were made for the forthcoming birth and Mom was thrilled with the modern and clean facilities she found at Clínica Calvo, a maternity hospital. They made arrangements with a Dutch nurse to care for her while she was there and met Dr. Calvo, a gynecologist who had studied in Paris for 15 years. Mom had worried she would be risking a birth in rough surroundings, but was reassured by the cultivated staff she found in Colombia's capital city. She wrote her folks:

> We North Americans come down here with a superior attitude, I'm afraid, and think nothing good exists outside the U.S. Well, when we walked into Dr. Calvo's office, our eyes bulged as though we were hicks coming to the big city for the first time. It was immaculate to the nth degree with ultra-modern gleaming silver instruments. The ivory telephone caught my eye. The doctor was efficient, inspirational, and

spoke English perfectly, having spent many months in London.

One thing different about hospitals here: we must take everything with us for the baby and me—diapers, shirts, wrapping blankets, nighties, baby oil, absorbent cotton, and powder.

At 10:30 p.m. on January 26, Mom announced quietly, "Bob, my labor pains are starting." He leaped out of his chair and quickly called a taxi. They arrived at the hospital, and Dr. Calvo said he guessed she had three hours to go. They had prayer, read Scripture, and talked jovially until midnight. As the clock struck twelve, the nurse announced, "the doctor wants Señora de Savage to come to the delivery room." As they wheeled her off, Dad felt very much alone in this foreign land, for unlike three years earlier when I was born, he did not have his own father to pace the halls with him. He steeled himself for several hours of waiting. But with this second baby the time was short and the news joyous: at 1:05 a.m. my baby sister Carol Elaine was here.

The nurse told Dad, "*Su esposa es guapa.*" Literally, that means "Your wife is beautiful" but in this context it meant "Your wife can take it" for she had not let out even one cry or moan during all her time of labor.

A week later, Mom wrote, "This is Carol's sixth day in the world and already she has made us captive to her charms. What a treasure. I guess I'm the luckiest girl ever. First I get the best husband, then a little son whose praise I've been known to sing, and now a precious little daughter."

During our stay in Bogotá, we met 61 missionaries we had not known before, and many others Dad and Mom had known as students at Wheaton College or Moody Bible Institute. At that time there were about 300 missionaries in Colombia, and Dad had become acquainted with 107 of them. It was typical of Dad to compile statistics like that. He didn't know "about 100" missionaries, but precisely 107. His focus on numbers was a driving force in his life. If the record attendance in Sunday School was 24, he was not satisfied until it reached 25, then 50, 100, 200, and 1,000.

There were five "gospel works" in Bogotá, and Dad had the joy of preaching in four of them. Missionaries often referred to a fledgling mission as a "gospel work" and did not call it a "church" until it had a good solid core of members and was officially chartered.

Mom was apprehensive about going back to Chinácota after the lovely days in Bogotá. She had been a gallant missionary and had faced angry mobs with equanimity. She had kept her attitude positive during the ordeals of hostility back in the small town in Eastern Colombia, but now that she was away from it, the thought of returning filled her with grim foreboding. She wrote her mother:

> I hate to leave Bogotá. I could be happy spending all my days here. However, there is work to be done back in Chinácota and that is where the Lord wants us at present. Humanly speaking I must admit that I dread going back to the fanaticism and opposition. I get such a queer feeling thinking of the hate continually manifested and what that priest back there is capable of doing. I guess Bob and I never will get to where we enjoy being detested.
>
> Do be praying much for us as we go back to Chinácota. We long to feel that our lives are bearing fruit for the Lord and we would be thrilled to see that fanatical place open wide to the gospel.

Despite her inner fears, Mom did not complain, for it was she who had first received the missionary call. She did not want to falter now. The story of her call to the mission field began in Romeo, Michigan, where Dad had his first pastorate at the First Baptist Church of Romeo. I was only six months old at the time.

Dad had sponsored a missionary conference at First Baptist and had invited several missionary speakers, including M. D. Christensen from Africa and Harvey Hammond from South

America.

Harvey Hammond's wife, Georgienna, had a meeting especially for the women. That night, Dad stayed home with me while Mom went to the women's missionary meeting.

When Mom came home, she said, "Bob, I don't know how to tell you this, but I've been called to the mission field. It was just so strong, the feeling, the impression. It was the Lord. He really worked on me tonight."

Dad hesitated, startled, then said thoughtfully, "Well, if He called you, Wilda, I guess He's certainly going to call me, too."

The next night M. D. Christensen was preaching, and as he issued his missionary challenge at the end, he dared each person to pray, "Lord, what dost Thou want me personally to do about the missionary challenge?"

Dad bowed his head and as pastor he thought of the young people in his church and began to pray, naming people who were there whom Dad thought would make good missionaries: "Oh, Lord, I pray for Mary, Art, and John. Lay this missionary challenge on their hearts and call some of these fine young people that I am pastoring into missionary service."

Christensen interrupted the prayer, "Wait a minute! I believe some of you are not praying the way I suggested. You are praying for others, and I asked you to pray for yourselves."

Dad was astonished. That's exactly what he had been doing, so he started to pray for himself, "Lord, is there something Thou wantest me to do about the missionary challenge?" In those days, Dad always addressed God in the formal "Thee" and "Thou."

His thoughts collided and he pleaded with God, "But Lord, Thou hast given me Thy long-range instructions, to pastor churches here in the homeland."

He suddenly became aware that he was arguing with God, softened his tone, and once again prayed, "Lord, dost Thou have something for us in the mission field?"

He came home that night, subdued, and said, "Well, Wilda, the Lord is working on me."

Mom was sitting at the piano, and began to play and sing:

Lord, send me, oh send me forth I pray,
The need is great; Thy call I will obey.
Thy love compels me, I must go.
I'm willing, ready, longing to go.

"Wilda, that's beautiful!" exclaimed Dad. "Where did you learn that?"

"I wrote it," she replied shyly.

"You wrote it? When?" he blurted.

"Just now," she replied.

"Why, Wilda, that's wonderful. You've never taken any courses on composing. That's a fantastic song. How long have you been working on it?"

"Just the last hour or so."

"Did you write the words first or the music?"

"It all came out together."

"Well, Hallelujah! This is surely a sign from God. He certainly wants us on the mission field," he shouted. Then he became quiet. "Honey, let's pray," he whispered, no longer in his usual booming voice, but subdued and pensive.

They got down on their knees, and Dad prayed aloud, "Oh Lord, we've been willing to go for a long time. I've told Thee that I would not buck Thy will, and I'd be willing to go to any part of the world, but I haven't been anxious to go. Now Lord, I'm not only willing, but as Wilda's song says, I'm ready and longing. Oh, Lord, let me be a missionary. Permit me. I would feel honored."

Now, two years later, in Colombia, the genuineness of their "call" was tested to its uttermost. The idea of being a missionary had once seemed exciting, even romantic. Now the reality of returning to a hostile environment provoked dread and anxiety.

We returned to Chinácota, and it was not easy. The delights of Bogotá, with its modern conveniences and friendly people, contrasted sharply with the primitive and remote village on the eastern slopes of Colombia. The reception was hostile and opposition to the gospel intense, determined, and fanatical. Dad visited several homes attempting to get acquainted. Most people rebuffed his friendly approach, and even refused to accept a tract. The effervescent Bob was taken aback whenever someone treated him frigidly, for he was always sure he could win anyone over with his cheery smile and loving disposition. But there were many in Chinácota who did not respond—not even to the magnetic Don Roberto Savage.

Dad spilled his emotions in an unusually gloomy letter to his mother:

You ask, Mother, if we had gotten discouraged and blue. We surely were when we left Chinácota the last week of December. The month of December was dreadful. It seemed that the little we had built up in October and November was falling completely apart. But these weeks in Bogotá have renewed our spirits and I'm anxious to get back into the fight.

I think often of the similarities between our work and the war in Italy. The Italian campaign has been described as an "inch by inch" effort. That seems to be the way with us. As the Allies must conquer Rome, likewise we must conquer Rome's influence if these people chained in spiritual slavery are to be freed. It is not my disposition to be an "inch by inch" soldier, but the Lord will give His strength and encouragement as long as He wants me to continue in this battlefield.

One note of encouragement in Chinácota was the rapid spiritual growth of Eduardo Gómez, the tailor who had been saved in November before the trip to Bogotá. He "grew in grace" so rapidly that he had already become a fine preacher by the time we returned. The missionaries used the term "grow in grace" to describe the process of Christian maturity as one becomes more familiar with the Bible, with doctrine, and becomes established soundly in the faith. They encouraged believers to memorize copious amounts of Scripture, word-for-word, and already

Eduardo quoted a lot of Scripture from memory. He showed a comprehension of the Bible that was remarkable. Dad and Mom began to pray that the Lord would lead him into full time Christian work.

Eduardo's wife, Pepa, had not yet accepted Christ, but gave a great testimony regarding his transformation, "I'm not an evangelical yet, but if the gospel can change a person the way it changed my husband it surely must be the true faith. Our home is completely transformed and Eduardo, instead of drinking and gambling every night, has become a wonderful father and husband."

Her enthusiasm did not last long. As pressures mounted from priest and neighbors, she, a fervent Catholic, turned on him and began to razz him and scoff at his efforts to serve the Lord. Dad shook his head and declared, "She should be the most grateful person in the world. Instead she's a constant wet blanket to his enthusiasm for the gospel."

Good news came from Pamplona. Señor Parrada, their brilliant language teacher in Pamplona, came to be "gloriously saved" while we were in Bogotá. He told Cora Soderquist and the congregation in Pamplona, "For three nights I was unable to sleep because I was so under the conviction of the Holy Spirit. Cost what it might, I had to come out for Christ." The cost was indeed great, for Señor Parrada lost his job as director of the school in Pamplona. The missionaries began to talk to him about attending seminary and becoming a full time pastor.

Dad began to think about getting Colombian nationals to take over the work of the church.

As a missionary I want to make myself as unimportant as possible. When a missionary permits a congregation to depend on him for everything—sermons, directing meetings, and running church business—that congregation's chances of becoming self-supporting and self-governing are seriously jeopardized. I'm going to use these Colombians almost entirely for public preaching services. I will teach a Bible class each week to give them correct doctrinal and Scriptural foundation, and will also spend one week each month visiting unevangelized towns.

The most casual conversation often produced opportunities for Christian witness. One Colombian friend asked, with innocent interest, "When are you going to baptize Carol?" Little did he realize this question would bring a profound theological discussion, for this gave my parents a chance to explain the differences between Protestant and Catholic views of baptism. Dad replied: "We feel our little daughter should accept Christ for herself when she becomes old enough to believe in Him as her own personal Savior. Then she can be baptized as a testimony of the salvation she has obtained through Christ's death for her on the cross."

"But what if she dies without being baptized," protested the worried friend. "She will go to Hell."

"There is no place in Scripture that says that," argued Dad, "and I don't believe an unbaptized little babe is eternally condemned. This is just one of hundreds of unscriptural teachings in the Catholic church."

While Dad struggled to win over one or two people in Chinácota, another Savage Baptist preacher, Grandpa Henry Savage, was having rousing success with Army camp tours. He reported over 2,600 conversions since his Army ministry had begun. Dad was agitated that his own results were not higher, and felt a tinge of jealousy, the kind of sin that afflicted even the pious Bob Savage. Sometimes he talked about what a sinner he was, and I asked him what he ever did wrong, for he seemed to me a perfect creature. He then told about his continual temptation to obtain glory for himself instead of his Lord. I thought it was that very drive that gave him so much energy and helped him achieve such splendid results. "Yes," he replied, "the Lord can use those qualities for His glory, but it's a fine line we walk, for those very same qualities can be used for self-glorification, and that's evil." Despite that sense of competition he cheerfully took pleasure in his father's success as he wrote: "Our hearts rejoiced when you told about the many conversions in your army camp ministry. I did not realize you were conducting five or six services daily. Part of your letter was deleted by censors, but the good news about your great ministry was left intact."

Opposition from the local priest, Padre Lorenzo Rivera, continued unabated. He wrote a letter to Don Juan, mayor of Chinácota, imploring him to take sterner action against the missionaries: "The authorities are obligated to discredit the Protestants' propaganda."

Padre Rivera told Don Juan that if he refused to act, the Catholic church would have to take the law into its own hands. If there were any conflict, declared the priest, it would be the Protestants' fault, for by their heretical teachings, they were instigators of lawless actions.

Fortunately for us, the mayor was no pushover. His main goal was to maintain peace and harmony in the town, and he took the opportunity to remind the priest of a shocking incident. The reverend father had encouraged a boy to throw a stone at the window of the Savage home. The mayor would not tolerate that behavior and wrote a formal note, laced with sarcasm, to the priest: "The boy and his mother both insisted that you had ordered him to throw the stone. As is natural, Your Reverence, I contradicted such an excuse, because I cannot think that an act of such a nature could be brought into being by your suggestion."

The mayor became so friendly with Dad that the two took language lessons from each other. He was a likable fellow, in his mid-30's, and when he came openly to our house for an English lesson, he made it clear by his bold action that he was not afraid to let people know he was associating with the Protestants.

Two more national workers began to emerge as leaders in the

local church. Pedro Esteves, from La Donjuana, graduated from the Bible Institute and preached in Chinácota. Manuel Durán from Pamplona came to preach. Whenever possible, Dad stayed off the platform, giving Colombians full responsibility for conducting the service and preaching. Even though he let them preach, however, Dad usually got into the act by playing his trumpet. His music was a big attraction to people in those rural communities with little entertainment. The blaring and enthusiastic hymns blasting out of Dad's trumpet were delightful though unfamiliar melodies.

Mom and Dad needed a meeting hall for their church, but most citizens of Chinácota were reluctant to rent to the hated Protestants. Finally, they found an absentee landlord who had little to lose—and much to gain, as he charged them a premium to rent his building. The first few meetings in the new little chapel produced total attendances of about 25 people but only four from Chinácota. Most worshippers were from the countryside, where attitudes were more open and the priest's influence less powerful.

It was not only dangerous for local citizens to rent a building to Protestants; it was risky to perform any services at all. The man who painted the sign "Casa Evangélica" was publicly excommunicated from the Catholic church. He had no association with my folks, and had taken it on only as a job, but the penalty was vicious social and religious ostracism.

Dad finally had a chance to baptize some new believers, and he did it his way, the Baptist way, as John the Baptist had done, so Dad believed, by immersion. Dad conducted the first baptism by immersion in the province of Norte de Santander when he and Wilf Watson baptized three people in the river called Río Pamplonita. A crowd of over 100 gathered to watch the fascinating ceremony.

Dad never lost an opportunity to talk about Biblical doctrines, and baptism was one of his favorite themes. He enjoyed matching wits with other missionaries from sister denominations. One day a traveling Methodist minister came through town and had dinner with us. Dad engaged him quickly in a discussion of the "right" form of baptism. The minister asked him, "Well, Brother Savage, would you say it would be enough water if you got someone wet up to the knees?"

"Oh no." Dad shook his head vigorously.

"Well, what if you got the person in up to his shoulders. Would that be enough?" prodded the Methodist.

"Nope," declared Dad.

"Well, what if you got him all the way under, but left the top of his head dry. Would that be enough?" asked the parson.

"No!" exclaimed Dad.

"So, in other words, the top of the head has to get wet, right?"

"Exactly!" affirmed Dad.

"Well, that's exactly what we Methodists do," grinned the traveling parson. "We get them right where you agreed it has to get wet—on top of the head!"

Dad roared with laughter. Although he believed passionately in immersion, he told this story often, lightening up conversations about baptism. Although he took baptism seriously, he took himself lightly. The jokes he told on himself were his most uproarious. Dogmatic he was, but his appreciation of a droll story never left him.

Dad's missionary colleagues affectionately began to call him the "itinerant Baptist preacher" as they referred to his travels by horseback through the mountains of Colombia. Mom did not join him on these treks, unsure about riding horseback. Dad, ever eager to get her to join him in everything he did, got her a horse of her own and encouraged her to mount. Ever so tentatively she tried him out. To her surprise, she found she liked the horse: "He's smooth riding...even for me. I think I'm going to become an enthusiast after all." She did ride with Dad a few times, on short outings, but never quite qualified as an enthusiastic horsewoman.

They often discussed where their lives could best be spent in the cause of missions. One night, Dad said to Mom, "Wilda, honey, I don't think this province of Norte de Santander is the place to spend too much time. It's cold and fanatical."

"It's definitely hostile to the gospel," agreed Mom.

"If other places are more receptive, why not try to reach them?"

"Maybe the Lord is judging our faithfulness rather than our results," suggested Mom.

"True, but I also want to use common sense. I'm not too sure it's His will for us to just 'grin and bear it.'"

"That's what most missionaries around here seem to do."

"Yes, and after five years they have little more to show for their work than after one year."

"We surely want His will above all else, and I know He'll lead," assured Mom.

"I'm praying much about missionary radio station HCJB, but have no definite leading from the Lord yet."

"Dad and Mom Savage keep writing us letters encouraging us to be patient."

"Let's pray about it," said Dad, "because I'm awfully discouraged and you know I'm not the kind to get that way easily."

In May 1944 there was revolution in Colombia, and Liberals took over from Conservatives. This was an enormous relief to my parents, because Liberals were in favor of religious liberty, and this gave them some assurance that they would have protection from the police.

It was not to be. May was the Month of the Virgin, the most important for the church in Chinácota. Each day in May, one neighborhood erected an altar to the Virgin. There was a daily procession, going from church to altar and back. This was accompanied by a two-week "Mission" during which Catholic devotion and loyalty were brought to a high tide. Everyone was encouraged to suppress and hate all influences that harmed the Roman faith. As a result, we got cold, hateful looks from people on the streets and kids shouted at us: "Long live the Virgin" and "Down with the Protestants."

One night was dubbed "anti-Protestant night" and many deliberate lies were told about the Protestant missionaries. The road leading up to the altar of the Virgin went past our home. Mom and Dad cringed as over 200 men marched with torches, chanting in minor tunes about the Virgin, accompanied by women and children shouting insults against Protestants. Dad wrote about the dramatic night and described it with indignation:

The darkness, blindness, and superstition of the people has never weighed upon me so heavily. How is it possible to free them from this condition? If God would only give us the apostolic power of making the lame to walk, or the blind to see, then perhaps these disillusioned, gullible followers of this perverted religious system would have their eyes opened to the truth.

I tell them, "Thus saith the Lord!" That should be enough. But it is not enough to convince them. I can present overwhelming evidence against the falsity of their system, but it doesn't mean a thing to them. If the priest says something, they swallow it hook, line, and sinker, even if there is nothing Biblical, logical, or Christian about it.

I was a blissful child, and none of these things affected me, oblivious to the fear and worry afflicting my folks. My life in Chinácota was a child's paradise, idyllic, with an abundance of fruits and vegetables, children next door who played with me, and a little sister who held my fascination. Dad wrote with gusto about his little family: "As a family, we've been the happiest ever. Ours is an absolutely perfect family. I share Wilda's exuberance over 4-month old Carolita. She possesses an indescribably sweet something that gets into your heart's depths and starts tugging. This afternoon Steve let his 'old nature' take over and hit his sister, for which he received the ping pong paddle punishment. Tonight he prayed: 'Oh God, bless me 'cause I did hit my bean on the post; and bless Carol for I did hit her on the head; and bless Mommy for she did spank me with the ping pong paddle.'"

Mom and Dad kept pecking away at this stone wall of fanaticism that had saturated the lives, culture, education, and activities of Colombia for over four centuries. A wonderful reward for their efforts came when Eduardo's wife finally gave in and joined her husband. "The glorious conversion of Doña Pepa has been a brilliant glow during these trying weeks," said Mom.

Violence in Colombia was due not only to religious conflict. Some of the fury was political, most was due simply to an absence of law and order. It was not unlike the raw and rough days of the opening of the West in the United States. Bandits in Colombia roamed freely, and robbery was common. Sometimes innocent missionaries became victims of a ferocity that agitated the entire nation of Colombia, robbed it of its productive potential, and terrorized Colombians and foreigners alike. On one trip Wilf Watson was almost murdered. The attack had nothing to do with his being a missionary or an American—it was simply the desperate act of a crazy bus driver.

Dad and Wilf Watson and eight other missionaries took a trip down the Magdalena River to attend a conference. To get to the river they had to travel northwestward over the Sierra de Perija, into Ocaña, and thence down into the Magdalena River valley. As the bus went down the perpendicular mountain sides, Dad peered out the window and realized there were only inches between bus tires and chasm—and no guard rails. Several times the passengers had to get out and walk over log bridges where the road had washed out, while the chauffeur coaxed his bus across. Finally the bus could go no further. A bridge had washed out. There was barely enough space for the bus to turn around and the driver had to jockey it back and forth, slipping in the mud as he went from forward to reverse and back. The ten missionaries got out, unloaded their bags, and prepared to transfer from bus to cable car to continue their journey.

Wilf was paying for all ten missionaries, and gave the driver 20 pesos per passenger, the price they had agreed on. The chauffeur demanded 30.

Wilf refused to pay saying, "You agreed on 20 pesos and that's what I'm paying you."

Without warning, the driver tore out a dagger and pounced on Wilf like a flash of lightning. As he thrust it into Wilf's shoulder, the handle of the dagger broke. Enraged, the chauffeur ran into a nearby house, grabbed an axe, and rushed back.

Wilf had hidden behind a shed, and as the mad driver rushed past, Dad hauled out his billfold and offered him the additional 10 pesos he wanted. But the man was so crazed that he scorned the money and continued to search for Wilf. Dad kept walking with the chauffeur as he continued his frenzied pursuit of Wilf. With words of calm and reason, Dad gradually quieted the madman. Eventually he took the money, clambered back into his bus, and drove away.

Quickly, Dad and the other missionaries grabbed Wilf and climbed into the cable cars that whisked them across the chasm. Wilf was bleeding freely from the wound on his back below his left shoulder, but no doctor was available until they got to Ocaña an hour and a half later. On the way, the missionaries said to one another, "It was a miracle the handle of the dagger broke, or Wilf would have been killed." Dad concluded, "It's better to get gypped than butchered." It was not a flip remark. Missionaries often agonized over the issue of bribery, the existence of which was standard daily fare in Latin America. Some felt it was simply part of the price one had to pay for goods and services, and even the strict-minded Bob Savage occasionally was inclined to pay an extra "tip" or "fee," usually after being coerced by a bland civil servant, such as a customs agent from whom he was trying to get clearance to bring possessions into the country, or an assistant consul from whom Dad needed a rubber stamp on his passport. In the case of Wilf Watson, it was truly a matter of saving his colleague's life, and Dad did not hesitate to pay the extra pesos, admitting he had been blackmailed, choosing it as the lesser of two evils.

Although Dad had faced angry mobs in Pamplona and Chinácota, he never had been physically hurt. However, Mom and Dad were both keenly aware that danger was always at hand, and Mom worried about her husband whenever he traveled. Her fears were not unfounded, for one of Dad's best friends was viciously murdered. Cecil Dye, co-publisher with Dad of the chorus book, *Cloud Club Choruses*, worked as a missionary in Bolivia. Dad had seriously considered working there with his friend and had been invited to be leader of a group that went into the Bolivian jungles to contact unreached Indians. One day, he was casually reading the Bogotá newspaper and was stunned to read that Cecil Dye and four of his missionary colleagues had been killed by those very Indians. Dad and Mom got down on their knees, prayed for the families of the martyred missionaries, and thanked God that Dad had not been part of that party. The entire missionary community was shaken, and each "soldier of the cross" realized more than ever how vulnerable his life was. Over the centuries since the birth of Christ countless martyrs had died for their faith, and the twentieth century was no exception.

Death came not only through martyrdom. Tropical disease was ever present, ominous, threatening. Most missionaries had bouts with malaria, parasites, yellow jaundice, and other diseases for which their bodies were ill-prepared. Harvey Hammond, who had helped inspire Mom and Dad to go to the mission field, paid the ultimate sacrifice of his calling as a missionary. He had gone on a trip to the Motiloni Indian tribes, in the hot lowlands of Eastern Colombia. He expected to be back in six weeks, but did not return. Many weeks passed while his wife Georgienna fretted and prayed. Finally a telegram arrived telling of Harvey's death 21 days earlier. Malaria had struck him down.

Again, it could have been Dad. He had considered going with Hammond's mission, the Evangelical Union of South America, and pondered in a letter written home in April, 1943: "It was a terrific shock to hear of Harvey Hammond's death. I might have been on that trip if we had decided to go with Evangelical Union of South America. The Motiloni section is considered by all missionaries as the most difficult to reach in this part of South America. Please rest assured that my trips will have no comparison whatsoever to the danger of going in to the Motilonis."

Dad's philosophy of missionary work continued to crystallize as he contemplated the example of the Apostle Paul who founded many churches rather than staying in one church. He wrote to churches in the United States that supported us:

> The popular missionary policy here is to secure one missionary for every small group of believers. Missionaries become pastors. The missionary is usually retained even after the local church has a national pastor.

> I feel a missionary's job is to found a work, then make himself unnecessary. I can't picture the Apostle Paul becoming the pastor of 20 or 30 believers and staying there forever as so many missionaries do today.

> If we adopt Paul's missionary policies, we should be able to found one or more new congregations every year. Jim tells me the *llanos* churches in Venezuela have been founded on this plan, and they have become healthier spiritually than groups dependent upon full-time help of a missionary.

> This conviction has influenced our plans for the coming year. We will let our Chinácota group run itself in the future, with the help of frequent visits by missionaries. By "abandoning" a work and leaving it to rely on its own resources, I think we are following the New Testament plan.

A generation later, the idea of a missionary turning the work over to nationals and establishing "indigenous" works became the norm. But in 1943 it was not common practice, and Dad's vision was years ahead of his time.

Despite his interest in developing the local church, Dad dreamed more and more about missionary radio station HCJB, with its powerful short wave transmitters, where he could be part of a worldwide ministry and get results in the thousands rather than dozens. He wrote his father:

> In Quito we could make profitable use of our musical gifts. Moreover, in a city Quito's size, there are many unevangelized sections presenting opportunities for Sunday Schools and branch works. One suburb of a city can present greater opportunities for spreading the gospel than a complete municipality like Chinácota.
>
> We are eager to work in Quito and feeling led that way. Maybe we were trying to rush the Lord last year. I feel that he wanted us to have this Chinácota experience, hard though it has been. We have learned lessons we couldn't have learned elsewhere.

Correspondence flowed often between Quito and Chinácota. Mom and Dad finally felt sure the Lord was leading them to the little country that straddled the equator. Once the decision was firm, their first order of business was to call on Eduardo and Pepa, our next door neighbors, best friends, and pillars of the young and struggling church. "Eduardo and Pepa," began Dad, "we are going to leave Chinácota and move to Quito in Ecuador."

Pepa gasped and began to cry. "But Roberto, you've just begun! There is so much more to do."

"Yes, Pepa, we've just begun, but from here on it is up to you. The church will grow and prosper under your leadership."

"But this is such a shock!" declared Eduardo. "We thought you'd be here for a long time. We love you and depend on you."

"That's why we must leave," said Dad, with voice choking. "We don't want you to depend on us, for you must carry on this work that God has begun. This is not Roberto Savage's work, nor is it Eduardo Gómez's work. Always remember, it is God's work. We will miss you, and we will love you always, but we must go."

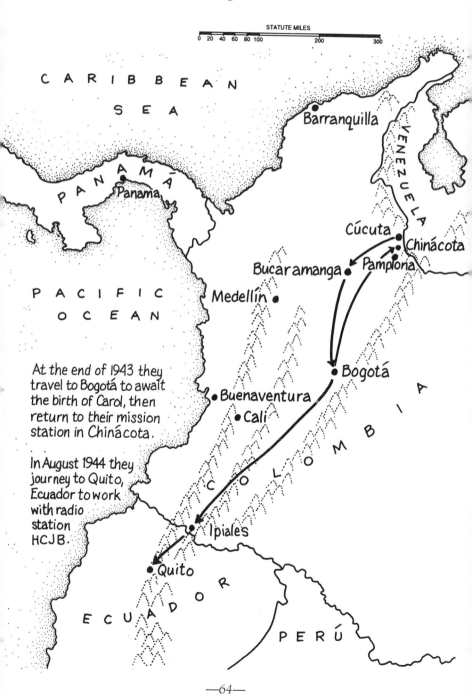

STATUTE MILES
0 20 40 60 80 100 .... 200 300

CARIBBEAN
SEA

Barranquilla

PANAMÁ

Panamá

VENEZUELA

Cúcuta
Chinácota
Pamplona
Bucaramanga

Medellín

PACIFIC
OCEAN

At the end of 1943 they
travel to Bogotá to await
the birth of Carol, then
return to their mission
station in Chinácota.

In August 1944 they
journey to Quito,
Ecuador to work
with radio
station
HCJB.

Buenaventura
Cali

Bogotá

COLOMBIA

Ipiales

Quito

ECUADOR

PERÚ

5

The Voice of the Andes

Faith is dead to doubts, dumb to discouragement, blind to
impossibilities.   —*Pocket Quips*, p.45

In August, 1944, a telegram arrived from Reuben Larson at HCJB
in Quito, Ecuador:

THE WAY IS CLEAR. COME IMMEDIATELY.

The four of us left Chinácota on August 23. But before we
could leave Colombia, we had to stop in Cúcuta to say goodbye to
our colleagues from the Scandinavian Alliance Mission. Wilf
Watson gave his friend a stout Scandinavian handshake and told
him, "I will always treasure you as my dearest friend."

The jolly Bob Savage was silent for a moment, then
brightened, assuring Wilf they would see each other again
someday. Then he added, "And if not in this life, Wilf, then let's
get together in heaven on the corner of Hallelujah Avenue and
Amen Boulevard!"

The next day we took a plane from Cúcuta to Bogotá and
stayed in the city of Carol's birth for a few days to get our family
passport renewed and extended to include Quito. Dad and I took
the trip by land from Bogotá to Ipiales, a town on the Ecuador-
Colombian border. Mom and Carol flew. Our overland trip was
filled with excitement for me, now nearly four years old. The first

day we traveled by train and had a mild wreck. Our coach derailed as the train pulled into the station. Luckily we were going slowly. The second day we got into a truck and traveled 18 hours, with six people crammed into the cab designed for four. The next three days, we changed modes of transportation from private car to bus to train, meeting missionaries in towns along the way. We visited the Christian and Missionary Alliance Bible Institute in Armenia, nestled between the western and central cordilleras, in the southwestern part of Colombia. The visit to the institute was a special celebration for Dad, for four students from Norte de Santander, the province where he had labored for two years, were now in attendance, preparing for life in the gospel ministry. He could leave Colombia satisfied that others were in place to carry on his work.

It took Dad and me five days to take the trip Mom and Carol made in three and a half hours in the airplane, but we enjoyed majestic scenery. Mom wrote that they spent most of their trip "carefully inspecting the sacks provided by Pan American Airways." Flights through passes in the high Andean mountain range called the Cordillera Oriental are about as rough as scenic mountain air can get.

At Ipiales, Dad and I boarded the plane and joined Carol and Mom for the last 45 minutes of flying to Quito, the place we would call home for the next quarter of a century. As the Douglas DC-3 flew down the valleys, over crystal blue crater lakes, between snow-capped mountains reaching up to over 20,000 feet, Dad peered out the window and gazed at the spectacular scenery, full of zeal for his new assignment and home.

The welcome we received in Quito was an outpouring of enthusiasm from the small staff of energetic radio missionaries. We were greeted in Russian, French, Swedish, Quechua (Andean Indian), Spanish, and English.

Mom and Dad were immediately caught up in the high-powered activity of the radio mission. They had barely unpacked their bags when Reuben Larson, founder of HCJB and station director, invited the young couple to sit in on an English radio program which was being broadcast live to the United States. Without warning Larson matter-of-factly announced into the microphone, "Now our newest missionary, the lovely young and talented Wilda Savage will come up to the microphone and give you a greeting."

Chagrined and flabbergasted, Mom turned pale. She had resolved never to speak on a radio broadcast, and had her speech ready to politely refuse the first time she was asked. But Larson had her on the spot. They were on live radio and she could hardly say no. She took a deep breath, stepped up to the mike, told the radio audience how happy she was to be in Quito and how much she looked forward to her ministry at HCJB. Then she announced, "I will now play a piano solo—'His Eye Is on the Sparrow.'" She walked over to the grand piano, sat down, and as she played out the sweet sounds, the song's words of comfort flooded her mind: "...if His eye is on the sparrow, then He'll surely care for you."

After the program, Mom sighed and had a moment of truth with herself: "The Lord certainly did care for me by getting me through my little speech on the radio. I never could have done it if I had thought about it ahead of time."

Mom and Dad were immediately assigned three daily broadcasts, one in English and two in Spanish. HCJB had been using 78-rpm records for 90 per cent of their vocal music; it was Mom and Dad's assignment to produce as much live music as possible.

Within three weeks, Dad was given the entire music responsibility, with over 600 broadcasts per month. Most were transcriptions of popular American programs, such as Charles Fuller's "Old Fashioned Revival Hour," Percy Crawford's "Haven of Rest" and the "Word of Life Hour."

Dad exulted as he began working with the two vigorous leaders of the World Radio Missionary Fellowship: Clarence Jones and Reuben Larson. For two years most of his enthusiastic and youthful ideas had been dashed with cold water and the comment,

"Brother Savage, we must not resolve these things too hastily." In Jones and Larson, Dad found two chiefs who not only gave him free rein to try his many ideas, but who pushed him to do even more.

Not only was my parents' task exciting, but their way of life enjoyable. They were impressed with living conditions enjoyed by many missionaries in Quito. After dwelling in simple and small houses in Pamplona and Chinácota, they were amazed to see how well a missionary could live. They wrote their parents: "The Larsons and Stearns have really ritzy homes, but we'll have to content ourselves with something humble for a while." The lovely and gracious Grace Larson took a one-month vacation and turned her house over to us—complete with her five servants, headed by Pedro, the amazing cook, who filled us with a constant array of marvelous cakes, pies, cookies, and desserts.

Dad was never quite sure what to make of this graceful style of living, for he had always thought being a missionary would automatically call for living in a rugged setting. However, in those days, a missionary could rent a nice home and hire a full-time cook and maid, at a fraction of the cost of similar help back in the United States. The missionary salary was modest—only $100 per month in 1944, but it covered all expenses, even the servants. However, servants were not considered a luxury. Missionary wives were expected to work hard at being missionaries. Evangelical missions in that era considered both husband and wife as full-time missionaries. It was a full generation before women in the United States were "liberated" from household duties. Who said missionaries were old-fashioned?! Indeed, before a couple was accepted for missionary service, the mission board carefully examined them both to make sure each marriage partner was genuinely called to this life. Therefore the mission encouraged its missionaries to hire servants, freeing up both spouses to devote all their time to real missionary work.

Dad wrote his father: "My desire to be busy has been satisfied. I come to the studio building at 8:00 a.m., finish up at 9:30 p.m., then listen to the English broadcast from 9:30 to 10:00 before heading home. I like it this way and am rejoicing."

They even got me, age four, involved in broadcasting: "Steve has been regularly broadcasting for several Sundays now and feels like a real big shot. He sings one solo on the Spanish Sunday School program on Sunday evenings at 6:00 p.m. He really lets out all the stops and has not shown a speck of mike fright."

Although Dad was immersed with radio broadcasting, he began to think of other ways to take the gospel to the people of Ecuador. After all, he reasoned, most people did not have radios. There had to be other ways. One idea was to get a "gospel truck" to travel all over Ecuador and take the gospel to various towns. The truck would have built-in sound equipment as well as movie projectors, so a service could be held wherever a crowd might gather.

The idea became crystallized and an army surplus truck was purchased. The back end of the enclosed vehicle was rigged with sound equipment, movie projectors, and a good supply of gospel literature and Scripture portions.

A new missionary couple, Abe and Dolores VanDerPuy, were scheduled to arrive soon in Quito, and Abe's first assignment would be to carry the gospel all over Ecuador in the sound truck. Dad began to picture what it would be like to work with Abe in this ministry as he wrote: "We will call it the *radio rodante*—the rolling radio." Dad looked forward to the arrival of Abe, whom he had known at Wheaton College. The dynamic Abe, champion debater in college and powerful preacher, would soon become an important part of Dad's life. The two would work together closely to spread the gospel throughout Latin America.

Although Dad was deeply involved with his gospel ministry, his love for sports did not abate, and he maintained a keen interest in what was going on back in the States. Around the first of October, he talked to Clayton Howard, HCJB's chief engineer:

"Hey, Clayt, any chance we could tune in the World Series?"

"Yes, I think we can pick it up through Voice of America or the Armed Forces Radio," replied the radio technician.

"Do you know if the Tigers have won the American League pennant yet?"

"I haven't heard," said Clayton.

"Well, keep me posted," said Dad, "because if the Tigers won, I'll be sitting in here wasting a couple of hours a day in the ungainful occupation of listening to ball game reports. But, if the Yanks won, I won't waste my time going near a radio."

Dad not only enjoyed reading about sports; he enjoyed participating. After two years with no opportunity to play sports in Colombia, he resumed his love affair with tennis and began playing every Monday. He wrote his mother: "I've been dedicating Monday afternoons to that terrible vice my father led me into. Dick Larson has a membership at a tennis club here, and it certainly seemed good to swing a racquet after a two-year layoff." The Quito tennis club boasted several red clay courts, surrounded by tall and graceful eucalyptus trees. I often accompanied Dad on Monday mornings in those pre-school years, chasing balls until my interest waned, then playing hide-and-seek with children of the Ecuadorian gardeners. We hid among thick hedges that lined the gardens of the club, and always knew what the score was, for Dad announced each point with a clapping bark, a yelp of glee whenever he or anyone else scored a point.

"Organ Interludes" became a popular program in Ecuador, as Mom played the organ and Marco Paredes, a Spanish-speaking announcer, introduced the hymns. Marco was not a Christian, and HCJB missionaries prayed for him daily, hoping his involvement with gospel programs would lead him to a personal saving knowledge of Christ.

HCJB did not use missionaries for Spanish broadcasts, preferring to use nationals like Marco who had perfect accents. However, when Dad preached at the local church, the service was broadcast and he preached in Spanish over radio waves for the first time. He wrote his father with enthusiasm: "Despite my imperfect Yankee pronunciation, when the invitation was given, seven fine young people publicly confessed Christ as Savior." Dad was being modest, for his accent in Spanish was actually quite good and getting better. He was elated with the experience of preaching to hundreds, perhaps even thousands, how many he could not tell for there was no way HCJB could statistically measure its audience. The only clue of their effectiveness was letters from listeners. Soon after his first broadcast in Spanish, Dad got a letter from an enthusiastic admirer, the first of hundreds he would receive from listeners across Latin America. This stream of correspondence continued, unabated, ever increasing, until it reached over ten thousand letters a year in the early 1960's.

The atmosphere in Quito was a dramatic contrast to Chinácota, and Mom wrote her mother:

> For the first time, we are not burdened with that overwhelming feeling of terrible oppression. I believe it is because there is such a strong group of Christians here together and we feel the presence of the Lord. In Chinácota we felt so alone. Had I not been there I would never have been able to understand what some missionaries go through and how Satan can hold such sway. A missionary in that position needs a furlough, not from overwork, but to save him from a complete breakdown due to that unexplainable something that comes upon him.

Dad reflected about Ecuador as it contrasted with Colombia:

> Quito is sloppier, dirtier, and less progressive than Bogotá, but Ecuador is more colorful and picturesque than Colombia. There were no Indians near Pamplona or Chinácota, but in Quito at least half the people are full-blooded Indians. They stroll down the cobblestone streets wearing blazing loud colors, funny hats, carry their babies on their backs, and herd their sheep and goats down the main street.

The temperature in Quito is about like October in Illinois. When you get up in the morning, the house feels about like that time of year in the United States when we debate whether or not to start the furnace. It is chilly, but when the sun gets going there is no discomfort. At mid-day we can have a picnic lunch outside, but at night a topcoat feels comfortable. Although we are only ten miles south of the Equator, the elevation is nearly 10,000 feet so the climate is moderate year around.

The busier Mom and Dad got, the happier they seemed to be. Mom declared, "We are as happy as any people you ever did see and everything has been working out wonderfully. I am so full of praise to the Lord to think He has let us be in missionary work, yet in the type of work we enjoy most."

Dad plunged into many events besides radio, and crammed his Sundays full of meetings, starting with early morning services in the jail, English worship at 10:00, and continuing with the Spanish service at 11:00 in the same building. Then he gamely pressed on with three broadcasts in the afternoon and evening.

He found his prison ministry fascinating. Each Sunday morning he went with a group of missionaries and Ecuadorian nationals to Quito's infamous *Panóptico*, the medieval fortress on the south end of Quito. After being admitted through a series of iron doors which clanged shut behind him, past cells stinking of urine, he emerged into the open-air courtyard in the center of the prison. Prisoners were usually standing around, some playing volleyball, others kicking a soccer ball. All Dad had to do was start blowing his trumpet and dozens of prisoners gathered round. He got them singing gospel songs, to their great merriment, then preached with his usual fervor. Each member of the team assisted, giving personal testimonies, passing out gospel tracts, and adding volume to the singing. Often, prisoners would make a profession of faith in Christ, and Dad hoped their commitment would stick.

His life was full. He had never been more content. The only

thing he missed was his horses, and he wrote, "I haven't been on a horse since leaving Colombia, and it 'makes me a lot of lack' as they say in Spanish."

In late 1944, HCJB began broadcasting on its new and more powerful 19-meter wave. Mom and Dad's *"Melodías Sagradas"* was the first program to go out on the new transmitter.

Reuben Larson was the superb administrator of HCJB while Clarence Jones was the sweeping visionary. Jones began to talk of establishing various radio stations around South America. He even talked of radio in Africa. He took a tour through Latin America to determine which countries should be targets for setting up additional local stations.

As the year 1944 ended, Mom wrote about how much she loved Quito and the work at HCJB: "Maybe we sound like we're putting it on thick, but we can't help but rave about Quito and HCJB. We are loving it, and oh, the Lord is showing more and more how definitely He was leading us. We are so thrilled over Marco Paredes, the fellow who was announcing our 'Melodías Sagradas' program. He accepted the Lord last week and said the program had been the means of convincing him of his need of a Savior. He gave his testimony on our program tonight."

Each person with whom my parents came into contact was a prospect for the kingdom of heaven, and nothing gave them greater joy than to see one of the HCJB Ecuadorian employees come to a decision to follow Christ. They would have preferred hiring people who were already evangelical believers, but the needs of a growing mission required the help of many skilled people, and they often had to reach outside the evangelical community to find the assistance they needed. Once hired, however, that person became a target of evangelism and it was rare to find an employee who could resist the daily witness of the missionaries whom he had joined as colleagues. Marco Paredes, with his splendid radio voice, had been hired to announce the news, then had been given a few spots on the gospel programs.

Now that he was genuinely converted, he was set free to work with the missionaries on a variety of projects, and he would soon prove his worth.

The year 1945 commenced with the publication of Dad's first book in Spanish, *Estudios Elementales* (Elementary Studies), a series of twelve lessons for new converts. Back in Colombia, Dad's colleague, Elof Anderson, who had spent hours arguing with Dad about the need to train new believers before baptism as the two rode horseback through the mountains of Eastern Colombia, declared happily, "Well, imagine that! Bob Savage wanted to save 'em and baptize 'em, but now he's got a regular course of studies—a catechism, no less—to get the new converts ready for baptism." Dad's eagerness to baptize new converts had not diminished, but he was now more aware of their lack of theology and saw a clear need to ground new believers in fundamentals of the faith.

Dad had modest expectations for the book and wrote to his parents: "I trust it will be a useful and helpful publication." He could not imagine that his little book would go through scores of printing runs and enjoy continuous use for the next five decades.

His plans for book publishing were not limited to books of Christian doctrine. He was already beginning to capture the vision of publishing a chorus book in Spanish, as he became aware of the small number of hymns that formed the body of hymnology in Latin American churches. He wanted to get going on the project immediately, but his missionary schedule was so hectic that he decided to wait until he went on furlough to the United States. His year of "furlough," scheduled for 1947, promised him the time required. Meanwhile, he began to gather music and organize the hymns and choruses that would form the book.

Grandma Ruby Johnson was scheduled to come and visit us, but the uncertainty of air travel in 1945 made her arrival date a suspense. We made six trips to the airport, only to be disappointed each time. Then, wouldn't you know it, one day Grandma suddenly arrived—but no one was there to meet her. She had been detained for several days in Panama and had sent several cables, but none had reached us.

When she arrived in a taxi at the radio station, confused and disoriented, Grace Larson, the lovely "grand dame" of HCJB, found her and escorted her immediately to the studio where Mom was in the middle of her program, "Organ Interludes." Mom caught a glimpse of her mother in the control room and could hardly continue playing. As soon as the red "on the air" light went out, she dashed out of the studio and into the arms of her mother.

The day after, Grace took charge of Grandma Ruby, sweeping her and our whole family through a tour to see the highly ornamented Roman Catholic churches of Quito. The most impressive was *La Compañía*, for its entire interior was inlaid with gold leaf. The gold was lustrous, the inside of the church ornate with intricate sculpture, filled with images of saints and grotesque medieval paintings showing condemned human creatures suffering in Hell, enveloped forever in flames, lashed, kicked, pummeled, and nailed to crosses by smirking, snarling demons.

Missionaries always liked to show this church to visitors, for it was not only impressive in its gilded beauty and gory art, but made a dramatic point: The Catholics, they said, had taken all that money from starving people of Ecuador, and instead of spending it on food, had squandered it on gaudy gold and worthless images. Dad could never look at the astonishing gold interior of *La Compañía* without emitting a "harrumph" of disgust. His loathing deepened as he considered the carved images of saints and observed devout parishioners kneeling before them, eyes full of hope, praying to the figures, which Dad considered nothing but idols. "Idolatry!" he exclaimed, "pure and simple. Right before our very eyes, the Catholics blatantly violate the first of the Ten Commandments: 'Thou shalt have no other gods before me.' What do they think those saints are if they aren't 'other gods.' Look at the way these poor people worship those images. It's awful, just plain awful."

We departed the church, shaken, and moved on to happier sights. We visited Quito's ancient Inca ruins, for Quito had been the northern capital of the fabled empire, and monuments to this sophisticated civilization still remained. Grandma was particularly impressed with the *Panecillo*, a hill that arose on the south end of the venerable city. Atop this mound, the Incas had built a magnificent temple, remnants of which still attested to the intelligence and industry of this splendid society. Again Dad could not help but comment with disdain how Spanish conquerors, goaded on by their priests, had mercilessly destroyed this sovereign kingdom.

Grandma enjoyed her six months in Quito immensely except for one thing: fleas. We had fleas; everybody in Quito had fleas. Fleas were a part of life there, aided by the cool climate from which fleas tried to flee. We had fleas in carpets, bedsprings, mattresses, and household pets. "The fleas are feasting on great banquets from my anatomy," cried out our scratching Grandma.

Dad tried to reassure her: "The first few months in Quito are doomed to be a time of suffering from fleas. After that, the fleas are still present, but your constitution gets immune and you don't notice them."

"I haven't gotten immune yet after two years," exclaimed Mother, blowing that bit of science all to bits.

The fleas were a nuisance, but a minor one, for living in Quito was a constant experience of beauty. From skytop Quito, we frequently beheld four or five snow-capped peaks towering toward the heavens in unexcelled majesty and grandeur. Grandma Ruby Johnson described it as "the most picturesque city in the world—and I've been in many countries."

Dad said, "Many people call it the 'land of eternal spring.'"

"I think 'eternal November' would be more fitting," added Mom.

"Yes," said Grandma, "the weather is perfect at midday but chilly in the evenings and early mornings."

"It's the kind of climate a football fan likes best on Saturday afternoon during the grid season," mused Dad, ever the sports fan.

"The sun sure gives kids rosy cheeks and healthy tans," remarked Grandma.

"There's not much atmosphere here at 10,000 feet to block the strong rays of the sun," said Mom. "I used to worry it might be too much, but they get used to it."

Grandma's visit coincided with a piece of legislation that hit the missionaries like a bombshell. The Ecuadorian Congress passed a law declaring that no foreigners be permitted to own or operate any newspaper or radio station. The HCJB staff gathered to pray, for the very survival of the radio mission was at stake. "Oh, Lord," intoned Dad. "before the mountains were brought forth, or ever Thou hadst formed the earth and the world, even from everlasting, Thou art God. Look down upon us today, we pray Thee, and gird us up with Thy strength. Soften the hearts of the legislators, and let not Thy work which Thou hast called us to do here in Ecuador be destroyed." Dad's prayers always sounded a triumphant note even in the midst of despair, and his sweeping vision of a grand and almighty God who was above and beyond the little problems caused by puny human laws, kept him always looking up, always positive, always rejoicing.

The events that followed seemed to confirm that the Lord had indeed looked down and was answering Dad's prayer. HCJB was popular with most Ecuadorians, so congressional opponents of the law used the missionary station as the focus for arguing that the law should be rescinded. Even proponents of the new law agreed that HCJB was performing a valuable service, and did not want it destroyed. Arguments hit front pages of daily newspapers and HCJB's prestige was enhanced as many favorable speeches were made. Furthermore, HCJB broadcast all sessions of Congressional debates—free.

The government of Ecuador had strong socialist tendencies and there was occasional talk of government take-over of all radio stations. Although the general attitude towards HCJB remained positive, the controversy kept the missionaries on pins and needles as they realized how precarious their status was. Many Latin American countries had passed restrictive laws making it difficult for missionaries. Perú required all gospel services to be held behind closed doors, and Ecuador had a law that no foreign *religiosos* were to be given entrance into the country. However, because the Ecuadorian government was friendly to HCJB, they got around that one by declaring its missionaries were not *religiosos* but *propagandistas*. Thus the work of HCJB carried on, and the Bible verse from Zechariah that formed HCJB's theme was once again confirmed: "Not by might, nor by power, but by my Spirit, saith the Lord God of Hosts."

Occasionally, my folks managed to slip away from their duties at the radio station and visit other parts of Ecuador. While Grandma Ruby was in town, we took her on several journeys, discovering for the first time, along with her, some of the wonders that made Ecuador such a very special place to us. The more time we spent in that equatorial land, the more fond we became of its people, geography, and history.

We had not seen many Indians during our two years in Colombia, for the descendants of the mighty Incas did not live in Eastern Colombia. My parents and grandmother were fascinated as we traveled into the northern highlands of Ecuador, to a town called Otavalo. As we drove north on the cobblestoned Pan American highway, we found a remarkable group of people, posterity of the noble Incas, who had their own culture nestled in the Andean Mountain *páramo*—high grasslands 8,000 feet and higher.

We took the train back home, an adventure that inspired Dad to write:

Otavalo is only five hours from Quito, but one feels like he has been transplanted to another country, situated in the shadows of Mt. Imbabura, a 17,000-foot extinct volcano.

Missionaries who work here must learn both Spanish and Quechua.

The men all wear long braids down their back, and at first I was puzzled as to who were men and who were women. But I soon learned that women could be distinguished by their jewelry, with ten or more strings of imitation gold and red beads covering their arms from wrist to elbow. Even when they are out hoeing corn, they wear their elaborate adornments.

You would have been particularly interested in their irrigation ditches, built by Incas before the coming of Spaniards over 500 years ago. I saw one ditch tunneled through the mountainside, a most remarkable engineering feat, accomplished several centuries before dynamite could blast through hard rock and surveyor's transits could point a level route for tunnels through mountains.

This Otavalo tribe of Indians is one of the most extraordinary people one could hope to encounter. They are primitive and happy to remain isolated from contacts with civilization, but put to shame most country folk I've seen in Colombia and Ecuador; their homes are better built, neater, and cleaner.

There is something romantic about visiting them and thinking of the grandeur and elegance of the civilization their forefathers produced centuries ago, before the Spaniards came to enslave them and grind them into pitiful submission. And the "whites" (in Ecuador, anyone who was not a full-blooded indian was called a white) still have that same cruel spirit towards Indians that Spaniards introduced centuries ago, a mindless bigotry in a land where color discrimation would seem the last thing one would expect.

Coming back on the train I saw scenes that made my heart ache. Second-class passage is in box cars, and benches are placed length-wise, seating four rows of people. Most passengers stand. At a couple of stations there was no room for many to get on, and if they were Indians the train officials kicked and abused them, taking their wide-brimmed hats and throwing them like boomerangs, to the amusement of others.

Dad was one of the least class-conscious people I have ever known. He showed equal interest in the lives of Indians and whites, rich and poor, educated and illiterate. They were God's creatures, and his friends. He brooked no prejudice.

Back home in Quito, Mom developed a sharp pain in her lower right abdomen. A local doctor diagnosed it as appendicitis and advised her to have surgery. Medical help was adequate in Quito, but not great. Mother had to have an appendectomy and the best doctor in Ecuador, or at least the one we Americans felt most comfortable with, was an American, Dr. Parker, who lived in the coastal city of Guayaquil, Ecuador's major port. Grandma Ruby was eager to see all the sights in Ecuador, and wanted to be with her daughter during the operation, so we traveled to the big, hot, steamy city. It was our first trip out of the mountains and the descent from 10,000 feet to sea level took us into an altogether different world. The coastal region of Ecuador is one of the world's most productive areas for bananas and cacao. Thousands of acres of banana plantations lined the road, and we bought delicious sweet bananas only minutes after they had been whacked off the tree. What impressed me most was cacao beans, because Dad told me they eventually became Hershey bars.

Mom's surgery was uneventful, but in those days a patient had to stay in the hospital for two weeks before release. Grandma Ruby spent several hours a day with her and Dad popped in on Mom frequently. His visits were always short, for he had a definite philosophy about hospital visits. As pastor, he always kept his hospital visits down to five minutes, enough time, he felt, to cheer up the patient and have prayer, but not too long to wear the hospitalized person (or himself) out. He was convinced enough about the correctness of this plan that he even applied it to his wife. She was happy with his short visits for he burst in often, always full of cheer.

Dad spent most of his time in Guayaquil visiting churches and missionaries in the sprawling tropical metropolis. He was fascinated with contrasts he saw between Quito and Guayaquil, and when he wrote his parents he compared mountain and coastal cities: "Guayaquil is hot, but progressive and modern. Quito is picturesque, but dirty, stinky, and backward. The two cities are of about equal size, but stores and streets of Guayaquil far outclass those of Quito. Guayaquil is one of the best spots for the gospel in all of South America. One of the two evangelical churches is the biggest gospel church on the west coast of South America. I have an invitation to preach there next Sunday."

Dad and Mom had arranged to have her operation coincide with an evangelical campaign. He had been invited to conduct a series of meetings at the Gospel Missionary Union church in Guayaquil. While Mom recovered quietly in the hospital, Dad conducted a campaign each night. He blew back to the hospital after his first meeting, exulting, bubbling over, for he had just finished preaching to the biggest crowds he had seen since leaving the United States. Between 250 and 300 were present each night and "the Lord gave us 45 conversions—mostly adult men."

Dad had some misgivings about accepting the invitation for a full week of meetings, for he did not feel he knew Spanish fluently yet. He accepted, however, thinking he'd be preaching only once each night. He was stunned when he found they had him scheduled for a daily chapel service at the Bible Institute, a half hour radio broadcast, plus music and preaching at night. Never one to say no, he gamely carried on, and even conducted instruction classes for those who had accepted Christ. He used his new book, *Estudios Elementales*, and said to Henry Klaasen, who pastored the Gospel Missionary Union church: "It doesn't make so much difference to me when we baptize new believers, as long as we start giving them instruction immediately after conversion instead of putting them on a year of probation before letting them become eligible for a catechism or baptism class."

"Yes," replied Klaasen, "it would be wonderful if every

evangelistic campaign would be followed immediately by several days of special classes for those who accepted Christ during their meetings."

"I for one," promised Dad, "intend to follow that idea."

We returned to Quito amid the heartening tidings that the Allies had entered Berlin. The savor of victory was exciting even to those of us who were far from our own shores, in another continent, another world. Grandma made plans to return to the United States to join Grandpa Lawrence, who would soon be getting out of the Army and returning to his civilian work as attorney for Hartford Insurance Company. But shortly before Grandma returned to the United States, the world was shaken with stunning news: our American leader, the one who had led us through years of depression and war, was dead. The Savage and Johnson families were rock-ribbed Republicans, yet the death of President Franklin Roosevelt affected them deeply. Mom was at the organ ready to play vespers when the news came at 5:00 p.m. A huge lump formed in her throat and she immediately changed her broadcast plans and began to play "Nearer My God to Thee."

Ecuador proclaimed three days of mourning, so even the Spanish programs took on a solemn nature. Our Ecuadorian friends shared with us their deepest sympathy, in their gracious and formal manner: *"Le doy el pésame por el fallecimiento de su amado presidente."* The English translation does not convey the style and grace of Spanish for it merely renders: "I give you my condolences for the death of your president." The word *pésame* is far richer than "condolence" because it expresses a deeper feeling of grief, a sharing of burden, and a sense of pain the English word doesn't capture. But it was not just the words that made the sympathy so loving. It was the way they said it. Latin Americans were not afraid to weep, or hug, or cry out in lament. They taught us stiff Anglo-Saxons how to feel, and as the years went by, we too became more passionate, more romantic, more open.

After Grandma Ruby returned to the United States, Mom and

Dad continued to explore the enchanting country of Ecuador, usually taking Carol and me with them. They were particularly fascinated with the Indians. They were aghast at the disregard the Ecuadorians had for the Indians. Sometimes it was worse than mere indifference; it could get downright cruel. One day as we rode the *autocarril*, a one-car train, we saw a horrifying sight: an Indian was desperately trying to pull his burro off the tracks as the train bore down upon them. The train's engineer made no attempt to slow, but plowed on, swiping the burro's rear end and sending the poor creature tumbling into the chasm below. Engineer and passengers laughed, but we looked back and saw the Indian with tears streaming down his face. He had lost not only his means of livelihood but his best friend. We were heartbroken by the scene and sickened by the evil and careless reaction of train driver and passengers.

Often Dad traveled alone, usually with the objective of preaching to a group of Christian believers in a remote area. One day he took a trip to the mining town of Macuchi. To get there he had to travel by train, truck, and mule. He described the exotic journey in a letter to the church back in Washington, D.C.:

...and of the three modes of transportation, the mule was the most comfortable. Trains were crammed tight. Even in first class, there were as many standing as sitting. On outdoor platforms between coaches, mobs paid the first class price. A big sign said "prohibited to ride on platforms" but 20 people did just that. On second class, they even rode on top in vast numbers.

The truck had two rows of seats in the front, with cargo in the rear. I chose to be part of the freight, figuring I could sleep better sprawled out on top of the baggage rather than crammed in with fourteen other people. I rode on top of the load from 4:30 a.m. until 9:00 a.m. When it got light I stood up to see where we were going. I looked for the road but couldn't find any. We were rumbling across unmarked terrain.

It didn't seem to bother our driver. He appeared to know exactly where he was going. I saw only an occasional track where another truck had gone.

We crossed a high *páramo* (mountain plateau) and I had on long underwear, suit, bathrobe, leather riding chaps, a poncho, and a big piece of oil cloth as a wind breaker—but still I shivered—and we live only a few miles from the Equator in the TORRID zone! It says so on the maps, and that's what I thought before I came to this land.

The truck driver was a wizard, nonchalantly lumbering through river beds. Often he would come to narrow spots in the road with perpendicular rock walls on each side. He wouldn't even slow down as the truck barely cleared an inch or two on each side. Some hairpin curves were too much for the truck so the chauffeur took half a turn, backed up, then calmly continued around.

For the first time in my life I saw llamas—hundreds of them, the most austere and sedate looking critters I've ever seen. They were used as pack animals, mostly to haul firewood. I watched them in amazement as they were loaded with several dozen logs hung on each side of their rugged backs, as they climbed up and down slippery and steep trails with sure-footed precision.

The mule trip was five hours mostly downhill through mud holes so deep that legends have formed about them. They told me a fellow was riding through some of this muck when he saw a hat floating on the water. He went over to pick it up and to his amazement found a man underneath it. He started to extricate the poor fellow from the mud, but the guy said to him, "Don't bother about me. I'm OK. I can still breathe. But, I would appreciate if you would help me remove the horse I'm riding."

At Macuchi, Dad got a warm welcome, not only from Ecuadorian Christian believers who were regular listeners to HCJB, but from 40 Americans who were "big shots" at the mine. Macuchi was chiefly a copper mine, although some gold was found. The lure of copper and gold had drawn many adventurers to this remote and lonely outpost.

While in Macuchi, Dad gathered together the small band of Christian believers, encouraged others to join, then played a few hymns on his trumpet to get everyone's attention. Several curiosity seekers wandered over. Dad welcomed them, thanked them for coming, and invited them to stay for the service. Several stayed, intrigued, while others slipped away inconspicuously.

Dad gave this little gathering of 25 souls the same vigorous meeting he gave to an audience of 1,000. He led them in singing, invited local believers to read the Scriptures and lead in prayer, then launched into his sermon. At the end, he invited those who had not yet done so, to accept Jesus as their Savior. Two responded affirmatively, and Dad stayed with them after the service, inviting experienced Christians to instruct new believers, for it was up to them to carry on the nurture of the work after he left. He offered the new Christians basic instruction in the faith, giving them a copy of *Estudios Elementales* (Elementary Studies).

On the return trip the truck was no longer running, so Dad spent two entire days on muleback, crossing the *páramo* with wind whipping and slashing, bitter cold and biting. Tired but uplifted he told us on his return, "Muleback is the only way to really see the country."

Carol and I played outside most of the time and our cheeks grew rosy in the Quito sunlight. Our house came equipped with a dog, monkey, parrot, and chickens. Our dog was a big mongrel named Jack who scared petty thieves from climbing over our wall and entering our house. We never worried too much about large-scale robbery, but everyone sought protection against the niggling thief who would sneak in at night and swipe one or two items. Most families, Ecuadorian and missionary alike, had high walls, festooned with colorful flowers, mostly geraniums, for they formed thick vines that crawled up the mud walls, splashing the barricade with joyous red florescence.

The high walls often had electric wire strung across the top, promising a good jolt to any thief that tried to storm the barricade. But the most effective protection was a snarling dog, and almost every family owned one. The only way a robber could overcome this final obstacle was to poison the dog. One morning I bounded out the door, then stopped, horrified, for there was Jack, lying dead in our walk in front of the gate. I cried loudly, "Mommy, come here!" She scurried out and put her arm around me. Dad followed a few seconds later. We looked at old Jack. The evidence was clear. In front of his mouth lay a piece of raw meat. Dad examined it.

"I believe it's laced with poison," he said sadly.

For me, the death of Jack was the first blow to my innocence, for up until then I had trusted everyone. Now I looked askance at every ragged person that walked by our gate and wondered if he were the evil creature that had killed our Jack.

Despite a tremendous amount of work at the radio station, Dad had a burning desire to establish churches in Quito and founded a neighborhood Sunday School near the radio station. They had a healthy start with 25 at the first meeting, and Dad began to encourage other missionaries to establish even more Sunday Schools: "We can't get too wrapped up in our radio work. We need four or five more Sunday Schools right away." Although other HCJB missionaries liked what Dad was doing, some felt their main calling was to be radio missionaries, and did not share his fervent desire to launch neighborhood Sunday Schools in Quito. Other missions, such as the Christian and Missionary Alliance, they felt, had missionaries in Quito whose specific job was to found churches. That didn't matter to Dad. He could think only of 200,000 lost souls surrounding him in Quito, and only 200 evangelical believers. There was a lot of work to do. He combed the neighborhood, visiting each home, passing out tracts, inviting all of HCJB's neighbors to come to church.

Within two weeks attendance had almost doubled—to 43 — and three men accepted Christ. One was a Colombian visiting Quito who had listened to *"Melodías Sagradas"* at home but had not made a commitment to Christ until he visited the radio station in Quito and attended Sunday School for the first time.

By autumn, the Sunday School Dad started in the summer had grown to 70 people crowding into a little room. The congregation began to dream and pray about building a new chapel, while Dad dreamed of starting other similar groups.

Work at the radio station continued to increase and Grace Larson asked Mom to help read letters that came in on the "Mail Bag" program. Mom was still shy about speaking on the radio and objected: "I sort of feel my place is in the music department."

"Oh yes, dear, I agree, but your speaking voice is just as beautiful as your lovely singing voice, and the Lord wants you to use all your talents." Grace was relentless and brimming with confidence, not only in herself but in her young missionary colleague.

"Well, I'll pray about it," promised Mom, as she hoped the Lord would lead her out of this dreaded assignment.

Soon, she found another task more to her liking for it got her involved with Spanish, and kept her from talking on the air. She began to read all Spanish mail. She logged each letter according to which programs the writers mentioned, and recorded excerpts of what folks said about blessings they had received. The many words of praise "encouraged my heart as I had not realized that so many, many people were listening." Reading the Spanish letters was a marvelous boost to her knowledge of the language. It gave her so much confidence that she volunteered to teach a Spanish Sunday School class using her well-worn and time-tested flannelgraphs. She had added to her collection of flannel characters, and told spellbinding stories of Old Testament heroes, affixing flannel images onto flannel board.

Of the more than twenty programs Mom and Dad had each

week, *"Adelante Juventud"* ("Forward Youth") became their favorite, for it was a program of inspiration and joy for young people in all parts of the Spanish-speaking world. A fine chorus of Ecuadorian young men, a girls' trio, a piano-organ-vibraharp combination, and visiting musicians united their talents to proclaim the gospel message.

Dad realized the younger generation in Latin America had many educational advantages not available to previous generations. The time was ripe to reach youth for Christ in Latin America. Many young people were fed up with Catholicism, but most tended to drift into agnosticism. The challenge for missionaries was to reach them with the gospel alternative before their minds and hearts were completely closed to any consideration of religion. It seemed they were making progress, because many letters came from young listeners praising God for the need this Friday night program was filling.

Over 50 per cent of radios in Ecuador were on the coastal lowlands but HCJB's long-wave transmitters did not reach that far. Short wave could be heard, but most radios in Ecuador were not equipped with these bands, so HCJB decided to set up a new transmitter on the coast. Reuben Larson told Dad, "We can double our Ecuador listening audience by setting up a long-wave station in Guayaquil. I'm going with Clayton Howard and Paul Shirk to set it up."

Dad replied, "Brother Larson, this is a wonderful first step, and I only hope we can establish three or four more stations in various parts of Latin America, such as Brazil, Argentina, and Mexico."

"Yes, I'm thinking along the same lines," replied Larson, "although another alternative is to keep increasing the power of our transmitters here in Quito."

Mom was asked if she would teach a religion class at the American School, run by the U.S. government. About 400 students attended the school, some Ecuadorian and some American, mostly children of embassy staff and employees of the Shell Oil Company, which was doing oil exploration on the eastern slopes of the Andes Mountains, in the headlands of the Amazon. This was a full generation before the issue of "prayer in public schools" had become a major political issue, and the U.S. government thought it fair to provide religious classes for those of Catholic, Jewish, and Protestant faiths.

She saw it as a marvelous opening for gospel witness and decided to take it. She had 23 students, the Jewish rabbi had 5, and the Catholic priest had the rest. Mom was nonplussed when they asked her to pose for yearbook pictures—between the priest and the rabbi.

That was not all for the reticent Wilda Savage. The Child Evangelism Fellowship asked each mission to appoint a member to their advisory council, and Mom was asked to represent HCJB. That assignment was not bad, but once the council met, she was asked to carry on the Teachers Training Course in Quito. She thought about her heavy program schedule, her Sunday School work, her duties at the American School, and her two children. It looked like a huge task, but as she prayed she felt the Lord was giving her strength. "Teaching others to teach" was desperately needed in Ecuador, and she accepted the job.

Dad continued to find ways to combine his international radio ministry with his local Sunday School ministry. He also wanted to focus on the entire nation of Ecuador in a series of revival meetings. He kept thinking of all those multitudes on the coast, receptive to the gospel, and longed to spend more time in that region. He was able to get away from HCJB for three weeks to hold a series of Youth for Christ rallies. The trip began with three nights of youth meetings in Guayaquil. Dad wrote that it was a "glorious time," terminating with a crowd of 850 people on Sunday night. Dad remembered how he had struggled with his one or two dozen people in Chinácota and Pamplona and relished the enthusiastic crowd. It was an inspiration and major encouragement to him. Mom was at the piano, Dad led singing, young people sang with gusto, and 27 were saved. Bob Savage was in his element.

Mom returned to Quito while Dad began a river trip with missionary Abe Dyck of the Gospel Missionary Union. Abe showed Dad his "missionary launch," a motorboat equipped with a sleep-in cabin, and sufficient capacity to haul Bibles, literature, and supplies for a river journey of several days. They worked their way up the Daule River, stopping at river towns along the way, gathering crowds into the village square by trumpet playing, then preaching in the open air. Abe and Dad distributed tracts, sold Scriptures, and during nine days held thirteen services. It was a journey that took Dad into parts of Ecuador he could never have reached by any other mode of transportation and the "gospel launch" gave him one more idea on ways to evangelize the world.

Dad was given charge of all Spanish gospel programs at HCJB and promptly increased the number of broadcasts from three to six daily. Whenever a visiting preacher passed through Quito, Dad recruited him to record a number of sermons. When Asdrubal Ríos came from Venezuela, Dad challenged him to set a new record and Ríos recorded over 100 messages, giving Dad a wealth of reserve material for several months. Dad then made it a habit to corner every visiting preacher, first invite him to speak in the flourishing Sunday School, then lock himself in the recording studio for a few hours and record the best of his sermons. It was an effective device, for HCJB began to build a huge library of sermons, catalogued both by speaker and topic.

The religious processions in Colombia had been frightening events, laden with threats on our lives, heavy with insults and taunts. In Ecuador, the Catholic church also had processions but they were not ominous for the Protestant missionaries, only sad, because they were besmirched with drunken revelry and little worship. Every December there was a massive celebration to the *Virgen de Quinche* (Virgin of Quinche), but this year it had to be postponed one week because elections were held the first Sunday of December and the government prohibited sales of liquor on election day. Dad commented wryly: "No festival to the Virgin could be complete without a free flow of liquor." Each year three or four families financed the gala affair, and often spent the rest of their lives paying the bills.

A few weeks before the feast a pilgrimage had been conducted to visit the home of the *Virgen de Quinche*, 30 miles north of Quito. Three hundred drunken pilgrims piled onto the one-car train designed to seat 50. They were crowded in, on top of, and about the car. Alongside a huge precipice the car overturned and 120 were killed. Dad considered this "licentious way of doing homage to the Mother of Christ," and concluded, "It is heart-rending the stuff that is pulled off in the name of religion. How these people need Christ!"

On Christmas Day, 1945, HCJB celebrated its 15th anniversary. To commemorate this milestone of the pioneer missionary broadcasting station, Dad and Mom joined Reuben Larson, Clarence Jones, and the rest of the HCJB staff to reflect on the achievements of this remarkable mission.

In 1929, Reuben Larson and Clarence Jones, unknown to each other and coming from different sections of the globe, both had been earnestly seeking a way to introduce the modern miracle of radio broadcasting into existing missionary methods. They met in Chicago and discovered the astounding similarity of their visions. In a small apartment at 3:00 a.m., they solemnly pledged themselves to the responsibility of bringing into reality their vision of missionary broadcasting. No one had ever attempted anything like this before.

Clarence Jones remained in the United States to raise funds while Reuben Larson returned to Ecuador to approach government officials and solicit a broadcasting license. They set out boldly, resolved to claim in a very personal way two promises of the Lord:

> Call unto me, and I will answer thee, and show thee great and mighty things, which thou knowest not. —*Jeremiah 33:3*

Not by might, nor by power, but by my spirit, saith the Lord of hosts.
                                                        —*Zachariah 4:6*

In 1930, Reuben Larson, assisted by fellow missionaries, the brothers Stuart and John Clark, approached the government for a broadcast license. Ecuadorian officials responded in a cordial and cooperative manner. A special decree of the President, confirmed by Congress, permitted the proposed station to be brought into the country. A charter was drawn up, establishing the right to broadcast educational, cultural, and religious programs.

On Christmas Day, 1931, HCJB broadcast its first program in inauspicious surroundings—a converted sheep shed with a tiny 200-watt transmitter. After a careful survey they found the total radio receivers in Ecuador numbered—six. With such unpromising beginnings, they boldly named the mission World Radio Missionary Fellowship, Incorporated. With vision for the future, they believed mini-powered radio station HCJB would grow in power and outreach. They also felt it would be the first of many more radio stations to come.

Within nine years, they had expanded from 200 to 10,000 watts and the President of Ecuador gave the inaugural speech for the new transmitter. HCJB had emerged from a tiny local station to a global broadcasting power, and by 1943 was broadcasting on four regular transmitters, one long wave, one intermediate, and two short wave. Programs went out in nine languages: Spanish, Quechua, English, Swedish, Russian, French, Dutch, Czech, and Yiddish. Between 1942 and 1945 the missionary staff doubled and so did the number of gospel broadcasts, totalling 820 per month.

The letters "HCJB" were the call letters assigned by the Ecuadorian government, but the imaginative Clarence Jones used them as an acronym in both English and Spanish. "Heralding Christ Jesus' Blessings" was the slogan broadcast to the United States, Canada, Great Britain, Australia, and New Zealand. "*Hoy Cristo Jesús Bendice*" ("Today Jesus Christ Blesses") was the motto in Spanish.

6

Breakthrough in the mountains of Ecuador

Guidance means I can count on God.
Commitment means God can count on me.

—*Pocket Quips*, p. 61

The twin-tailed, twin-engined Beechcraft circled over Quito's Mariscal Sucre airport and Dad exclaimed, "That's it! That's the little TACA airliner. Let's hope they're on the plane."

Excitedly, we waited while the 15-passenger plane taxied in. Carol and I pressed our faces against the cyclone fence and when I saw their faces peering through the airplane's windows, I exclaimed, "Carol! Look! It's Grandpa and Grandma, and Aunt Helen!"

Seventeen-year-old Helen stepped off first, her cheerful smile spreading across her ashen face as she staggered down the short stairway, a classic study of happy reunion mixed with wretched airsickness. Grandma Bessie Savage followed, just as happy and just as sick, waving feebly, smiling wanly. Then Grandpa Henry Savage emerged, his six-foot frame stooping low to get through the small oval door, placed himself on the footstep, and waved vigorously. The turbulence had not bothered him a bit.

"There they are!" shouted Dad. "Welcome to Quito! Amen, amen, amen!"

In 1946, customs procedures were relaxed and the Savages from Pontiac, Michigan, United States of America, were able to stroll over to the fence to hug and greet us before entering the terminal to present their passports and clear customs.

Grandpa exuded his profound feeling on arriving in the place his son had come to work for the Lord: "Bob, I'm so thrilled to be here to be able to see your work at first hand. This is wonderful." Grandpa had reared his son to love and serve the Lord. Nothing in life was more important than to win souls to Christ. Nothing gave Grandpa more satisfaction than to see his son, right there, in the mission field. Jesus said, "Go ye into all the world and preach the gospel to every creature." That was the Great Commission. Dad was fulfilling it with all his might. Grandpa was proud.

After a couple of days during which Grandpa, Grandma, and Helen acclimated to Quito's thin atmosphere, we took a trip to Otavalo, the Indian market five hours north of Quito. We were joined by fellow missionaries Clayton and Helen Howard. Everyone piled into the HCJB station wagon to follow the Pan American Highway, a 20-foot-wide cobblestone road which led north out of Quito.

On the way we stopped for lunch at the town of Cayambe, nestled right at the foot of Mount Cayambe, a beautiful snow-cap through which the line of the Equator passes. As we sat around the table a man rode a horse right into the dining room, chatted with the head waiter, turned around, and rode back out. Grandpa laughed merrily and said, "This reminds me of the old days back in La Junta, Colorado!" La Junta was the town seven miles west of the Savage homestead where Grandpa had grown up. Cayambe did, indeed, have those hearty and rugged qualities, the free spirit, the frontier spontaneity, that made us think of the Old American West.

We continued on, northward, another hour on the cobblestoned highway, past the crystal-blue crater lake, San Pablo, until we arrived at the small town of Otavalo nestled at the base of Mount Imbabura. Every Saturday, there was an open air market in Otavalo, and Indians from all over the region arose at 2:00 or 3:00 a.m. to lug their wares to the market. Many of the Otavalo Indians were weavers and brought their brightly-colored ponchos, scarves, and tapestries. Others wove rugs, with intricate and ancient Inca designs hooked by hand. Most Indians had a burro to serve as beast of burden but others carried 100-pound loads on their own backs. From all over the highlands they descended into the valley, chose their spots in the block-size plaza, laid out hand-woven mats, and piled their goods for all to see. The place was busy by 6:00 am, and the air was filled with delicious aromas of pork cooking over charcoal braziers next to small kiosks. Everyone chattered excitedly, with sellers pleading for passersby to examine their merchandise, and buyers arguing for lower prices.

At the Otavalo Indian market, Grandpa bought a beautifully fine-woven straw Panama hat and was surprised to learn that all "Panama" hats were woven in Ecuador. This inspired Dad to lead us in a song as we drove back home: *"Los sombreros que llevan los gringos son tejidos en el Ecuador"* ("The hats worn by the gringos are woven in Ecuador.") Dad sang it over and over, and even after the rest of the family had grown tired, continued to sing. He did not wear down easily.

The Howards invited us for dinner and Henry Savage began to regale us with his latest repertoire of jokes. After each joke, everyone laughed politely, but Dad roared with pleasure, while Helen Howard gently kicked her husband under the table. They smiled at each other knowingly—for they had heard exactly the same jokes from Dad only a few weeks earlier.

Jokes were always a part of the conversation when Dad and Grandpa were present. All their jokes were light, and they often poked fun at themselves. They enjoyed nothing more than Baptist jokes. Grandpa would tell one and Dad would add another. The evening went on like that, back and forth.

Grandpa said: "You know, there are Baptists north of God and

Baptists south of God. There are even Baptists independent of God."

Dad roared loudly, then quickly came back with: "Do you know how the Baptist church began? Some people say it began with John the Baptist. But no. It got started long before that. It started way back there with Abraham and Lot in the Old Testament. Remember that story? Abraham said, 'You go your way and I'll go mine.' And that's how the Baptist church began."

On it went. They never ran out of jokes.

In those days, the staff at HCJB was small and intimate and each visitor was treated with great respect. Ecuador was also small, and it was not unusual for us to have contacts with high government officials. During Grandpa's visit, Reuben Larson pulled out all the stops and arranged an audience with President Velasco Ibarra. After all, reasoned Larson, the president of Ecuador ought to get acquainted with the president of the Conservative Baptist Foreign Missionary Society. Larson also wanted President Ibarra to meet the man who had pioneered gospel radio broadcasting in 1926, only four years before HCJB had begun in Ecuador.

Both Dad and Grandpa were introduced to Ecuador's mercurial president, known both fondly and derisively as *el loco*. Ibarra was gracious and cordial, and Dad translated as the President chatted with his father. Grandpa told Ibarra how impressed he had been with the majestic beauty of Ecuador, and the president said, "Please tell your friends back in the United States that Quito is a civilized city, and that we are not a bunch of head-hunting Indians!"

"I will do just that," promised Grandpa, but he also had a request for Ecuador's president: "This is a Bible, the Word of God, and I would like to give it to you as my way of saying thank you for your hospitality. Will you please read a chapter each day?" Ibarra promised he would.

After they left the presidential palace, Larson and the two Savages got in the car. Before starting the motor, the three men bowed their heads in prayer. Dad prayed, "Oh Lord, we thank Thee for this marvelous contact Thou hast given us with the President of this wonderful republic we call our home. May he take that Bible and read it. May he come to a saving knowlege of Jesus Christ and may he be used for Thy glory."

The visit of the Savages lasted a month, so Dad kept his father busy. He got Grandpa involved in a series of meetings, and translated for him whenever he spoke to an Ecuadorian audience. They ministered together, father and son, at every opportunity. Grandpa not only preached in the evangelical churches in the area, but assisted in open-air street meetings, prison services, and special revival meeetings featuring gospel movies.

Dad also took advantage of Grandpa's presence by asking him to record a series of messages for the radio. By the time Grandpa and Grandma left, there were 50 new messages in HCJB's tape library, to be used in English broadcasts beamed to the States, Canada, England, Australia, and New Zealand.

After Grandpa, Grandma, and Helen left Quito, they flew to Venezuela and spent a month with Jim and June Savage, participating in the missionary work in that country. Grandpa savored the satisfaction of having both his sons working in the calling he considered most glorious of all: full-time Christian service in a foreign missionary field.

Helen had already dedicated her life to missionary service even before her trip to South America. The energy, vigor, and devotion of the missionaries she observed only reinforced her commitment. She had spent two years studying Spanish in high school. Now as she prepared to follow in her brothers' footsteps and attend Wheaton College, it was with the specific goal of preparing herself to return to South America as a missionary.

Shortly after the Pontiac Savages left Quito, Dad took another trip to Guayaquil, where he had lined up a series of meetings in the bustling coastal metropolis. This time, however, the rallies were not as well-attended and upbeat as the first exhilarating series had been. Dad was extremely disappointed. The reason for the letdown in attendance was not anyone's fault; it was simply the weather. Heavy rain storms cascaded on Ecuador's port city of Guayaquil in February, 1946. Only about 150 people were present Friday and 250 Saturday, compared with over 800 a few months earlier. Even though attendance was down, "four fine young men accepted Christ," and that made Dad rejoice. If only one person had been gained for the kingdom of heaven, the trip would have been worthwhile.

Dad wanted to continue from Guayaquil to Manta, another port city farther up the coast, but heavy rains made the Manta airport too muddy for airplanes to land, and Dad described himself as "fuming in Guayaquil."

Back in Quito, Dad had lined up another series of meetings scheduled for the week before Lent. However, he had failed to take into account a major event that took place at this time each year. It was time for Ecuador's annual craziness: Carnival. Carnival season in Ecuador took place for the five days leading up to Lent. The chief activity was water-throwing. Water fights were continually in progress everywhere. Girls stood in little balconies that overlooked the streets and threw buckets of water at fellows who passed beneath. The fellows in turn bought dozens of little balloons filled with water to throw back at the girls.

Traveling into town was an adventure, for streets were lined with boys holding buckets of water. Dad declared, in the tone of a prophet of old, "Woe be unto you if your car window is busted for you will surely get soaked." It was a serious problem, for in those days car windows were not shatter-proof, and the force of a bucket of water thrown directly at a window would sometimes smash the window. Then the longsuffering bus riders not only got wet but pierced with glass fragments. The only solution was to leave all windows rolled down and endure the cold dowsing of water. To make matters worse, there was lots of flour thrown around and people got plastered with flour all over hair, face, and clothes—becoming paste when they were further engulfed with water. In some instances the tricks got more damaging. Ink was thrown, fist fights ensued, and each year several people died of pneumonia as they caught chills with their soaked bodies in Quito's cool March night air.

My friends and I thought carnival was wonderful, and played it with great zeal. We tossed balloons at each other with great gusto. A bag of 144 balloons cost only a few *sucres*, so water bombs were in copious supply. It was fun for children and young people, aggravating for adults, but dangerous for old people. It became barbarous at times, completely out of control, and the only defense for most people was simply to stay at home.

Dad had scheduled a week of revival meetings in the little Sunday School he had founded near the radio station and as they began he said regretfully, "It was a mistake to line them up during Carnival." Surprisingly, however, the meetings were worthwhile. Guillermo Sotomayor, a young fellow from the Bible Institute in Guayaquil, did the preaching and two young men stepped forward to make decisions for Christ. Their public commitment rejoiced the hearts of my parents and they concluded, "We'll never slate another week of meetings during Carnival, but the Lord blessed us anyway, and we know it will have eternal results."

After Carnival, the family traveled to Riobamba, where Dad was scheduled to conduct a series of Youth for Christ meetings. Riobamba was a mountain town of 40,000 people nestled in the lap of Ecuador's highest mountain, the fierce and awesome Chimborazo. It was a fanatical town, fervently pro-Catholic and anti-evangelical. It reminded my parents of Pamplona in Colombia, both in its picturesque mountain setting as well as its sullen attitude towards the Protestants. They prayed that the Lord would use the Youth for Christ ministry to break down walls formerly unyielding to the gospel message.

Missionaries had worked in Riobamba for nearly 50 years, and although they had a small congregation, it was made up mostly of folks who were converted in other towns and had moved to Riobamba. The Riobambeños themselves were intransigent and closed to the gospel message. Several missionaries had worked in that cold mountain city, cold in climate and cold in its response to the gospel. It was a desolate and unrewarding post of duty. When we went in 1946, missionaries Ken and Eunice Lewis of the Christian and Missionary Alliance were assigned to the forlorn post, and were cheered by Dad's three-day campaign.

People were afraid to enter and sit in the seats, but gathered in the doorway by the dozens. Dad pondered the situation and finally hit on a solution. One night he announced, "I have a free calendar for everyone who is seated" and they rushed for the seats. When it came time for singing, he abandoned his usual custom of asking the congregation to stand for singing, because, as he remarked wryly, "I wasn't about to give them a chance to get away." Two accepted Christ as Saviour, and the Lewises rejoiced, for they were the first two conversions in years for Riobamba.

On the way back to Quito, we crossed the high plateau that stretches north and south between two ranges of fierce snow-capped mountains, the road climbing and descending between 8,000 and 13,000 feet. After a few hours we arrived in the lovely town of Ambato. Ken Lewis made this drive each week, for he had meetings in the open-air market. He asked Dad to join him this week, so Dad happily pulled out his trumpet and began to play until a crowd gathered. He preached in that huge assemblage, where Indians came on foot from miles around to sell and exchange their wares. After it was over, and we continued our drive to Quito, Dad talked about the splendid freedom he had felt to preach to that crowd. He told us about restrictions other countries had on open-air services and commented: "How we ought to praise God for the privilege of preaching in the open air here in Ecuador."

One of Dad's concerns was the fragility of religious freedom in Ecuador. He exulted in the liberty to conduct the open–air meeting in the Indian market in Ambato, and frequently thanked God for the freedom they had to continue broadcasting in Ecuador. He was aware, however, that the position of evangelical missions in Ecuador was fragile, and that restrictions could be slapped on them at any time. He could not help, therefore, but be intensely interested in the political fortunes of Ecuador's leaders.

When we had arrived in Ecuador in late 1944, Velasco Ibarra had been president for four and a half months, and many were predicting that a revolution was imminent. He confounded experts by weathering several attempts to overthrow him. In April 1946, Ibarra arrested some army and political leaders, charging them with conspiring to overthrow the government. When Dad went downtown to cash a check he found the streets full of people and mounted soldiers. While in the bank he heard shots fired. As he emerged from the bank, he found out that 200 University students were demonstrating against *el dictador loco* (the crazy dictator) and demanding he be put out. Dad slipped away quietly, boarded the bus and returned to HCJB, safely nestled in the north end of the city. Meanwhile, the cavalry was called and demonstrators commanded to cease. Instead they started tossing chairs and tables out of windows and onto police and soldiers. Shots were fired into the air and students arrested. The army dispersed a mob with tear gas, and many of Ibarra's enemies were expelled from Ecuador. The army had its tanks and machine guns well distributed throughout the city, so Ibarra was able to maintain control.

Although HCJB was careful never to choose sides in the constantly changing political landscape, the private opinion of most missionaries was that Ibarra was a friend, pro-HCJB, and they hoped he would stay. He had given Grandpa a cordial reception, and Dad couldn't help but like him, so quietly hoped he would hold on to his power.

Although missionaries had considerable latitude in conducting religious services, there were still formidable barriers. Dad wanted to rent a huge auditorium to conduct a series of meetings, but found that it was almost impossible to get anyone to lease a building for an evangelical meeting. Despite his boundless optimism, he began to despair of ever getting a big enough location for a huge rally.

He found help from an unlikely source. Marco Paredes, Ecuadorian announcer with the melodious voice who had made a decision for Christ after working at the radio station, now proved his worth another way. He had many contacts with Ecuadorian government officials, and he was also a man of optimism and bravado. Dad had talked with Marco about renting a huge auditorium for a series of gospel meetings. With a confident grin, Marco told him, "We'll get the best place in town. Wait and see."

One day Marco came into the HCJB studio with a big grin on his face and announced, "Don Roberto! We finally have the papers to rent the *Teatro Sucre!*"

"The *Teatro Sucre!*" exclaimed Dad. "That's the best place I can imagine. Are you sure we've got it?"

"Positive!" declared Marco, as he showed Dad the signed papers.

"Praise the Lord, Don Marco!" whooped Dad. "How did you do it?"

"It took weeks. The theatre is government-owned and there was a lot of red tape."

"This is a miracle," gloried Dad.

"Yes, it is," replied Marco, "it is a miracle they would rent it for religious services—especially evangelical. They kept putting me off and giving silly excuses for not renting it, but finally it went through."

There was one condition, though: admissions must be by ticket only.

The *Teatro Sucre* was the national theatre of Ecuador, and seated 900. Strategically situated in downtown Quito, it was the concert hall where world-renowned musicians performed when they came to town. Now, evangelical missionaries had an opportunity to preach the gospel in a prestigious location, one that would hold large crowds.

At first Dad thought the ticket requirement would be a handicap, but the optimistic Marco grinned and said, "It will prove to be a blessing in disguise. You watch—people will be eager to get a ticket, whereas they would scorn a hand bill invitation."

Dad printed 9,000 tickets and visited high schools and colleges, offering tickets to school administrators and students. At military barracks, he presented free New Testaments along with tickets to the youth rallies.

Dad fretted, wondering, "What will be the result? Have we been over-zealous contracting for such a big place? Would it be wiser to secure a smaller place? If only 200 or 300 people attend, will it put the gospel into disrepute?"

They planned a musical program consisting of a young men's chorus and a young ladies' trio: Delores VanDerPuy, Peggy Jo Larson, and Wilda Savage. They also had an instrumental trio of Hammond organ, vibraharp, and piano.

John D. Clark, one of the most loved missionaries in the Republic, would be speaker and Reuben Larson master of ceremonies. The *Vozandes* orchestra would play the first fifteen minutes.

On opening night, 30 minutes before the curtain was to rise, Dad asked all missionaries and national workers to gather behind the stage to kneel as he led them in prayer: "Oh Father in Heaven, we praise and thank Thee for securing this place for these rallies. It is a worldly theatre, but tonight it is Thy temple and we dedicate it to Thee. May we magnify and glorify Thy name tonight, and may our words and music bring people to the feet of our blessed Savior, Jesus Christ."

Every few seconds, Dad peeked through the curtain to see if anyone was arriving. They were. Dozens, then scores, then hundreds. Just 30 seconds before the curtain arose, Dad looked out for the last time. As he looked out on the audience, he saw to his astonished delight that practically every seat on the main floor and the three galleries was filled and silently lifted his heart in praise to the Lord for "having shown us great and mighty things."

He whispered to J. D. Clark, "Probably 80 per cent to 90 per cent have never attended a gospel service."

At 6:15 p.m. the curtain went up as the young men of the chorus combined with the ladies' trio to sound out the testimony chorus, "*Gozo tengo en mi alma hoy—porque sé que Cristo me salvó.*" ("I'm so happy, and here's the reason why—Jesus took my burdens all away.")

The Hammond organ and vibraharp were the only two instruments of that kind in Ecuador. These amazing and unknown musical wonders had been featured in all the publicity and created intense interest.

When J. D. Clark began to preach, the audience fell silent, for here was an Englishman with imperfect Spanish accent but perfect command of the language's rich vocabulary, with impeccable grammar and intricate knowledge of Ecuadorian history and literature. Not the least flamboyant, the quiet and earnest Clark kept the audience's attention through his eloquent unfolding of Scriptural stories most had never heard. They were moved by this humble man, who continually apologized for his inadequacy as a speaker, and thus endeared himself to his listeners for his understanding of good manners in the best Latin American tradition.

The first night was successful beyond their most vivid hopes, and as they wended their way homeward, they praised God. Dad still worried, though, for he did not know what to expect on succeeding nights. He wondered, "Now that people realize it's 'just a gospel service' instead of a program of entertainment, will they become indifferent and stay away?" There was no cause for misgivings, for on the second night, not only were the seats again completely filled, but many had to stand. By closing night over 1,100 were seated and standing.

Dad wrote:

> I certainly didn't have the faith to believe it was possible, but tonight I've seen it as a glorious reality." This was the expression of Ruth Clark, one of Ecuador's veteran

missionaries as she left the National Theatre after the closing meeting of a four-night young people's rally—an occasion that drew the biggest crowds in the history of gospel missionary work in Quito. Over 1,000 people crowded into the renowned building each night, 900 seated, 100 standing, a truly amazing testimony.

In Dad's view, the four nights at the *Teatro Sucre* constituted the most potent testimony for the gospel Quito had ever witnessed. Only a small percentage of those attending had ever been inside an evangelical church. One of the things that most pleased Dad was that the audience went across class, racial, economic, and educational lines: rich and poor, whites and Indians, professionals and workers, university students and illiterates. A former candidate for the presidency of the republic attended all four nights.

Because of restrictions placed upon them, the missionaries were not able to give their usual public invitation for people to come forward to accept Christ as Savior. However, many people signed "decision cards" which were used for follow up visits. Dad concluded:

> God has used this victory in the National Theatre of Quito to inspire our faith and enlarge our vision to include not only future rallies of the same sort in Quito, but also in other parts of Ecuador. For the future we are determined as never before to put into practice China missionary William Carey's old motto: "Attempt great things FOR God. Expect great things FROM God."

The *Teatro Sucre* campaign whetted Dad's appetite for evangelism on a large scale. He wanted to initiate similar events all over Ecuador. His work at the radio station remained full, but somehow he always figured out a way to leave for a few days of meetings. He traveled again to the coast, this time without the family, and finally reached Manta, where the airport runway had been too muddy a few months earlier. Five days in this coastal fishing village resulted in record crowds with many young people attending and 19 conversions.

While on the coast, Dad continued on to Guayaquil. He had been invited to open the school year at the Bible Institute. He gave two messages a day on "Principles of Power." The Institute director, Harvey Bostrom, had asked Dad to combine Bible teaching for the 23 students along with a revival effort. The plan worked. Youth rallies resulted in seven conversions and 17 "dedications for life service." Dad encouraged the institute students to follow up by nurturing new converts and guiding them in their new beliefs.

For weeks after the successful meetings at the *Teatro Sucre* in Quito, Dad thought about ways of duplicating this performance in other cities. The problem in most towns, however, was finding a place big enough to hold the meetings. He wrote his father: "Since the Teatro Sucre meetings I've been dreaming dreams and seeing visions. I'd like to secure a big tent seating 500 people and use it all over Ecuador conducting campaigns."

A tent, Dad thought, would attract a big crowd any place they would go, and "provide a means whereby we could start reaching multitudes instead of poking along with mere handfuls."

Mom, ever the pessimist, cautioned, "Wouldn't you be under constant danger of having fanatics cut the tent to pieces with their machetes?"

"Yes, that's a danger, but it doesn't dim my ardor," replied Dad, ever the optimist.

The idea of a gospel tent remained in the back of Dad's mind. Meanwhile, he had to conduct meetings as best he could, wherever he could, in the best facilities possible.

His vision for evangelism extended beyond the borders of Ecuador and he often thought of Colombia, where he had first ministered. He was pleased when Bill and Mary Gillam, who worked with the Overseas Missionary Crusade in Medellín,

Colombia, invited my parents to come and conduct a conference.

Dad blazed through five services each day, preaching and singing, while Mom played the piano.

Mom and Dad were pleased to be back in Colombia, and were impressed with its modern facilities compared to quaint old Ecuador. "We thought Colombia was backward when we first came here, but now after being in Ecuador it seems like a really progressive place. I'm afraid Ecuador is an awfully poor little place and way behind most."

Economically, Colombia was way ahead of Ecuador, and we were thrilled to be able to buy essentials like U.S.-grade underwear, of fine quality unavailable in Quito. We stocked up on these mundane items, but they seemed like luxuries. Few of our friends in the United States could ever imagine how exciting it could be to receive a pair of well-knit, well-fitting shorts.

From Medellín, we returned to our original stomping ground, traveling to Cúcuta to attend the Annual Field Conference of the Scandinavian Alliance Mission. Even though my parents were no longer official members of the mission, the old ties remained, the bond eternal, and they were welcomed to come to the meetings. It was great to see old friends like Elof and Isabelle Anderson, Ken and Ardis Bystrom, and Wilf and Elizabeth Watson. But Dad wrote that the biggest thrill of all was to find that Issachar Parrada, the language teacher from Pamplona, for whom Mom and Dad had prayed faithfully, "had come out 100% for the Lord." He was a natural enthusiast and now directed all his enthusiasm into the Lord's channel. Dad wrote: "He got kicked out as superintendent of the public school in Pamplona after he became a Protestant, but soon got a much better job with the oil company in Cúcuta. He even got some of the U.S. fellows at the oil company interested in going to church."

Another rousing event was our trip to Venezuela to visit my uncle and aunt, Jim and June Savage. Venezuela had loosened its restrictions on tourists, and we obtained a three-day permit. We got to know the Bible Institute that was the focus of Jim and June's activities. A few months earlier I had asked Dad the question children so often ask, "Who's your best friend?"

Without hesitation Dad had replied, "My brother, Jim."

Now, that friendship became apparent to all of us as the two brothers prized each other's company, sharing their triumphs and discouragements, regaling each other with stories and jokes, laughing hilariously, rocking the house with booming noise. Uncle Jim's voice was not as loud as Dad's, but it had plenty of force. When the two heehawed together, with Jim's tenor cackle joining Dad's baritone bellow, the hullabaloo was uproarious.

The flight back from Bogotá to Quito was the roughest Mom had ever experienced, as the plane continuously fell out from under her stomach, plowing through whirling Andean wind fluxes. This time, however, Mom smiled confidently, and her hand never reached forward to grab the airsick bag. She had a new weapon, Mother Sills Pills, and was proud to report, "I was not even the slightest bit sick the entire trip."

While in Colombia, we heard many stories of the violence that was growing all over that lovely nation, marring its tranquillity, affecting not only evangelicals but many of Colombia's regular populace. Much of the violence was political, so all citizens were vulnerable. But some of it was religious, directed against Protestant evangelicals. Many Christian believers were stoned, hounded out of their jobs, ridiculed, and bullied. Homes were burned, churches vandalized.

Upon his return to Quito, Dad's schedule intensified. Field Director Reuben Larson was in Guayaquil establishing a new radio station. Larson assigned Dad to take on his duties of administration in Quito, including English programs and personnel.

Dad was now working 12 to 14 hours per day, exuberant, but pushing the outer edge of his enormous energy and efficiency. It seemed that he could do no more. But he would—for the swirl of activities dramatically increased its tempo when Clarence Jones arrived. Dad wrote:

> Whew! A human dynamo has taken over here, named Dr. Clarence Jones, and it is some changed place. We are thrilled, but working like horses. He is certainly some leader.
>
> Jones has been producing several programs and it is an education to work with him. He knows what makes the wheels go around and all of a sudden this place is electrified.

Jones began to beam additional programs to England, Australia, and New Zealand. To handle the extra programs he asked more of each member of his missionary staff, often getting them up in the middle of the night for live broadcasts to Australia and New Zealand where it was prime time.

Dad and Mom may have felt underworked in Colombia, but now they put in more hours than ever—and Jones did not let up the pressure. He even got Mom to do more talking on the radio. He appointed her to announce one morning a week. She wrote her Mother, "I wasn't scared but just so plum embarrassed I didn't know what to think." Mom did not realize how good she was; she always tended to take a dim view of her talent. Despite herself, with prodding from her vigorous husband and the indomitable Jones, she found herself ever more in the public eye, performing successfully. People always complimented her, lavishing praise on her piano skills, her pretty alto voice, and her soft speaking voice. She appreciated the tributes, but never quite believed them.

7

The gospel tent

❖

The only thing worse than a quitter is the man who is afraid to begin. —*Pocket Wisdom*, p.105

By November, 1946, we had completed our first four years of missionary work in South America. A four-year "term" was followed by a one-year furlough in the United States. "Furlough" was a misnomer, for it was by no means a time of rest. Most missionaries spent the year in intensive travel, visiting churches, promoting interest in missionary work.

My parents talked eagerly of our trip "home," although that word did not describe the United States as it used to. They told us, "Ecuador is beginning to feel more like home than the U.S."

I had just finished my first semester of first grade at the Alliance Academy, the school for missionaries' children in Quito, with a total of 60 students in the entire school, primary through high school.

We flew Avianca Airlines from Quito to Barranquilla arriving at 3:50 p.m. on a Sunday afternoon. It was there in Barranquilla, on Colombia's northern coast, on the shores of the Caribbean, where we had first landed on the South American continent four years earlier. We were tired from the long journey and when Dad said, "Let's go to church," we all groaned. Dad had never missed a

Sunday, not one, not a single Sunday in his entire life, and he was not about to mar his record. He dragged us all to the Southern Baptist Church that night.

The next day, we flew on Pan American Airways to Miami via Cuba and Jamaica. It had been a two-day journey, one which is now routinely flown non-stop by jet in three hours. From Miami we flew on Delta Airlines to Chicago.

We spent the first six months of our twelve-month furlough in Wheaton, Illinois, in the home of my grandparents, Lawrence and Ruby Johnson. Grandma Ruby was a devout Christian, but Grandpa had a bemused view of the Christian faith. He was sympathetic with the missionary work to which his daughter had dedicated her life, but he did not "speak the language" of the evangelicals. He knew the lingo, to be sure, for his father had been a Swedish Methodist minister, but during his college and Army years he had gradually lost interest in the church. Now, with his daughter and son-in-law constantly bubbling over with talk of Christianity, he could hardly ignore it. If asked "Are you a Christian?" or "Have you accepted Jesus Christ as your Savior?" he would always agree "yes, of course," thus avoiding discussion of the issue. But Mom and Dad were troubled, sensing he was not really "committed." Besides, he smoked. He never smoked around us, but often went out for walks. We all knew why he wanted to walk, for when he returned, the cigarette smoke odor was obvious. I rather liked the smell, for it was uniquely Grandpa's, but it was the smell of sin for fundamentalists, and we continued to pray for his salvation.

We prayed for him every night, and my nightly routine sounded something like this: "Now I lay me down to sleep, I pray Thee Lord my soul to keep; if I should die before I wake I pray Thee Lord my soul to take—and please help Grandpa Johnson to soon get saved. Amen."

Grandpa was able to deflect most of the troublesome issues with his special brand of humor. Once during the blessing, he looked around the table while Dad was eloquently thanking the

Lord for the food. After Dad's resounding "Amen" Grandpa mumbled, "Stevie had his eyes open!" I quickly replied, "How did you know, Grandpa, unless you had your eyes open, too?" Dad laughed nervously, wanting to be pleasant, but eager for everyone to understand and feel the seriousness of prayer. For him, closed eyes were important, for thus were all distractions removed, and one could concentrate solely on communion with God.

One day Dad called on me to say the blessing. I closed with a phrase often used by evangelicals: "...and bless our conversation around this table. May it be to Thy honor and glory. In Jesus' name, Amen." Grandpa muttered, "Well, that sort of limits the conversation." Mom giggled, Dad laughed nervously, then Grandpa added, "Can't talk about the Democrats, can't talk about Notre Dame, can't talk about the Yankees. What are we gonna talk about?" We all broke into uproarious laughter and as usual Dad laughed loudest of all.

Grandpa's biggest enthusiasms, besides his family, were Northwestern University's football team, the Chicago Cubs baseball team, and the Republican Party. It was not a happy choice of passions, for Grandpa's causes lost a lot more than they won. He hated Notre Dame, for they usually beat Northwestern, and besides, they were Roman Catholic. To be sure, Grandpa was not an avid evangelical, but he was fundamentally a rock-ribbed Protestant, a Mason, anti-Catholic. Once Dad announced with great excitement that one of the players on Northwestern's football team had just accepted Christ as his Savior. Grandpa's immediate response was, "Humphh! Hope it doesn't mess up his game against Notre Dame on Saturday." Dad heehawed despite himself.

Grandpa was worried that a Christian football player might be too nice to the opposition. Dad had no such fears. He described his view of Jesus: "Pops, I want you to know that my idea of Christ is not a pale, anemic sissy like you see in those awful medieval paintings. I like to think of Christ as the muscular carpenter, who chased the money changers out of the temple. Christ is a man's man. If this fellow understands what being a Christian is all about, he'll play with vigor, he'll play to win. Then, when it's all over he'll thank the Lord for helping him play his best. He'll also congratulate his opponent for a job well done."

Grandpa grunted, "I can go along with most of that, but I don't know if I'd want to congratulate a Notre Dame player for anything."

Grandma Ruby had been an English teacher and constantly corrected our grammar. She was meticulous, not only in her speech, but her housekeeping, and she was always in motion, picking up, arranging, and fretting aloud about projects left undone. She puttered around, every few minutes asking each of us if we were hungry, cold, or uncomfortable. She never seemed to sit still, and even when we had all begun to eat, she kept getting up and down, asking us all, one by one, if we had everything we needed. Finally, exasperated, Grandpa would command, "Ruby, sit down and eat!" That got her down for a minute or two, but soon she'd be up again, scurrying from kitchen to dining room.

While in the U.S. we had to get our dental work completed, for dentistry in Ecuador in 1947 was primitive. My earliest recollection of pain was in the dentist chair of Dr. Peñaherrera in Quito, who used a slow-speed drill, and required three agonizing visits to complete one filling.

In Wheaton, Mom introduced us to her old family dentist, Dr. Henry. I dreaded going. Grandma assured us that things were better now because Dr. Henry used a high-speed drill. He also used Novocaine. Even though that eliminated the pain, the shot itself was an ordeal. In the end, I accepted a few seconds of terror to avoid an hour of torture.

We were sitting in Dr. Henry's reception room. Another patient asked Mom, "Where are you from?"

"Quito, Ecuador, in South America," replied Mom.

"South America!" exclaimed the man. "Amazing! What does your husband do?"

"He's an ambassador," responded Mom.

"Ambassador! It must be wonderful to represent the United States government overseas."

"Oh no, you see, my husband represents an even more important government than the United States," emphasized Mom.

"More important than the United States! You must be fooling me. What country does he represent?"

"He represents the King of Kings and Lord of Lords. My husband is a missionary, an ambassador for Christ."

"Oh," murmured the patient as he returned to read his magazine.

I glanced quizzically at Mom. She had been dead serious, but an impish grin crept over her face as she realized how she had disappointed the other patient. Later, in the car, I asked her why she had called Dad an ambassador. She told me that an assignment as a missionary was the highest calling a person could receive, and she really did consider Dad to be an ambassador of highest rank.

Dad's "furlough" was packed with projects. He began working on his first Spanish chorus book. He also took an 18-week radio course at Moody Bible Institute in Chicago. But his main project was to visit churches across the nation, describing the work of HCJB, urging young people to enlist as volunteers in the Lord's army, to join forces in the great cause of evangelizing the world.

Dad had conducted many youth rallies in Ecuador, often under the banner "Youth for Christ" ("*Juventud para Cristo*"). A young organization of the same name, Youth for Christ International, had its headquarters in Wheaton, Illinois, and was growing rapidly throughout the United States. During our days in Wheaton, Dad had many conversations with Youth for Christ leaders Torrey Johnson, Robert Evans, and Billy Graham. They asked him to take over as Vice President for Youth for Christ in Latin America. He thought about it, prayed, and talked with his seniors, HCJB's Clarence Jones and Reuben Larson. They all agreed he could divide his time between the radio station and evangelistic campaigns.

During the summer we stayed at Maranatha Bible Conference with Grandpa and Grandma Savage. Maranatha, this special place on Michigan's western shores, was a focal point for our family. For us children, it was a time of fun, to play on the beach, attend children's chapel, or walk in the woods. For my parents, it was holy ground, for it was on the sand dunes of Maranatha that Bob proposed to Wilda.

Grandpa Savage was gone half the time. During the summer, he spent three-day weekends at his church in Pontiac, then drove to Maranatha for the mid-week services there. In his absence, Grandma Savage presided over the "Savage tribe" at their beautiful home in Maranatha. She was the grand dame of Maranatha and played her role with vivacious warmth. She was exuberant and friendly, a gracious hostess, splendid cook, a perfect complement to her often taciturn minister husband. She made our visit that summer a jolly and memorable time. After a day at the beach on Lake Michigan, we often came home to find Grandma sitting on the couch in front of the picture window, looking out at the channel waters that connected Mona Lake and Lake Michigan, her Bible open, meditating upon God's Word. She told us she was praying for each member of her family, individually, by name.

In the fall we moved to Pontiac, Michigan, to be near Grandpa and Grandma Savage. Grandpa's presence was commanding, and it was hard for me not to stare at him. He had an air of majesty and a sense of self-assurance that often intimidated people. His august manner sometimes scared me, especially when Grandma prepared a magnificent T-Bone steak dinner as a welcome for the "Savages from South America." Her dinner service was elegant, with her best silver, linen tablecloth, and fine napkins.

After I had cut as much steak as I could, there were still some tantalizing juicy strips clinging to the bone. I looked at Grandma and said, "May I pick up the bone in my fingers?"

Grandma wanted the occasion to be a perfect time for all of us. She looked worried. Everything in her face said "yes" but she said nothing and looked over at her husband, "Henry, what do you think?"

"Nope," was the stern reply.

Nothing more was said, and I left those marvelous little slivers of meat uneaten. After a few minutes, dessert was over, and without further ado, Grandpa pushed his chair away from the table, got up, and left the room. I thought he was displeased but Grandma assured us he always did that. He participated in family conversation only to the point where his interest remained intact. He was often gracious, friendly, and funny, but a part of the lonely Colorado range never left him.

My first three semesters of primary school were in three different schools. Mine was not an unusual lot for an "MK"—a "missionary kid." In the fall of 1947 I began second grade at my third school: Baldwin School in Pontiac, where my father had attended primary school.

While we were in Pontiac, the Baptist churches in Washington, D.C. sponsored "World Missions" week and invited Dad as speaker. Congressman Leonard Allen of Louisiana, staunch member of Metropolitan Baptist Church, and a good friend of Dad's from the days when he was assistant pastor, arranged a meeting at the White House for 32 missionaries. Allen introduced each one to President Harry S. Truman and when he came to Dad, announced, "This is Bob Savage, from radio station HCJB in Quito, Ecuador."

"Well, you come from way up on top of the world, don't you?" remarked Truman.

"I'm delighted you know your geography!" complimented Dad. "Most people think South America is nothing but steaming jungles."

"I've spent many hours staring at maps of South America," added Truman, "thinking about those majestic Andes Mountains. Quito must be a beautiful city."

"Yes, I believe it's one of the most spectacular places on earth," said Dad.

Truman addressed the entire gathering of missionaries: "I consider missionary activity one of the most important factors in efforts to obtain peace throughout the world. I compliment each of you for your efforts as gospel ambassadors. I believe a basic requirement for world peace is to get people converted first."

Later, Dad told us, "I think the President would make a good preacher. He made as good a missionary speech as most of us do."

But Grandpa Johnson retorted, "Don't forget he's a Democrat."

Dad roared with laughter. "OK, Pops, you don't have to worry. Truman was attractive, but he didn't change my politics."

While in Washington, Dad told Congressman Leonard Allen about his vision for a gospel tent. Allen paid close attention. He asked Dad how it would be used, and Dad told him about the success of the *Teatro Sucre* meetings. "But there are not many places like the *Teatro Sucre* in most towns, and the only way we can have a big meeting is to erect a tent."

The next day, Allen made a few phone calls, tracked down an Army surplus tent and called Dad, "OK, Bob, you've got your tent."

Dumbfounded, Dad replied, "You say I've got my tent? Where did you get it?"

"The Lord dropped it from heaven," laughed the Congressman.

"How big is it?"

"It's huge—40 by 80 feet. Bob, you'll really be able to pack 'em in!"

"Well, praise God!" shouted Dad, and Allen had to hold the phone away from his ear. "This is a marvelous answer to prayer. Thank you, thank you, thank you, a million thanks."

"Oh no, Bob, don't thank me. Just thank the Lord and use the tent for His glory."

"Fine, fine, fine, Congressman, but I'd like to ask you one more favor. Let's have a service of dedication and you lead us in prayer."

"Sure, come on over to my office and we'll do it."

Dad invited five other missionaries to join him as they went up to Capitol Hill, entered the office of Congressman Allen, and there, overlooking the Capitol dome, they bowed their heads as Allen led in prayer: "God, use this tent to the salvation of souls and the stirring of revival fires in South America."

Then Dad prayed: "Oh, Lord, may that great harvest time sweep over South America. May multitudes of people attend meetings in this tent. Bring us the best preachers, the finest musicians, and go with us everywhere. May thousands of souls be won for Christ, in whose blessed name we pray. Amen."

As our furlough year drew to a close, Dad told us during our family devotions: "A few months ago we prayed around this table and asked the Lord to help us recruit scores of young people for missionary work. Well, He has answered our prayer, because we've presented the missionary challenge to 160 different groups in 14 states, and 300 young people have made decisions to offer themselves for missionary service in foreign fields." Dad often shared these types of statistics with us. I was fascinated with the numbers and thrilled with his accomplishments.

Despite Dad's intense travel schedule, he was still able to accomplish the primary goal he had set for himself: the publication of his first chorus book in Spanish, titled *Adelante Juventud (Forward Youth)*. He had not yet discovered many authentic Latin American songs, so this first book was mainly translations from English. However, most of them had not appeared in print in any other Spanish hymnal, so it was an important first step in expanding the richness of Latin American evangelical hymnology.

Our second departure for the mission field was no easier than the first. Even though our grandparents had visited us in Quito, the distance was great, and four years was long. We planned to drive from Pontiac to Miami, stopping in Cedarville, Ohio, to visit our greatgrandparents, Charles and Ada Steele. As we began to say goodbye, Grandpa suddenly said, "We'll drive down to Cedarville with you. Stevie and Carol can come with us in our car." Grandpa was not ready to say goodbye.

After a few hours visiting with the Steeles in Cedarville, Grandpa and Grandma reluctantly got up and said, "Well, we've got to get back to Pontiac." He stood, faced his son, shook his hand, then began to weep, unabashedly, just as he had at the train station four years earlier. Father and son, both men of iron will and strong self-control, held each other and sobbed. Grandpa's tears expressed two overwhelming feelings tumbling in his soul: towering pride in the work his son was doing in South America, and staggering grief as he let him go for another four-year term of service.

We continued our drive from Cedarville to Miami, then boarded a Nicaraguan airliner, TAN *(Tranportes Aereos Nicaraguenses)*, an old bloated-body World War II C-46, twin-engined troop transport to Costa Rica, then on Panagra's (Pan American Grace Airways) DC-3 to Quito.

Carol and I pressed our noses against the window and as we circled over the Quito airport I squealed with delight, "There they are! The HCJB station wagons!"

As we stepped off the plane, the entire crowd of missionaries and Ecuadorian nationals cheered and burst into song:

There's a welcome here,
There's a welcome here,
There's a Christian welcome here.

Before entering the terminal building to clear customs, our family of four paused at the bottom of the stairway and stood together waving at our assembled friends, Carol and I jumping up and down with excitement. With tears streaming down her face, Mom said to Dad, "A year ago we said we were going home to the U.S., but I think today we've really come home." And Dad shouted to the crowd, his huge voice drowning out their cheers,

"We're home, folks, we're home! Praise the Lord, we're home!"

It always took a couple of days to adjust to Quito's 10,000-foot altitude, and we were encouraged to sleep longer, take naps, and move slowly. We kids ignored all the advice, and promptly got reacquainted with all our old buddies, both American and Ecuadorian. Carol and I had forgotten our Spanish, but within a few weeks we were once again speaking it easily. Our parents marveled at how quickly we children could forget and relearn the language that had demanded of them so many years of arduous study.

Mom and Dad also ignored the common wisdom, and did not take it easy the first few days in Quito. They plunged immediately into the whirlwind of HCJB activity. Mom had a heavy schedule of radio programs, and got back into her Child Evangelism and Sunday School responsibilities. Dad participated in several radio programs, was appointed Program Director for all programs, supervisor for new apartment building construction, preacher at various church services, and director of jail services.

Both Mom and Dad had gained a lot of weight during our year in the United States, with plenty of rich food and constant invitations to eat out. Quito's rarefied altitude and the frenzied work schedule took a lot of weight off Dad, but Mom said, "I seem to retain my tonnage in spite of everything."

Dad's primary duty was his work at the radio station, but because of his intense schedule, he was concerned that he couldn't properly prepare for each radio program. One day at family devotions he prayed, "Oh God, enable us to go before the microphone at each broadcast with a fresh, Spirit-filled message from Heaven."

Dad never hesitated to pray on the spur of the moment, and frequently would stop the conversation for a quick sentence prayer. He sensed the presence of Christ clearly, and could talk with his Lord at any moment.

Up until that point, evangelistic services were conducted in churches and rented halls. The gospel tent had still not arrived from the United States. It was coming the slow way, by boat. But even before the tent arrived, Dad began to experience some exciting results, right in the downtown church. In May he enjoyed the most fruitful week of his missionary experience to date.

The week began as Dad preached in the downtown church and 22 people responded to his invitation to accept Christ. On Monday, he began instruction classes for them. On Friday and Saturday, he conducted two Youth for Christ rallies and wrote with enthusiasm: "My, what an outpouring of God's Spirit was experienced. Friday night 24 came forward to accept Christ as Savior. Saturday morning we prayed that the Lord would give us 40 more decisions that night. Instead, He gave us 48.94 conversions in three services in one week. Praise the Lord!"

There had not been a two-night harvest of souls like that in the history of missions in Ecuador. The preacher for the two youth rallies was a young Ecuadorian, Paco García. He had graduated from Bible Institute a year earlier and was pastor of the church in the coastal town of Manta. Paco was an inauspicious-looking fellow, thin as a rail, homely, short, with two front teeth missing. Although age 23, he looked 17, but as Dad wrote, "...when he starts preaching—my, what a power he is for God. He's got the most spizerinktum I've yet seen in a national pastor."

It was Dad's standard practice to get Latin Americans to preach at most of his campaigns. Although he was a spellbinding and effective preacher, he never tried to make himself the focus of attention. He was content to be the sparkplug, the catalyst that made the meeting possible. He usually led the singing and thus was in the public eye. But his biggest contribution to the evangelistic crusades was behind the scenes. It was his energy and vision in the weeks preceding that made these meetings happen.

When the gospel tent finally arrived, Dad was ecstatic. He planned a big series of meetings for July, using the massive tent, featuring Bill Gillam from Colombia and Jim Savage from Venezuela as musicians. Ramón Cabrera from Cuba was to be the featured speaker.

Dad found an ideal site for the gospel tent, easy to reach by various bus lines, in a prominent location. He inquired about the owner, to ask permission to use the empty lot, and was surprised to find that it belonged to Bolívar Avilés Alfaro, grandson of Ecuador's turn-of-the-century president.

President Eloy Alfaro was the liberal who had made it possible for the first Protestant missionary to enter Ecuador in 1890. Alfaro had been overthrown by the conservatives and his life was ended ignominiously as he was dragged through the streets of Quito, tied by his feet to the back of a cart, his head bouncing on the cobblestones, bloodied and bludgeoned to death.

Alfaro's descendants became outstanding Ecuadorian citizens and successful businessmen, and were sympathetic to the work of the gospel in Ecuador. His great-grandchildren attended school with me at the Alliance Academy. The Alfaro family lived one block from the HCJB missionary compound and were evangelical believers. Bolívar was head of the Land Rover dealership in Quito and Guayaquil.

When Dad asked if he could rent the lot, Bolívar replied, "Why, of course! You may use it for your rallies, and I wouldn't think of charging you any rent."

Plans were further enhanced when Marco Paredes secured the *Plaza de Toros* (bull fight arena) for the Sunday afternoon meeting. The tent held 1,000 people, but the Plaza seated 3,000, and it was Dad's dream to fill it up. He rented the entire arena for $16 (U.S.).

The gospel tent was portable, sort of, but it took an enormous effort to erect it. All the parts were unfolded and laid out in logical sequence. Six-foot-deep post holes were dug and two telephone poles were installed, the main supports for the thick canvas structure. Dad organized a crew of 15 missionaries and nationals who labored intensely for three days to get the tent erected in time for the first meeting. Crowds gathered to watch as the crew sweated, grunted, lifted, pulled. Children thought a circus had come to town, and were disappointed when told it was merely a gospel meeting. But Dad was quick to encourage them: "There will be movies, singing, performances by musicians, and exciting speeches. Come! And invite your neighbors." Then he went back to work, directing the laborers, helping them, until their perspiring bodies were streaming.

Putting the tent up was the biggest job, but there were others: building a platform, getting programs printed, rehearsing the chorus, installing electric wiring, setting up a public address system, distributing thousands of tickets, transporting 600 seats and a grand piano to the tent, and setting up a security system to keep the tent from being slashed by vandals.

Dad contracted with the Quito Municipal Band to play for the Sunday service at the Plaza de Toros. Permission had to be granted by the mayor of Quito, who was considered a staunch Catholic, and when the approval came through, Dad exclaimed, "The Lord is working! Amen! Amen! Amen!"

But a few snags remained. On the night of the grand opening, only two of the five key participants were in place. George Poole was on hand to sing bass, and Dad was baritone for the International Gospel Quartet. But no one else had arrived. Dad got one cable after another, each with discouraging news. His brother Jim could not get a permit to travel from Venezuela and Bill Gillam could not get clearance from Colombia to Ecuador. The featured speaker, Ramón Cabrera, was unable to get his flight from Los Angeles to Panama.

"Satan is fighting us every inch of the way," declared Dad, "but we're not going to let him stop us."

He wired Malcolm Brown, missionary in Guayaquil with the Gospel Missionary Union, and asked him to come to Quito to sing tenor in the quartet. Brown promptly dropped everything to join the campaign in Quito.

On the first night, missionary D. S. Clark gave the message. Abe VanDerPuy showed color slides, a big event in the city of Quito in 1948, for not many people had the chance to see anything in color. Most movies were still black and white, so even though the slides had no action, the vivid color fascinated the public, and turned out to be a big drawing card. When Clark issued the invitation, scores of people came forward, and Dad told Abe, "The Lord undertook in our weakness, and the results are beyond what we imagined."

The second day, Bill Gillam arrived from Colombia, and Dad exclaimed, "We're gaining ground! Satan won't win this one!"

Ramón Cabrera had not yet arrived, so the next night Abe VanDerPuy preached and showed pictures of the prodigal son. Once again, dozens of people came forward, and after the service, Dad said, "Abe, I believe you and I will be working together on many campaigns like this. You were inspired by the Holy Spirit and I could not be more happy."

On Sunday, everyone had a huge amount of work to do, transferring equipment from tent to bullfighting arena. The tent itself was left in place, with a crew to guard it, for they would return to the tent for the final meetings. Cabrera had still not arrived, so Dad said to Bill Gillam, "Be ready to give the message."

Bill protested, "I came here to sing, not preach! I'm not sure I can handle a crowd that large."

"You can do it, Bill," comforted Dad. "The Lord will help you."

At 11:00 a.m. Sunday a cable arrived from Cabrera saying he was in Panama and due to arrive in Quito at 12:30 noon. He had to transfer planes in Cali, Colombia, but as Cabrera's flight from Panama touched down in Cali, the plane to Quito was already taxiing down the runway. The pilot of Cabrera's plane radioed ahead and the Quito-bound plane taxied back to the terminal building. That was back in the days when Avianca, the Colombian airline, used DC-3's, schedules were relaxed, and airline operations were controlled by polite human beings instead of monster computers. No airliner today would return to a terminal, but in that era, they came back. Cabrera hastily boarded and arrived in Quito at 12:45.

Dad raced with Cabrera to the downtown arena, and the two watched solemnly while over 2,000 people entered the Plaza

Belmonte for the largest crowd that had ever gathered in Quito to hear the gospel. Cabrera, short of stature, but impressive with white shock of curly hair and bushy black eyebrows, was magnificent.

After the service, Dad told Cabrera, "in the very arena where crowds had gathered to witness the bloody and sadistic spectacle of toreadors matching their agility with fierce bulls, there now echoed melodies of gospel songs and preaching of salvation from sin."

They returned to the gospel tent for the last meeting, but the final night was threatened with cancellation. After the mayor of Quito had approved the Quito Municipal Band for the Sunday meeting, he had received abusive criticism, and tried to appease his critics by cancelling the final tent meeting, claiming Dad had not gotten his permit from the right source.

Dad spent all day going from one government office to another, pleading, charming, cajoling, as one officer after another told him "no, no, no." At 4:00 p.m. he was told by one official he absolutely could not hold the meeting in the tent that night. Persisting, he went to another office, showed his police permit and assured the administrator that all was in order. Finally, at 4:30 p.m. the authority said "yes." Dad quickly said thank you and left before the director could change his mind.

The last meeting was best as the tent was packed and there was perfect attention. The meeting ended at 8:00 p.m. after 50 people came forward to accept Christ. Dad and the other team members joined Cabrera to counsel the new believers. They stayed until 10:00 p.m. talking to the newly converted, reassuring them, and cementing their new faith.

In one week, over 200 people had made commitments for Christ, in a city where the total evangelical population had been less than 200.

The seasoned missionary D.S. Clark said to Dad, "The number of believers in Quito has doubled in one week, after more than 50 years of gospel work in this city."

"Yes, D. S., praise God, this is a marvelous victory, but we are merely reaping the harvest. We must be thankful for the pioneers who have sown the seed and nurtured the crop over these past five decades." Dad always admired the courageous Nineteenth-Century missionaries who had opened the doors for gospel work in Ecuador and who had labored faithfully for many years, preaching the gospel without seeing the fruits of their labors.

The gospel team left Quito for Guayaquil, and that same morning Jim and June Savage finally arrived from Venezuela. June stayed in Quito with Mom while Jim hurried to join the rest of the team in the port city.

In Guayaquil they did not need the gospel tent, for they had secured a splendid location: the same coliseum where the Olympic basketball championships for South America had been held. Guayaquil had always been more open to the gospel than Quito and 4,000 attended the first night.

Dad told Cabrera, "Brother Ramón, I believe that's the largest crowd that has ever attended a gospel service in the northern half of South America. Only in Argentina and Brazil have there been larger crowds."

Over 100 new converts enrolled in the instruction classes which were organized in Guayaquil's two churches, and the *"Cuarteto Internacional"* ("International Quartet"), with Cabrera, moved up the coast to Manta, the post of duty for Ralph and Ruth Emery of the Christian & Missionary Alliance. June flew from Quito to play the piano for the Manta meetings.

The bulky gospel tent, folded into a dozen huge bundles of canvas, arrived from Quito by train and was set up within a few yards of fishing boats nestled in Manta's quiet harbor, with waves of the Pacific Ocean lapping gently as background music to the gospel services. The 40' x 80' tent had been considered suitable for 500 people when Congressman Allen secured it for Dad, but in Manta over 1,500 people crowded in, with 300 seated and the rest standing.

After the Manta meetings, Ralph Emery asked Dad to conduct

some tent meetings in the nearby town of Jipijapa (pronounced hee pee hah' pah) for there had never been a real crusade in that dusty village.

The tent was erected in only eight hours, for by now they had gotten quite good at it. There was only one thing missing: benches. There were no wooden benches in Jipijapa so the gospel crew hastily constructed benches made of bamboo. They were crude, but were satisfactory...at least for the first few minutes. The evening service was filled to capacity, and rather than sit on the "benches" the people stood on them. All at once a whole row of people disappeared. The bench had collapsed. As the service continued, one bench after another cracked and split. Each time the crowd laughed, and Dad laughed with them. In the end, they were all standing on the ground itself, packed in tightly, a good-natured crowd.

Dad reviewed the month of July, 1948, with gratitude and astonishment: "This one month has been the most thrilling of my ministry. God has brought into reality a harvest in South America that would have seemed preposterous in by-gone years. Praise God from whom all blessings flow."

Dad ran these campaigns in his official capacity as vice president for Youth for Christ for Latin America. The Youth for Christ home office in Wheaton, Illinois, had promised $2,500 to aid in the cost of the series of campaigns, but had sent only $250. The young organization was having financial troubles of its own. HCJB had advanced money for travel, and Cabrera had paid for his flight from the United States out of his own pocket. Dad got the team together and they knelt in prayer: "Oh Lord, we have felt Satanic opposition every hour of this month, hindering travel plans, complicating requirements for official permits, and creating multitudinous delays and obstacles. Now we have no money. We plead with Thee, Oh God, to touch the hearts of thy servants so we may continue in this work Thou hast laid on our hearts."

Over the next few months, donations came in from family and friends so Dad was able to repay all campaign debts but was in a quandary: could he count on help from Youth for Christ for the proposed rallies in November? Bob Cook took over the helm at Youth for Christ and wrote Dad an encouraging letter, assuring him that they planned to back up the South American team. Heartened, Dad said, "Wilda, it looks like things are going to move now."

Still there was no money, only a promise. Plunging forward on faith, Dad went ahead with his plans and left on November 1 for Pereira, Colombia. On November 12 he wrote with ardor:

The blessings continue. Revival fires continue to spread. Great numbers of souls are being saved. Never has there been such a wonderful harvest of souls in Colombia. Jim said to me the other night, "Bob, I'm afraid I can't take many more such blessings—I'm just going to bust with joy." In our first 11 days of meetings, 240 have been saved, and we pray for 500 for the entire month.

Colombia is more fanatical than Ecuador, the Catholic clergy is more in control, and stonings and persecutions are common. Yet God is blessing us with marvelous results. We have encountered no physical violence on this trip, but we must be prepared for it.

Although we have not been harmed physically, we have had other difficulties. In Pereira we had a theater rented but the owner was the most cantankerous fellow you can imagine. Our meeting was scheduled for 5:30 p.m. and crowds were waiting to get in, but he started a show of his own and wouldn't let us in until 7:00 p.m. Four hundred people waited two hours, then listened attentively to the sermon by Colombian preacher Henry Parra. Just as he gave the invitation, the owner came up to the platform and told us we'd have to get out, as he had another show ready to begin. We asked those who wanted to accept Christ to walk to the missionary's house—and twenty sincere seekers did so.

The last night, Parra was preaching on the theme, "How shall we escape if we neglect so great a salvation?" As he was wrapping up his sermon, the theater owner let in a crowd of young boys who rushed in yelling, whooping, and whistling. Even in the midst of such a distraction God gave us 14 souls who accepted Christ.

Here in Cali, just as we started giving the invitation, the lights went out. Satan tried to cause unrest but God overruled as 14 people groped their way forward in the dark to take their stand for the Lord.

Back in Quito, Dad accepted responsibility for several monumental tasks and Mom wondered how he could keep going as program director at HCJB, coordinator of Youth for Christ campaigns in various countries, and pastor of a new church. She became concerned about Dad's frantic schedule, for he began "checking the news" at 6:00 a.m. and often didn't finish announcing the last program until 2:00 a.m. Throughout the day, there was a constant stream of activities, and Mom told him, "Bob, honey, I'm worried about you. You've lost weight, you're working 16 hours a day and you're trying to do it in Quito's high altitude."

Dad said, "Thanks for checking, Wilda, but I enjoy every minute, and I feel terrific. Don't worry about me."

She sighed, "Well, I'm not complaining, because it's wonderful to be in the Lord's service, but I do sorta wish we had more personnel."

Dad's radio ministry was worldwide. His evangelistic campaigns were continental. But he also loved his local ministries in Quito: Sunday School, jail work, and development of a new church. The Sunday School he had founded in Iñaquito, near the HCJB compound, was now overflowing with over 90 people crowded into one small room. They needed to build a church, so both Dad and Abe VanDerPuy set themselves to find the right site. HCJB was in the northern part of the long city of Quito, and the Christian & Missionary Alliance church was in the south. Dad sought a location in the strategic center.

Dad's prayer was that God would give them a church of 100 new members each year or 1,000 members in 10 years. His request was one of great magnitude, for at the time, there were less than 1,000 active members of gospel churches in all Ecuador.

Great Grandpa Jenson sent Mom and Dad a check for $50 and asked them to do "anything they wanted with it." Mom wrote back, "If you really want us to do with it exactly what we want most, well, we don't really need anything, but there is something that would please us more than anything. We'd like to put it toward the property for our new church. That's the main thing Bob dreams about and same with me, and your check would mark the first contribution to our effort."

It was typical of Mom and Dad to take a personal gift and turn it over to the church. They had very few needs. We lived comfortably but modestly. By Ecuadorian standards, we were rich. By U.S. standards, we had the typical comforts of a middle-income home. They did not crave more. Dad sometimes quoted Philippians 4:11: "I have learned, in whatsoever state I am, therewith to be content." He was content with his standard of living; his only dissatisfaction was with his accomplishments for the Lord. He wanted more, always more, and seldom rested, for he had to achieve great things for the Lord.

Back in the United States, Maranatha Bible Conference held a special missionary meeting to address the need of the new Quito church and Amy Lee Stockton laid the challenge before the people. Over $8,000 was pledged, $5,000 coming from Dr. and Mrs. Bell of New Orleans. Sallie Lee Bell was a well-known Christian writer at the time. The work of establishing the new church could now go forward in earnest.

Although a permanent site was at least a year away, Dad and Abe began to hold meetings every Sunday afternoon. They got together with some of the leading church members, and told them: "A church is not a building but a congregation of believers. Let's become an organized church now. Later we'll find a building we can call our own."

The new church, called *El Centro Bíblico* ("The Bible Center") was organized in October, 1948. The organizational meeting was simple, yet impressive, as each charter member walked to the front to sign the covenant and statement of faith. Dad was named co-pastor along with Abe VanDerPuy, and Abe led in a communion service. Until the church building could be constructed, the newly formed congregation would rent a hall in downtown Quito.

The church did not have a piano, and Mom played on a little pump organ. She longed for a piano, so she could give Dad's robust gospel songleading equally vigorous accompaniment. Events took a sudden turn in the life of her parents which would soon provide her with a piano: After the Second World War had ended, Grandpa Johnson had returned to his home in Wheaton from his military post in Boston, and resumed his work as a lawyer for the Hartford Insurance Company. But in 1948, he was offered reinstatement in the Army. He eagerly took the position, and wrote that he would spend a few months in California, followed by a tour of duty in Japan.

I was concerned and asked, "Won't Grandpa get killed?"

"No, there's not a war going on right now," assured Mom.

The piano Mom had played throughout her growing-up years was still in the home of her parents in Wheaton, but as they prepared to sell their home and move to Japan, they shipped the piano to Quito. Mother was ecstatic, and planned to install it, not at home, but in the new church. "You are such swell parents, for you not only gave me a great musical opportunity in encouraging me to have the best classical lessons over the years, but now you've provided me with the instrument to serve the Lord in our new church."

Mother's touch on the piano could be both light and dramatic. She learned the Latin beat so well that no one would have guessed an Anglo-Saxon was playing the piano. She was able to transpose from one key to another with ease, and worked closely with Dad to make a service peppy and effective. Sometimes she would be asked to play a piano solo, and her classical training came forth as she brilliantly played arrangements of gospel music which transformed them into gorgeous compositions of concert caliber. Then she could quickly fade into the background, to play a soft and gentle accompaniment to missionary Jeanne O'Dell's rich contralto voice.

During Dad's travels and hectic schedule, Mom kept our family going. A few glimpses into our family life show what it was like for an American family in Ecuador in 1948. We children got an allowance of 2 *sucres* (12 cents U.S.) each week. That was enough to buy some candy and gum, but now that I was age eight, Mom began to give me jobs so I could earn more money. My favorite task was waxing floors, for I loved to see results of my labors. The shining wood gave me great satisfaction.

A big event for our family was the day pasteurized milk came to Quito. No longer did we have to boil our milk, because a sanitary plant had been set up and we began to receive bottled milk daily. The taste was so splendid that I drank three glasses the first day. Dad drank four. The word "cholesterol" was not a part of everyone's vocabulary in those days, and Dad drank milk with relish.

Dad and Mom both disciplined me with spankings. Mom used her hairbrush; Dad used his slipper or belt. They were of the old school: "Spare the rod and spoil the child." But they also had creative ways of punishing me and none was more effective than putting me in my room for an hour, sitting in a chair or standing in a corner. One day I wanted to walk barefoot and asked Mom's permission. Ever the pessimist, she worried that I might catch cold, step on a nail, or pick up some germs. She said "no."

A few minutes later I saw Dad and asked him if I could go barefoot and he cheerfully said "sure!" Not long after, Mom and Dad compared notes. I was immediately ushered into the august presence of my father, who told me that never again was I to play him off against his wife. It was such a serious offense that it earned both a spanking and an hour standing in the corner.

As I think back on my spankings, I feel they were well deserved and do not hold any grudge against Dad for giving them to me. But when they were administered, it was awful. The spankings hurt, but worse, there was a grim time of preparing for them as Dad attached ceremony to the event. He held a strong belief that he should never strike any of his children when he was angry. He believed that a spanking was a just punishment that should be delivered only after deliberation and discussion. Often I wished he would get it over with quickly, but he would discuss the issue, explain why he felt a spanking was in order, take me out to the back room, pull off his belt, and whack me hard across the buttocks.

One time I stole a flashlight from a store. When Dad asked me where I got it, I told him the store owner had given it to me. Unconvinced, Dad checked out my story. I was caught red-handed. After lectures regarding theft and lying, as well as prayer and forgiveness, we went into the bedroom, whereupon Dad pulled off his belt and gave a dozen swats. After the terrible ceremony was over, Dad told me how much he loved me and how he hoped I would learn from this punishment.

I did. I never stole again.

Mom asked me to write a letter to the Junior Church at the First Baptist Church in Romeo, Michigan, which took care of my support. All missionaries wrote frequent "prayer letters" to their supporters back in the United States, and since the Junior Church contributed money to support me, Mom figured I should write a missionary prayer letter as well. The substance of my "missionary prayer letter" was, "Douglas and I had some frogs. They are dead. They stink." The letter was mailed to Romeo and read to the children in church. It was one of the more interesting missionary letters received by the church that year.

Although Dad traveled a lot, we did not usually feel deprived for Mom made sure our lives were full of activity. When Dad was home he was a powerful and joyful force. His absence did have an effect, however, and little Carol expressed it eloquently. Dad was in Colombia during November and when Thanksgiving Day arrived, Carol said, "Mommy, tomorrow is Thanksgiving, isn't it?"

"Yes."

"Is Daddy coming back?"

"Not until Saturday."

"Then how can it be Thanksgiving?"

8

How much can one man do?

"May we be a twentieth century Good Samaritan, having compassion on those who have fallen into difficult situations, lifting them up and caring for them."

—*Pocket Prayers*, p. 25

The new church, *El Centro Bíblico*, had been in existence only three months. We still worshipped in a downtown rented hall, and a permanent site of our own was still a dream, but by January 1949 we were already enjoying attendances exceeding those of the only other evangelical church in Quito, which had been ministering for 25 years. Dad reported, "Prayer meetings are wonderful and Sunday afternoon rallies glorious. I don't believe two fellows could be happier in a ministry than Abe and I are. We work together in perfect harmony and oneness."

Abe VanDerPuy and Dad were becoming close friends, for they toiled jointly in many capacities: radio, evangelism, and co-pastors of the church. Their evangelistic ministries took them all over Ecuador using both gospel sound bus and gospel tent. Some missionaries began to refer to them fondly as "the David and Jonathan of the HCJB staff," a reference to the Biblical characters whose profound friendship became a classic model of two men working together in a common cause, with deep affection for each other, in which the combined efforts of two were greater than the sum of the individuals.

One project the two colleagues accomplished together was the construction of a baptismal pool. Until the new church could be built, there was no proper place to baptize new converts, so the two friends had an outdoor baptismal pool constructed right on the HCJB property, under the tall towers which broadcast programs to every continent on earth. The first baptismal service was held, and the most eloquent account was written by the effusive Grace Larson:

What a day, O glorious day of blessing never to be forgotten here at HCJB. For some weeks now, those blessed boys, Bob and Abe, have been building a baptistry. The spot they chose is right in front of our garden gate. Very thoughtfully and artistically they have arranged the steps to lead right down into the water, passing through curtains that hang in the arch of the garden gate.

I will never forget Bob in his white suit there in the water, the pool surrounded by lilies, and then by groups of people washed whiter than lilies by the blood of our Lord. Abe led the singing and precious Wilda played the little pump organ.

The rain that had been falling in torrents in other parts of the city held off until dear Bob buried the last candidate in the watery grave and with glory in his face, brought them up to newness of life in Christ Jesus.

At the close, fifteen knelt to confess their sin and find grace and pardon at the feet of Jesus. One whole family wept their way through to peace. This I have never witnessed in all the years we've been here.

Bob and Abe's smiles were so bright I almost needed dark glasses. It was glory in their precious faces. Thank God for these chosen instruments who are in God's place at God's exact minute. Surely they have come into the world for just such a time as this.

Grace's husband, Reuben Larson, was present at the baptismal, as was his colleague, D. S. Clark. The two senior missionaries looked on with pleasure at the baptismal ceremony, but an unspoken worry nagged each of them. They treasured the talents of Abe and Bob, and feared they were getting too distracted from their radio ministry. Their fear was not without foundation, for by May, the *Centro Bíblico* had become the third largest church in Ecuador, and Dad dreamed of its becoming the largest in Latin America. They were still meeting in a rented hall in downtown Quito, and Dad was eager to get on with purchasing property and building the church. He had selected a site he considered ideal, across from the University, on a main thoroughfare.

But the project stalled as Reuben Larson and D. S. Clark voiced their concerns that Abe and Dad were getting distracted from their primary task—radio evangelism. The elder missionaries asked the two fiery young evangelists to join them for a meeting. Reuben Larson, with his massive square head and authoritative deep voice, declared, "I am deeply concerned that Bob and Abe are liable to give priority interest to the church to the detriment of our radio ministry."

Dad replied, "I agree the church could take me away from my work at the radio station, but I deeply feel that God wants me to do both."

"But how can you have time for both?" wondered the venerable D. S. Clark, with his soft and distinguished British accent.

"Well, I'm still hoping I can be relieved of my duties as program director so I can devote more time to evangelism and church work," said Dad.

"But, Bob," replied Reuben, "you're one of the best organized people I've ever known and you do a wonderful job of staying on top of all those details."

"Well, Reuben, I've got a confession to make. I may be good at administrative details, but I don't like them. I think the Lord has called me to be a preacher and feel I should spend more of my time performing on radio programs and less time organizing all the little details that consume so much time."

"Mmmmm," murmured Reuben. "This is probably not the best time to bring it up, but I was thinking of appointing you Field Director when D. S. goes to the States."

"I'll do whatever I'm asked to do, but my heart is in evangelism and church development," replied Dad.

Then D. S. Clark presented his vision of the radio ministry: "My brothers, God has vouchsafed to us of the World Radio Missionary Fellowship a unique and sublime ministry of reaching the regions beyond by means of radio. This holy calling should always be paramount in our hearts and all auxiliary efforts, even though of great importance, must be subordinate."

Dad protested, "I don't feel these efforts should be classified as 'subordinate.' Abe's sound-bus work, our new church, and the revival campaigns all merit just as high a rank of value as the radio ministry."

"I agree," chimed in Reuben, "but the point of the discussion is not which ministries are more valuable. The point is that we have a specific ministry here at hand, radio, and if we spread our energy too thin, we won't do our radio job well."

"Our job is to preach the gospel," rejoined Dad, "and radio is one way of doing it. I think my radio ministry will be more fresh and effective if I am working in my own back yard."

"I am very eager to keep HCJB non-sectarian, a servant of other missions," averred D. S. Clark.

"Agreed," said Abe, "and our vision for this church is that it be strictly an evangelical church, with no denominational labels."

"I'm afraid it would become a denomination all unto itself," fretted Reuben.

"We will fight to keep it simple and uncomplicated," vowed Dad.

"My hope is we will have a national pastor within five years," added Abe, "and Bob and I can step aside. The church must become self-governing and self-supporting."

"Amen. Amen. Amen," concurred Dad, in triplicate, as was his manner.

"One thing that makes me praise God," interjected Abe, "is that we can have sharp differences of opinion, yet discuss them with love and harmony."

"Indeed, this is a miracle," said Reuben. "I doubt if many organizations could solve their problems in this manner."

"We must wait on the Lord so He will give us wisdom," counseled D. S.

Dad's idea of "waiting on the Lord" was to wait for a couple of hours, pray earnestly, figure out what to do, and get moving. He did not see any need to "wait on the Lord" for weeks and months. Discouraged by delays in moving ahead with the church building, and anxious to keep momentum going, he prayed the four of them would soon reach a consensus agreeable to all.

A few weeks later, no conclusion had yet been reached, so Dad looked at the bright side by admitting the delay might have been useful. A different location might be advisable, farther away from the University, but closer to major arteries where bus lines could bring people from all over Quito.

The four men joined together once again for another discussion about the church. Reuben and D. S. told Abe and Dad, "We've prayed and talked, and now it's time to move. We would like to take our hands off, and let you do what you think the Lord wants you to do."

Almost in unison, Abe and Dad replied, "Praise God!"

Men of vision, working together for a common cause, found ways to blend their differences of opinion. They agreed on one thing above all: they were called to advance the cause of Christ.

Throughout his years as a missionary, Dad's love of being a pastor held a central position in his ministry. He often said, "I have a pastor's heart." Fortunately, those wise men, Reuben Larson and D. S. Clark, found ways to satisfy this love, yet channel his energy in a multitude of ways in the radio ministry of HCJB.

Dad finally secured a site right across from the *Colegio Espejo*, Quito's newest high school, a few blocks from the University of Quito, right on a bus line, and two blocks from the main avenue that ran north and south through the long valley in which Quito lay.

The price for the 443 square meters was $7,000 (U.S.) or 119,000 sucres. This was higher than comparable properties in most American cities in 1948. Although property prices were higher, labor costs were considerably lower, so the ultimate cost of the church was about $15,000.

Meanwhile, the gospel tent was put to good use. A campaign was scheduled for the lovely mountain town of Ambato, 66 miles south of Quito, a bastion of Catholic conservatism.

Over 2,000 people came to the services in Ambato. Never in the history of evangelical work in Ambato had such crowds listened to the gospel message.

From Ambato, Dad moved on with Abe VanDerPuy and missionary musician Bob Beukema to an even more exciting campaign in Ecuador's northernmost port, Esmeraldas, named after emeralds mined in the area.

The journey to Esmeraldas took two days, a 12-hour trip by truck to Quinindé, followed by a nine-hour voyage by canoe. The canoe almost proved disastrous. While coming through rapids, a huge wave splashed into the narrow craft, filling it half-full of water. Suitcases, sound equipment, film projectors, and the gospel tent were immersed. Clothes were drenched. Dad's first fear was, "The slides! The color films! They're ruined!"

As they pulled the canoe ashore, and began to unload it, the unflappable canoe polemen told Dad this was normal, and not to worry. Sure enough, as he examined the metal containers, Dad was relieved to find the film had not been damaged. There on the beach he led the group in prayer, "Oh, Father, we thank Thee for preserving these films which have been dedicated to the furtherance of Thy gospel. May they be used to convict people of their sin, and bring them to Thy son, our Saviour, Jesus Christ, in whose name we pray. Amen." They reloaded the canoe, pressed on down the river, and arrived in Esmeraldas a few hours later. Missionaries, cameras, clothes, and gospel tent all made the trip intact.

The crowds in Ambato had been large but subdued, typical of mountain people in Ecuador. But Esmeraldas was a different world. Often referred to as "Little Africa," most *Esmeraldeños* were coal black and full of exuberance. The gospel tent was filled to capacity each night, with hundreds standing. It was difficult to maintain order as most had never been to a gospel service, and considered the tent meeting a circus.

It was uplifting to have a joyful audience, but it had drawbacks. Because of the festive mood of the jolly crowd, Dad hesitated to give a normal invitation to come to the altar to accept Christ, fearing everyone would swarm forward just for the fun of it. Instead of asking people to come forward, Dad invited those who were interested to remain behind when others left. Unsure whether this approach would succeed, he was pleased when dozens of people stayed every night, and in a more quiet setting, he was able to explain fundamentals of the faith and lead them in prayer.

The return from Esmeraldas was by a different route. They decided to take a boat ride down the Pacific coastline to the port city of Manta, then fly to Quito. The boat carried a load of cattle. With horns attached to outrigger poles on the canoe, the poor beasts were forced to swim out to the boat which was anchored in deeper waters. A block and tackle hoist was used to lift them out of the water onto the deck. Dad's stomach turned as he watched the way the stevedores brutally manhandled the hapless animals. By the time they were flopped on the deck they were exhausted from the swim, but it was necessary to get them up so they could walk into the pen in the hold of the deck. To motivate a cow to stand up, the men broke their tails. Dad looked at Bob Beukema and grimaced. After the cows were all on board a sailboat came alongside with a load of pigs. They were thrown squealing on top of the cattle. This made the cattle unhappy and they bolted in unison, pulling boards off that section of the ship.

The missionaries moved to their "stateroom," with its tiny window and five-foot bunk beds. The ruddy Abe VanDerPuy was blistering with sunburn and organist Bob Beukema was nauseated, both from the swelling seas and the disgusting scene he had just witnessed. Both were startled to see Dad calmly carving up an onion. As he put the slice between two layers of bread, he said, "This onion sandwich will cure whatever ails you! Have one." He ate alone.

It was time to hold another gospel tent meeting in Quito. For Dad, the occasion was especially exciting because it meant a reunion of three of the four members of the Evangel Male Quartet, who had sung together at meetings across the midwest during Dad's years at Moody, Wheaton, and Maranatha. Howard Schoof and Clyde Taylor traveled to Ecuador to join the meetings. Russ Case was unable to attend, but HCJB missionary George Sánchez filled in as the fourth member.

A gospel tent meeting in Quito was risky business. Every evangelistic campaign was clouded with the fear that violence could break out at any time. To make matters worse, the Catholic church in Ecuador sponsored a Eucharistic congress that same week and delegates from all over the country converged on Quito to attend the conferences.

When Dad and Abe had scheduled the meetings in the gospel tent, they had been unaware it coincided with the beginning of the Eucharistic congress. The timing was bad; the tent's location even worse. It was set up in the Ejido Park, directly across from the stadium where Catholics were preparing for their meetings. It was a location almost guaranteed to cause trouble, almost as though the evangelicals were defying the Catholics, challenging them to a confrontation. This of course was not their intent, but it seemed that way to the Catholics. There was always an underlying current of tension between evangelicals and Catholics, but passions were usually restrained when everyone kept a polite distance. Now, however, the gospel tent stood there, audacious and conspicuous, drawing attention to itself and to the meetings taking place under its rooftop.

The first meeting was tense. Everyone was fidgety. During the entire service, the congregation was disturbed by "haunting, weird-sounding, minor music" produced by a procession passing by, celebrating the entrance of the "Virgin of Quinche"—a small idol two feet high considered by many Ecuadorians as the most miraculous of the virgins. Despite the disturbance, Dr. Walter Montaño, the converted Spanish priest known as "The Monk Who Lived Again," preached, arresting in his passionate delivery, and the crowd ceased to notice the distractions outside the tent. Dad reported, "God gave us a marvelous harvest of 40 souls. It was the greatest sermon I've ever heard preached in Spanish." Montaño's sermon, however, was not without interruption. For about ten minutes, he preached in darkness, as someone cut the light wires. Somehow, this rumpus served only to inspire both preacher and crowd, as they sat upright, determined, defiant, and finished out the service with uplifted spirits.

The minor commotion of the first night was but a foretaste of things to come. It got much uglier. The second night, the evangelistic team members quietly slipped into the back of the tent, lifting their hearts to the Lord, "We plead your blessings upon our efforts tonight." The quartet sang two numbers and Washington Padilla, a young Ecuadorian preacher, led in prayer. Suddenly a mob of young men outside the tent began to chant, "Down with Yankee imperialism," "Long Live the Virgin," and "Destroy their Bibles." Because many evangelical missionaries were from the United States, the gospel was often associated with everything people disliked about the United States, so it was not uncommon to hear denunciations of Yankee imperialism mixed with diatribes against the evangelicals.

Dad asked the congregation to rise and announced the hymn, "Stand Up for Jesus." The mob of young Catholics countered by singing "*Ave María.*" Both groups sang louder and louder, but the crowd in the tent easily outsang those outside. The mood turned uglier as Catholic young men marched inside the tent yelling "Down with the Protestants" and "Let's burn their Bibles."

Attackers moved closer and closer to the platform but Dad kept the music going. Suddenly the tent started to fall down. Outside, angry young men were hacking away at the guy ropes. The sides of the tent fell, lights went out, stink bombs went off, but Don Roberto Savage kept them singing. Mom was playing the piano, terribly frightened, but Dad turned to her, smiled broadly, winked, formed his thumb and forefinger into the "OK" sign, and kept pumping his arms vigorously. Mom was heartened. The crowd's mood seemed to change as well, for their singing became bolder, heartier. Dad paused between verses, complimented them on their singing, then said, "That was pretty good, but this time let's turn up the volume and let everyone know how much we love the Lord." As he said "turn up the volume" he twisted his hand as though turning a radio dial. Then, as he set the beat, he stomped his foot on the platform and ordered *Cantemos!*" (Let's sing.) The audience responded with *brio;* their singing became robust and brawny.

Within 15 minutes, police arrived, order was restored, and lights came back on. To his great surprise, Dad looked over the crowd and noted no one had left. He congratulated them for their courage as a group of evangelical young men patched ropes, drove in stakes, and re-erected the tent.

After the service, Dad discovered some of the Christian young people in the back of the tent had been attacked and bruised. Víctor Guzmán came up to the front with blood streaming from his lips. With intense emotion he wept and said, "Don Roberto, these few wounds aren't very much. Christ suffered more than this for me. I suffer gladly for my Lord. I would give my life for Christ." Víctor had known the Lord only five months, yet this was the second time he had been beaten for Christ's sake.

Later, Dad wrote, "Did our people flee to their homes for safety? Not one! They stayed on the spot, more firm in their stand for Christ than I had ever seen them before. How I praise God for them. My heart swells with pride as I think of their staunchness. I never heard such victorious singing as resounded in the tent as we commenced anew the rally."

Not all Christian believers were as devout as Víctor. After the high spiritual fervor of an evangelistic campaign, there were often some disappointments and letdowns. Nothing discouraged Dad more than to see Christian believers slip from their bedrock of faith. One of the Spanish announcers at HCJB, a founder and deacon of the new church, was caught stealing funds from the radio station. Church members who were pillars of the faith got involved in extra-marital affairs. It enraged and bewildered Dad, who could not imagine why a Christian would go astray once the truth had been clearly implanted in his mind. He wrote: "At present I am doing a series of Sunday messages on 'Sin.' I feel deeply burdened with the necessity of awaking a real sense of shame and conscience in regard to sin. Fornication, adultery, lying, and deceit are so common there is hardly any consciousness about it."

As the year 1949 drew to a close, our personal lives were touched with extra joy, with plain and simple pleasures that meant little or nothing to those in the United States. When missionaries returned from the United States, they often brought gifts from relatives back home. Shortly before Christmas, the Larsons returned and brought delights like scotch tape, canned goods, and packaged goods. We were thrilled to get Dentyne and Blackjack gum, and an assortment of American candy bars. Grandma Savage sent Dad ties, wool socks, sport shirt, and a maroon jacket. He wrote his mother saying, "I'm strutting around like a peacock. Whoopdeedoodendoo."

These simple items formed part of our Christmas gift exchange and we smacked each treat with relish. But the best gift for Carol and me was found in a little envelope lying on a branch of our Christmas tree. We tore it open and read the announcement:

A BABY BROTHER OR SISTER IN MARCH

We giggled with glee when we read the news. From then on we talked about it daily. I wanted a little brother and Carol hoped for a sister. The idea of a new baby was so compelling I could not wait until March, so I visited the home of missionaries Bob and Marion Clark, who had two small children. I looked in on four-month-old Marjorie nearly every day, and played with two-year-old Bobby. All the while, I was thinking, "I hope I'll get a brother, but any baby would be fine."

9

Multiplied ministries

"Almighty, Victorious God of Glory, You formed the mountains with your mighty strength."

Pocket Praise, p. 58

1950

Baptism by immersion was often scary for the person being baptized. There was the fear of the water, the cold, and most of all, of being submerged. I never saw anyone do a finer job of baptizing than Dad. He once baptized a huge 250-pound man, 6'4"—towering over Dad's 5'9" frame. I thought surely Dad would lose his grip on the giant once he was down in the water, but Dad had a technique that never failed. He simply bent his knee as he lowered the person into the water, so his upper leg was firmly planted under the person's back. This solid stance, combined with the buoyancy of the water, made the procedure smooth, flowing, and graceful.

The doctrine of baptism splintered many Protestant denominations. Some preferred sprinkling and others immersion. But the method of baptism was not as fundamental as its nature and timing. What exactly was baptism anyway? When should a person be baptized, when he's a baby or an adult? Many Protestant denominations practiced infant baptism, whereas

Baptists like Dad believed it was an act of obedience that should be performed only by a person who had already freely chosen Christ as his Savior. Baptism was a testimony of the transformation which had taken place in the life of a believer, the outward expression of an inward change. The Christian, in baptism, was identifying with Christ's death, burial, and resurrection.

Dad felt the "sprinkling" technique did not do justice to the symbolism of baptism. Immersion, on the other hand, described it perfectly, for in descending into the water the Christian was buried symbolically with Christ and in arising he was raised with Christ.

Nothing was lovelier than baptism in a river for that was how John the Baptist baptized Jesus. Dad baptized people in rivers, lakes, and the shores of the Pacific Ocean. Usually, however, it was done in a baptismal pool, where the water was about three feet deep. In Quito's cool climate, he made sure the water was heated ahead of time.

Dad would enter the water, followed by the candidate for baptism, both wearing robes with weights in hems to keep robes submerged in water. He then asked, "Do you believe in the Lord Jesus Christ as your own personal Savior?" After the candidate's affirmative reply, Dad gently put a handkerchief over the person's nose and carefully lowered him backwards into the water until he was completely submerged. This represented being buried with Christ. Then Dad lifted him so the individual once again assumed a standing position. This symbolized being raised with Christ.

Many Protestant denominations that practiced infant baptism considered the sacrament an act of family dedication, similar to the ancient Israeli practice of circumcision, a visible symbol of the covenant the family had made with God. In baptizing an infant, they were "sealing the covenant," vowing to God to raise their child in the "nurture and admonition" of the Lord.

Although Dad did not practice infant baptism, he was not totally opposed to the concept. Many of his colleagues at both the Scandinavian Alliance Mission and radio station HCJB came from

Presbyterian and Methodist backgrounds. Many of the faithful at Maranatha Bible Conference were from western Michigan's Dutch Reformed Church. All these denominations practiced infant baptism, and although Dad would have been happier if they had practiced adult immersion, he did not consider it a strong enough issue to divide the church. He felt he could have good Christian fellowship with people of these denominations and work joyfully with them in the same organizations. His approach to the issue was positive: he preached in favor of adult immersion, but not against infant sprinkling.

However, the Roman Catholic view of infant baptism went way too far for Dad. The Catholics not only baptized their babies, but considered this sacrament essential to get the baby into heaven. Nothing caused more anguish for a Catholic family than to have a baby die without being baptized.

Dad heartily believed in adult baptism, but there were strict standards for the person to achieve before baptism. First and foremost, he had to be saved. This meant acknowledgement that he was a sinner, repentance, acceptance of Christ in his heart, and a public profession of his faith in Christ. Then, a person had to have some grounding in the fundamentals of the faith before baptism. It was up to the pastor to decide if the person was ready. That was not always an easy judgment call.

A new convert named Pedro, age 30, wanted to be baptized, but Dad suspected he was living with a woman out of wedlock. He decided to confront Pedro. "Are you living with a woman?"

"Oh, yes," answered Pedro, unabashedly.

"Don't you think you'd better get married?" asked Dad.

"Impossible, Don Roberto. She has such an ugly disposition, we could never get along."

"Is this the only woman you've had?"

"Oh my, no."

"How many have you had?"

"Oh, Don Roberto, they are uncountable. At least twenty."

"Well, Pedro, I can't baptize you if you are living out of holy wedlock."

"No problem, Don Roberto. I'll move out."

A few weeks later, Pedro came to Dad once again and reported, "I'm not living with a woman, I love the Lord, and I want to be baptized."

"That's fine, Pedro. I hope the Lord will enable you now to establish a real Christian home and have a Christian wife and family."

"Excuse me, Don Roberto, but now I'm not interested in any woman. My prayer is that the Lord will let me go to Bible Institute. I want to get trained to serve the Lord. Then it will be soon enough to think about establishing a home."

Dad gulped. It was not exactly what he intended. Although he was glad the man was no longer living out of wedlock, and although his aspirations to go to Bible Institute sounded noble enough, Dad did not in any way want to discourage anyone from Christian marriage. However, he had to admit Pedro had followed, to the letter, the advice of Don Roberto Savage. Therefore, he was baptized.

Baptism was only one of many theological issues that missionaries discussed in great depth. Another was even more fundamental: who is saved and who is lost? Underlying the whole purpose of missions was the status of "heathen" who had never heard the gospel. Sometimes we discussed the eternal destiny of those who had not had a chance to make a decision for or against Christ. Dad felt that once a person had heard the message, and had been presented with the invitation to follow Christ, he was responsible for his eternal lot from that point forward. Rejection meant eternal death; acceptance eternal life.

But what about those who had done neither? What about jungle Indians who had never heard the gospel? How about the person who had followed his conscience to the best of his ability? John Calvin taught that we were all sinners and all deserved eternal death. It was only through the grace of God that anyone was saved at all. The heathen would perish and they deserved it. It was a harsh view, but held by many.

Dad did not go that far. He trusted that God in His mercy would look with favor on those who had done their best with the knowledge they had. He considered the ancient Incas who used to worship the sun. Their prayer was, "We worship Thee, oh Sun, and if Thou art not the true God, we worship Him who made Thee."

"What else could they do? They must be saved!" I pleaded, in my best ten-year-old theology.

"Well, I'm not sure," mused Dad, "but I wouldn't rule them out."

How about a person who was just "at the edge of the kingdom of God," who had done everything within his conscience to follow the light, who was on his way to the path of the cross, but who died before he knew the full story? Was that man destined to eternity in Hell? Consider the case of Salomón Ramos. In the remote mountain village of Quinchibana, Salomón wanted to buy a Bible. He did not have enough money, so he sold some of his scarce food supplies and bought one. Then he invited HCJB missionary Frank Cook to come with the gospel sound bus and show a gospel film.

While the film was being shown, a couple of shots were fired from the darkness. It startled the missionaries, but the volleys did not sound too close, so the movie went on. Then a hail of shots rang out, this time closer. Worried, they stopped the picture and began to pack up the sound bus. Suddenly, more shots were fired. Ramos fell to the ground, clutching his chest.

The missionaries quickly laid Ramos in the back of the bus and drove as fast as the gasping gospel sound truck could go, bumping over cobblestone roads, until they reached the hospital in Ambato. Doctors worked frantically over him all night, but at 5 a.m. Salomón Ramos died.

All HCJB missionaries were shocked and grieved for his death.

They also worried that Ramos had not yet been saved, and wondered whether he had made it into the heavenly kingdom. After much thought, Dad concluded, "Ramos never took a public stand for Christ, because the open-air service in which he was wounded was the only gospel service he had ever attended. But I feel anyone who had shown the interest he had and done what he did, must have been a believer in his heart whether that belief had crystallized in a public profession of faith or not."

There were missionaries more doctrinaire than Dad, even though he considered himself a strict fundamentalist. Some would have argued that Ramos was lost, tragically and irredeemably, for he had not truly accepted Christ. Dad was willing to consider the special circumstances under which Ramos had died. However, Dad still considered himself a "hard-liner" on this issue. For him, the doctrine was settled clearly in the Bible, for Jesus said in John 14:6: "I am the way, the truth, and the life. No man cometh unto the Father but by me." It was up to God to decide the fate of Salomón Ramos, reasoned Dad. In the meantime, it was his job to make sure everyone heard the Good News of salvation. He averred, "It's not up to me to decide the fate of an individual; it's simply my task to tell that individual about the fate that awaits him if he neglects to surrender his life to Christ, the only way to the Father."

It was this task for which HCJB and all other evangelical missions existed: to preach the Word of God, in obedience to Christ's Great Commission: "Go ye into all the world and preach the gospel to every creature." For HCJB, there were many ways to preach the gospel, and several distinct "ministries" were formed to that end, each ministry designed to reach unsaved souls for Christ.

A long and continuous rainy season gave Dad one thing to cheer about. He had fretted about delays in getting the church built, but now had cause to rejoice: "The property we were so enthused about right across from the university would have been a fatal mistake. For the last three months it has been completely flooded. I tremble when I think how we had the contract all drawn up and ready to sign, but praise the Lord He turned us from that decision."

A new location had been chosen and the new church was finally completed and inaugurated. A three-week revival service was planned. Abe VanDerPuy, co-pastor along with Dad, was featured speaker the first week. Ramón Cabrera, who had stirred thousands in Quito in the campaign in the bullfight arena, preached the second week. The indomitable, effervescent, and musical Alfredo Colom preached the third and final week.

Dad supervised all details of the three-week campaign, all this while continuing his work at HCJB as program director, and radio musician. He was not about to let Reuben Larson down, for he had assured the elder missionary he could handle both jobs, radio and church.

Then he went even further, loading himself up with more work, when he took on an added assignment and taught English at the Alliance Academy every morning from 8-9 a.m. He felt each HCJB missionary with children should assist in teaching, for the school was providing an education for their children. He never complained of overwork, but cheerfully carried out each task with animation and liveliness.

He also had a series of chapel services at the Academy. I still remember some of his sermons. Most had three points. The most memorable one had four: "Ho, go, woe, and lo." He based it on four Scripture verses:

-Ho, everyone that thirsteth

-Go ye into all the world and preach the gospel.

-Woe unto him who builds his house by unrighteousness.

-Lo! I am with you always, even unto the end of the world.

The sermon left an indelible impression on me because of the way he shouted out the four key words, over and over, HO, GO, WOE, LO.

Not only were his sermons interesting, but his performance riveting. He had a habit of standing right on the edge of the platform, rocking on his heels, for maximum closeness to his audience. We children watched in horror, wondering if he'd fall off.

At 6:45 a.m. on the morning of March 24, I heard the phone ringing. I rolled back over in bed, assuming Mom or Dad would answer the phone. It rang and rang. Neither Mom nor Dad answered. Disgusted, I finally staggered out of bed and picked up the receiver. It was Dad, calling from the hospital. "Stevie," he hallooed, "you've got a baby brother!"

"May I see him?" I shouted back.

"Sure, come on over," said Dad, "and bring Carol."

I banged on Carol's door. "Get up, get up. We have a baby brother. Get dressed fast. We're going to go see him."

I dashed to my room, put on my clothes, and tore back to Carol's room. "Ready?" I called.

"Not yet. Wait a minute."

"Can't. You come when you're ready. I'm going."

"Wait."

"No."

The HCJB clinic was only two blocks away, so I ran the whole way. Dad met me and took me to the window where we peered at my little brother, a hefty 8 pounds, 4 ounces. "Are we still going to name him Jimmy?" I asked excitedly.

"Yessir," said Dad. "James Lawrence Savage—after Uncle Jim and Grandpa Lawrence."

Mom had fed me "by the book" with a rigid feeding schedule but with Jimmy she was more relaxed. She said, "It's so nice to just enjoy my third baby. I now realize it isn't so terribly important if he gets fed a little earlier than the book says. I used to make Stevie wait until 6 on the dot even if he got hungry at 5:50. Poor little guy!"

A month later the Korean War broke out and we were all immediately concerned about Grandpa and Grandma Johnson who were living in Kobe, Japan. Mom wrote to her mother, inviting

Grandma Ruby to come instantly to Ecuador.

"Will Grandpa get killed?" I probed.

"I think they're safe," replied Mom, "but this old world is in a real mess. I feel the time must be short."

"What time?" I asked.

"The time of the Lord's return," she replied.

"Why do you think it's time?" I quizzed.

"Because the Bible says that in the last days there will be war, rumors of war, and persecution. Also, Christ will return after the nation of Israel has been established once again. They are now a nation, ever since two years ago. I really believe the Lord is coming soon."

"How can I be sure I'll go to heaven?" I worried.

"Do you believe in Jesus as your Savior?" she checked.

"Yes," I assured her.

"Then you have nothing to worry about."

Deep inside, however, I continued to worry. I knew I loved the Lord, and was quite sure I was saved. At age seven I had knelt and sincerely prayed, as Dad coached, "Jesus, I am a sinner. I repent. Forgive me. I accept You." Yes, I was saved. However, stories about Christ's return always frightened me. I heard messages about Christ's parable in which He described his Second Coming. Two people would be working together, and "one shall be taken and the other left behind."

How could I be sure I wouldn't be left behind? One day I came home from school and yelled, "Mommy!" No answer. "Daddy!" No answer. "María!" No answer. The house was silent and I panicked. The Lord had come and I had been left behind. I looked out the window. The cobblestone street that ran between our house and the HCJB mission compound was deserted. The silence was eerie and I prayed, "Oh, Jesus, I love you. I believe in you. I trust you."

Suddenly the most beautiful sight filled my eyes as Kreky, the one-eyed, wiry missionary radio technician with the gnarled and kind face, walked by. "Kreky!" I gasped to myself. Enormous relief swelled through me because I knew that when Christ came back to earth for the great rapture of the redeemed, the saintly Kreky would certainly be among the first to be taken up. I was safe.

My life was full of color and activity. I raised chickens, collected stamps, and began to take trumpet lessons from Dad.

We boys made racing carts. We couldn't buy ready-made soap box derby racers, so built them ourselves. We cannibalized wheels and axles from broken wagons, or made wheels out of wood, using a jig saw in the shop at school. I worked for weeks on my racer, sawing, pounding, and painting. When it came time to race, I was the driver, and David Miller my mechanic. We lugged our carts up the hill behind the radio station, on the slopes of Mount Pichincha, and raced down. David gave it the initial kick, and I steered it with my feet. Every time we slowed down, David kicked for extra propulsion. There were about eight carts, and each time we had a race, at least one cart lost a wheel and there'd be a wreck. Often the winner was not the fastest driver, but the one who avoided an accident by keeping his cart intact all the way down the rough hill.

When I was not racing cars, I was raising chickens. My Spanish teacher, Señorita Eudolfilia Arboleda, gave me two chickens, Rhode Island Reds, and I placed them in the coop with my other mongrel chickens. I was stunned next morning when I went to feed my chickens, for the new little hen had no feathers on her head—and her scalp was bleeding. The older chickens had pecked at the head of the intruder all night. The poor thing had taken an awful beating and I was sure she would die.

We separated her from the older, larger chickens, and were heartened to see her continue to eat and grow. We were daily amazed as, gradually, her scalp feathers grew back.

My chickens started to lay two or three eggs a day and provided enough eggs for our family's use. Soon, however, the novelty of chickens wore off, and I no longer did a good job of looking after them. Finally, I sold them. Then I proceeded to find animals that would not require so much care. I bought a rabbit, but had to bury it when it was killed by a dog. Carol bought another rabbit, but it got sick and died. Then we bought three guinea pigs, but two died. Life was full of small tragedies.

My relatives in the United States often sent me books, and they could always be assured of my delight. Mom said, "Steve gobbles up his books and you can be assured every one is appreciated."

I got the entire set of Zane Grey books and read them all with intense interest. I devoured *The Black Stallion* and *Treasure Island*, *Huckleberry Finn*, *Tom Sawyer*, and *Arabian Nights*. These classics were the only books around, so my ten-year-old mind was filled with only the best literature. I have often felt my life in South America was much richer than that of the average boy growing up in the United States, with television, programmed activities, and other stimuli to keep him entertained.

Then I decided to read through the Bible. Dad suggested I start with the New Testament, but I wanted to go from cover to cover. I plowed through Genesis and Exodus but when I got to Leviticus became anguished as I read all the strict dietary and sanitary regulations. It seemed unfair to treat people as "unclean" when they had sores or diseases. I asked Dad, "Why does the Bible say a woman is unclean when she has an issue of blood?" and "What is an issue of blood?" Stumbling, at a rare loss for words, Dad once again encouraged me to read the New Testament first and save the Old Testament for later.

Soon I learned I could use my Bible reading as an excuse to keep my light on late at night. Mom said, "Stevie, time to turn your light out and go to sleep."

"But I'm reading my Bible," I proclaimed.

Mom could hardly insist that I quit reading the Bible—and I was allowed to leave the light on.

The highlight of the year was my two-week trip with Dad on

an evangelistic campaign that went from the mountain town of Riobamba to the jungle villages of Sucúa, Huambi, and Macas. The Alliance Academy gave me permission to miss two weeks of school, and I rode in the back of the HCJB pickup truck as Clarence Jones drove with his family up front, to join Dad in Riobamba. We traversed the Andean *páramo* to drive past Ecuador's most majestic snowcaps. We left at 5:00 a.m. and as the sun began to rise, it burst gloriously in dramas of screaming pink behind the Eastern slopes of Mount Cotopaxi. Sometimes called the "Fujiyama of South America," it had a nearly perfect cone and at 19,347 feet was considered one of the world's highest active volcanos. It had erupted more than 25 times in the last 400 years, and the last explosive eruption had been only eight years earlier—February, 1942.

It was cold in the back of the pickup, and even though there was a top over it, the canvas flapped in the wind. As we climbed up to over 12,000 feet to cross the high plateau, I bundled up in sweater, jacket, and blankets, then peered out at the awesome mountain hovering above me. I shivered with cold and fright and imagined lava and hot ash causing snow on the flanks of the cone to melt rapidly, sending big flows of mud pouring down the mountainside over our forlorn little pickup.

An even greater sight awaited me, and this at the end of the day, for as we approached Riobamba, the sun began to set in the West and cast its glow over Mount Chimborazo, highest of 30 Andes peaks that form an "avenue of volcanoes" in Ecuador and Perú. Rising to 20,561 feet, the mighty mass dominated the entire sky. The Ecuadorian man riding with me in the back of the pickup told me the legend of the mountain: several thousand years ago it was twice as high, and had been part of the adjacent mountain, Carihuairazo, which had blown its top to form "Chimbo." I shuddered to think of anything bigger than this towering, dreadful beast, and in a childlike way sensed why the Indians had worshipped this mountain as their god.

After the meetings in Riobamba, we drove to Shell Mera,

gateway to the jungle. Once a jungle outpost for the Shell Oil Company, it now served as the hub of missionary activity for it was the headquarters of Missionary Aviation Fellowship.

We were entertained by Nate and Marj Saint. We had met Nate two years earlier when his Stinson Voyager had crashed upon takeoff from Quito's 9,200 foot high airport, after encountering a severe wind gust. Nate broke his back and spent a few months in Quito convalescing. I came to look upon him with awe for he was not only a pilot, but a mechanic, inventor, artist, and devoted Christian. He gave a series of messages in our school, during chapel, and I enjoyed his chalk drawings and illustrated stories. He took a keen interest in me, and helped me build model airplanes, showing me how to shape the camber of a wing, carefully curving sandpaper over balsa to form a graceful shape that would lift as air rushed over it.

Nate's wife, Marj, was one of the most hospitable people we had ever known, and she made us feel totally at home in her jungle haven. I felt it was one of the finest houses I had ever seen, and dreamed of the day when I might live in the jungle, and have a dwelling like the Saints with no glass windows, only screens, and with no foundation except cement posts set in oil to keep insects and rodents from crawling up into the house. They had mastered jungle living, and made it gracious.

I had always enjoyed flying in commercial airlines, in DC-3's, but the thrill of my life came when I jumped up into the Stinson Voyager for my flight to Sucúa. The small, single-engine airplane had been purchased with donations from many supporters of the Missionary Aviation Fellowship. The Stinson was fabric-covered, painted yellow, with four seats. It could haul a load of over 1,000 pounds, including fuel, passengers, and baggage. With its 125-horsepower Lycoming engine it cruised at 115 miles per hour. Now regarded as antiques, the few Stinsons still flying are treasured by their owners, an utterly honest little airplane.

Nate loaded our luggage and some components of the gospel tent in the back seat and luggage area, but told us he would have to make several trips to get the entire tent transported.

As the little Stinson pranced down the gravel runway I sucked in my breath with delight. We climbed out over the Pastaza River, and I watched as it undulated slowly eastward across Ecuador, eventually to join the Amazon. Nate pointed out the many sandbars and told us any one of them would provide a safe landing spot if the engine failed. He noted he no longer flew to Quito, for the plane's performance was marginal at high altitude, and gusty winds in the high Andes precarious. Here in the jungle, however, with landing strips between 1,000 and 3,000-foot elevations, the Stinson performed gallantly and reliably.

Looking off to our right we could still see the Andes and we began to comprehend the drama of their geology. The mountains plunged eastward from 20,000 to 3,000 feet in only 60 miles. Then the mountains tapered off into mere foothills, gently and lazily descending from 3,000 feet to sea level across the entire South American continent, as dozens of other tributaries like the Pastaza and the Napo joined the Amazon in a journey of 3,000 miles.

We flew south for 40 minutes, and circled over Sucúa. Nate told Dad and me this trip used to take missionaries eight days of weary trodding through jungle muck.

We were greeted in Sucúa by the robust Mike Ficke and his gentle wife, Ella. Their son, Jack, was a year older than I, back in Quito at school. The Fickes had been in Sucúa for eight years, and their mission, the Gospel Missionary Union, had established a missionary station in this region in 1901. Mr. and Mrs. Freeland were the first missionaries. Despite nearly 50 years of gospel work, there were few believers.

Sucúa was in the southern jungle of Ecuador, in the heart of Jívaro country. The Jívaros were the so-called "headhunters" for they had become famous for their practice of shrinking skulls of enemies killed in battle. Although the practice was dying out, the shrinking process was still passed on to younger generations of Jívaros, and it was a closely guarded secret. The only thing outsiders knew was that they used heated stones and hot sand, but other details remained a mystery. The eventual result was a coal black skull with hair, about the size of a fist. It was mysterious that the hair remained undamaged, and even eyebrows were perfectly preserved during shrinking.

Jívaros had remained indifferent to the gospel message, and the missionaries worked diligently for many years in the face of almost total apathy.

Mike Ficke used the occasion of the revival campaign to inaugurate the delightful chapel he had built with his own hands. He had sawed the boards on his own sawmill, from jungle trees. With its open-air windows, and long hard benches, surrounded by thick jungle and sweet tropical scents, it was a perfect place to worship. Dad told him, "Mike, I've been all over Ecuador, and I must tell you that despite your jungle location there are very few Ecuadorian churches more commodious."

Abe Dyck and Frank Drown joined the campaign. Both were missionaries with the Gospel Missionary Union. Abe was the missionary who had taken Dad on his memorable river trip up the Guayas River in the GMU gospel launch. Frank Drown had taken over the new mission in Macuma, and had gained respect for his facility with the Jívaro language and his sensibilities for Jívaro customs. He described to Dad and me how Jívaro women washed their babies. They got a mouthful of cold river water and swirled it around in their mouth until the water was warm, then sprayed it on the child's body. The kids loved the bath—and Dad loved the story.

But Dad did not like another story Frank told about Jívaro women, for it was the custom among Jívaros for women to do all the work in the field. This was in addition to all their responsibility for children and meals. Dad grimaced, "That is deplorable."

"Yes," agreed Frank, "it illustrates the effects of paganism."

"I have never known a Jívaro woman to live past 45 or 50 years," added Ella Ficke.

Services in the gospel tent were successful—but not with the Jívaros. The meetings were well-attended by the "whites"—Spanish-speaking people, but only a few Jívaros showed up.

The town of Sucúa consisted of 25 or 30 houses, surrounding a square that had been hacked out of the jungles. The gospel tent was erected right in the square, and Mike Ficke was thrilled when over 200 people came to the meetings. He figured nearly every person in and around Sucúa had come.

Each night, Dad and I played trumpet duets, and the novelty of a ten-year-old *gringuito* (little gringo) playing a duet with his father was one of the unexpected features of the campaign. I was not a great trumpet player and could not reach high notes. Dad always played melody and I played alto. The people didn't seem to care that I wasn't a virtuoso; it was enough that a child was playing trumpet with his dad in the remote jungle town where entertainment of any kind was scarce and thus appreciated.

Before our trip to Sucúa Dad had given me a new hunting knife. One day I went out behind the Ficke's house with my knife and slashed at tall grass the way I had seen Indians do it. After whacking off several yards of tall grass, I missed the next clump and swung the knife right into my left knee.

Bleeding profusely, I hobbled up to the Ficke's home, where Ella Ficke bandaged me up. She said, "If you were back in Shell Mera, they'd give you a few stitches, but I'll just tape this real tight and hope it holds."

The next campaign was in Huambi, and I had to miss the trip because of my injured knee. Only the roughest road existed between Huambi and Sucúa, a road accessible only by Jeep, and there was only one Jeep in the area. It belonged to the Catholic priest, Padre Lobo. It had been flown in to Sucúa on the Ecuadorian Air Force C-47.

Everyone on the road between Sucúa and Huambi was astonished when they saw Protestant missionaries driving the Catholic priest's Jeep, hauling the bulky gospel tent across mud holes and over rocks. Then the word got around. Mike Ficke was the only person in the area capable of fixing the priest's Jeep. As they bounced along the road, Mike gleefully chortled, "The priest has loaned us the knife to cut his throat."

While Dad and Mike were in Huambi, I stayed in bed for a day, trying to keep my knee immobile, then got up and limped around the next. By the time Dad and Mike returned, I was eager to join them on the next leg of the journey—to Macas, capital of the southern jungle province of Santiago-Zamora.

From Sucúa to Macas we plodded through mud trails by horseback. My lame leg dangled helplessly off the left side of the horse, and I worried it might split open the wound. To the contrary, the joggling seemed to do it good, for it loosened my knee, and by the time we had sloshed through slurpy clay for five hours, I dismounted in Macas with a remarkably improved leg.

Once again, I joined Dad for nightly trumpet duets and the crowd of 500 roared with approval.

The messages in Macas were the most productive of the three towns, as eleven people made a profession of faith in Christ. A year earlier, Dad might have claimed 70 saved, because that number had indeed remained behind for counseling. But Dad decided to impress them with the seriousness of the decision, and talked about what it meant to be a Christian: "You must take up your cross and follow Christ. You must renounce sin, change your life, become a disciple. It is not easy, but once you make the decision, it is a glorious and happy life." By making his listeners think about what was at stake, he eliminated those who might make a careless and thoughtless decision and remained with eleven stalwart souls.

At the end, Dad said to Mike, "I want to thank you for all the preparatory work you've done. You are as rough and ready as they come, and you are one grand fellow to work with."

Mike responded, "Bob, I'm so impressed with your willingness to come to our humble mission station like this. You're a 'big shot' at HCJB, but you come with your joy and exuberance to help us out here in the jungle. These have been great days, and you've been a great sport, sleeping on boards and eating jungle food. Nothing was too great a sacrifice."

Dad concluded, "Well, thanks, Mike, but I think you folks are the real heroes in missionary work. Every atom of your sinewy 190 pounds is completely dedicated to the Lord. We live in relative luxury in Quito, so you are the ones who have really made a sacrifice. It's been a pleasure to get a glimpse of this type of missionary work, and I hope you'll invite me back."

"We will!" guaranteed Mike,

As we returned from Macas to Shell Mera, Dad had similar words of admiring praise for the work Nate Saint was doing. "Nate, I've been talking to the other missionaries out in the jungle and I don't know a single one who does not lift his voice daily in praise to God for Nate Saint. With your Stinson, you have completely transformed the whole complex of jungle missionary work. You are every inch a missionary and the most meticulously careful pilot I've ever seen."

"Well, Bob," said Nate, "I love the Lord, and I love to fly, so it's nice I can be doing a little bit of good."

"A *little* bit of good!" exclaimed Dad. "Nate, the campaign we just conducted would be absolutely impossible were it not for the time-saving, energy-conserving ministry of your missionary aviation program."

As we left Shell Mera for the long drive back to Quito, I thought about Nate Saint with boyish hero-worship and decided I would be a missionary pilot when I grew up. Then I told Dad about my dream. "Amen, amen, amen. That's swell," exuded Dad, ever supportive, especially when his son said he wanted to be a missionary.

10

The music man of Latin America

Bleeding hands of Jesus, crucified for me,
Hands that suffered torment, pain and agony,
Pierced by my transgression there on Calvary:
By his Blood I'm ransomed and from sin set free.
                    —Alfredo Colom, Guatemalan Songwriter

In March, 1950, Dad met the man destined to make a major impact on his ministry in Latin America. Alfredo Colom, Guatemalan evangelist, first came to Quito to conduct a series of meetings at our church. Alfredo was tall for a Latin American, about 5'9", same as Dad. He combed his hair straight back, but because it was curly, it did not lie flat but flowed gracefully backwards. He was loud, almost deafening, in his speech and song. His spirit was bubbling, his personality outgoing. For once, there was a person whose voice was as loud as Dad's, and whose exuberance matched his own.

Dad called him *Señor Aleluya* ("Mister Hallelujah") and Mom said, "He is the most bubbling-over Christian I have ever seen." When Alfredo and Dad talked, a crowd gathered, for it was a noisy, boisterous occasion. They laughed, joked, and prayed. Alfredo had the same penchant as Dad for spontaneous prayer. And when someone else prayed, Alfredo encouraged the Lord and

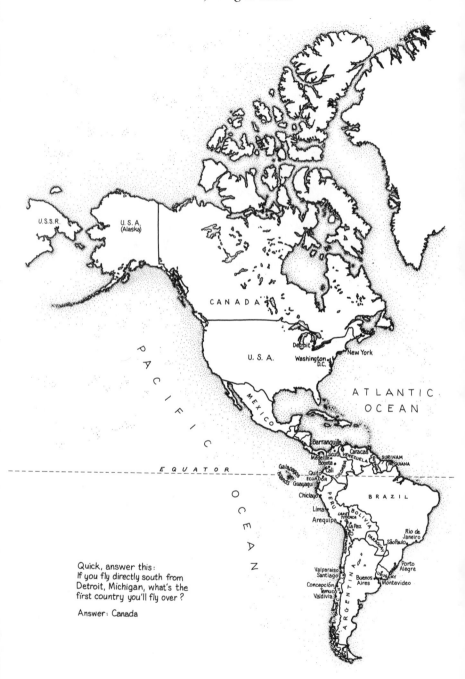

Quick, answer this:
If you fly directly south from
Detroit, Michigan, what's the
first country you'll fly over?

Answer: Canada

the petitioner by loudly shouting "Hallelujah" and "Amen" frequently throughout the prayer.

As if his spirit were not gift enough, Alfredo played the accordion and often led the congregation in singing, playing the buttons on his accordion with his left hand, and leading singing with his right. I often watched his accordion, fascinated, as he expanded it explosively and contracted it with an implosive shove. It seemed sure he would tear open the bellows as he pushed maximum volume out of his instrument, stretching it to its outer limits until it must surely burst. When Alfredo Colom and Roberto Savage shared the platform, the audience was galvanized into enthusiastic participation in song, prayer, and praise.

There were many musicians who could sing with sweeter tones, and play their instruments with greater skill. But no one sang or played with more passion than Alfredo and Roberto, and the fervor of their music infected their audiences.

These two men were called to be preachers, and they saw themselves in that role. Music was secondary: it supported and contributed to the message. Little did Alfredo and Roberto realize that their meeting would be historic, that their ultimate legacy would be their music.

Alfredo Colom, evangelist, poet, and musician, became one of Dad's closest friends. Dad had the joy of learning hundreds of songs born in Alfredo's heart. Dad arranged and published these songs. When he sang them on his radio program, and taught them to his audiences in gospel campaigns throughout Latin America, they were received with enormous enthusiasm. Alfredo's life, ministry, and music had a tremendous impact on Dad and upon his efforts to bring into being an "indigenous hymnology" for Spanish-speaking believers. Dad often referred to him fondly as *la fábrica de himnos y coritos* ("the factory of hymns and choruses").

Dad's first three chorus books in Spanish had been published in 1947, 1948, and 1949, but were mostly translations from English, focusing on English songs never before published in traditional hymn books used in Latin American churches. The main hymnal in those days was published by the Christian and Missionary Alliance, filled with classics that made English-speaking Christians happy, such as "Onward, Christian Soldiers" and "Holy, Holy, Holy." Although these hymns were well-received by Latin American believers, the Latin toe taps to a different tempo than the Anglo. Something was missing.

The change began when Dad published his fourth Spanish chorus book, *Preludios Celestiales (Heavenly Preludes)* in 1951. Featuring many songs by Alfredo Colom, the book also contained songs by other Latin American Christians, each tune with a distinctly Latin melody and rhythm. Some songs had become popular but no one knew who had written them. Dad gave credit to the author whenever he could but sometimes he could only print "author unknown."

Several of Alfredo's songs lamented the wounds of Christ's body, and were written in the minor key. Three songs that quickly became "hits" among Latin American believers were "Bleeding Hands of Jesus," "Divine Feet," and "Divine Eyes." The words and music had a weird ring to the ear of North American and British missionaries. Some missionaries objected that they sounded too much like Roman Catholic Gregorian chants, with haunting, minor sounds.

No Latin American believers objected, and when they sang Alfredo's songs, their eyes closed, and they sang with reverence and deep feeling. Often tears ran down their cheeks.

One hymn became widely popular throughout Latin America, for it had the Latin beat, minor key, and words of poetic passion that sounded distinctly Latin. The title was "Jesus, I Fully Surrender." Its English translation barely conveys the intensity of the Latin soul:

Jesus, my Savior, I fully surrender!
O Lord, I pray Thee,
Cleanse this temple made of clay.
I want to please Thee, O how I love Thee,
All on the altar, humbly now I pray.

Each hour I need Thee to gain the victory,
Pure, clean and holy I long to be.

The song was made even more dramatic by the piano accompaniment, with deep bass notes rocking solidly in a contrapuntal beat evocative of the most poignant Latin songs of love and joy.

It was widely assumed this hymn had been written by Alfredo Colom or some other Latin American hymn writer. However, anyone noticing the name of author and composer was amazed to discover it had been been born in the soul of a North American missionary, the same person who had written that touching missionary song, "Lord, Send Me." This magnificent and moving Latin hymn was the work of none other than the self-effacing Wilda Savage.

Dad asked Alfredo to come to Ecuador for a few months to conduct a series of evangelistic campaigns throughout the country. He replied, "I'd love to, brother Roberto, but I can't be away from my family that long."

"Bring them here," thundered Dad.

"I will. Hallelujah!" shouted Alfredo.

Sara Colom brought her five children to Ecuador, and I struck up a fast friendship with ten-year-old Elí who was my age. Dad arranged for living accommodations and helped the children enroll in school. With everyone settled, the two preacher musicians began a tour of Ecuador, effects of which are still felt.

Dad's evangelistic work had focused on the three northernmost countries of South America: Ecuador, Colombia, and Venezuela. But he wanted to conquer the entire continent for Christ, and in 1951 planned a sweep southward.

While Alfredo Colom continued his crusades through the northern countries, Dad assembled the old team. Bill Gillam and Jim Savage flew to Quito to join Dad. They flew south from Guayaquil, over the northern coast of Perú, and Dad was struck by the stark desert, dotted with oil fields. To his left he saw the towering Andes and to his right lay the Pacific Ocean. But the land between ocean and mountains was barren, for rain seldom fell in this part of the world. Across the mountains, directly east, lay the steaming Amazon rain forest, but the northern coast of Perú was an arid, unending stretch of sand-blown barrenness.

As the Panagra DC-4 descended into Chiclayo, they were welcomed by the refreshing sight of green oasis, for irrigation ditches brought water to this coastal town of 40,000. They were greeted by missionaries from the two gospel churches in Chiclayo—one Nazarene and the other Pilgrim Holiness. The two churches cooperated beautifully in sponsoring the Youth for Christ team.

Dad's vision was that all Protestant churches in Latin America would become known as "evangelical" churches rather than by their denominational identities. In each of his campaigns he strove to present the gospel of Jesus Christ in its basic simplicity, so those who accepted the message could feel at home in any church.

The only churches Dad did not feel comfortable with were those he deemed "liberal" or "modernist." He could happily cooperate with almost any pastor in any Protestant denomination as long as that pastor believed in a few basics: the Bible as the inerrant Word of God, salvation through faith in Christ, belief in a historical Jesus, with a literal virgin birth, crucifixion, resurrection, and ascension. If a pastor "wobbled" on any of these issues, Dad could not feel free to send a new convert to worship in that church. Furthermore, he wanted to be assured that the church taught "separation" from the world, and encouraged its members to radically change their worldly habits, renouncing drinking, smoking, dancing, gambling, and most of all, sexual immorality. Most churches saw eye-to-eye with him on this issue, for it was from the fundamentalist branch of Protestant Christianity that most missionaries had been sent.

With the missionaries in Chiclayo, Dad felt totally at home, because they were doctrinally "sound" and definitely "separated."

The Nazarenes taught "sanctification." A person first became saved, then sanctified. Dad had no problem with this view and often preached the same general theme, although he called it "consecration" or "rededication."

The Pilgrim Holiness church was "charismatic," although that term did not come into widespread use until the 1970's. The word "charisma" came from the Greek *kharisma* which meant "divine gift." The Pilgrim Holiness folks put a strong emphasis on the baptism of the Holy Spirit, an event accompanied by the "gifts of the Spirit", especially the gift of "speaking in tongues." Dad had never experienced the gift of tongues, but rejoiced with others who had received it. He enjoyed Christian fellowship with them. Dad sincerely felt he had indeed been baptized by the Holy Spirit but, as he put it, "the Spirit has not chosen to give me the gift of tongues."

Some Protestants could not deal with each other if one believed in speaking in tongues and the other did not. But for Dad, it was no problem. He was quite fascinated with the experience, and showed great interest when missionaries talked about it. He knew he could send converts from his Youth for Christ meetings to the Pilgrim Holiness Church, knowing they would receive biblical instruction from godly people.

Lima was the next stop, and Dad gasped with wide-eyed wonder as they drove from airport to city. "This is the most beautiful city I've ever seen," he declared, and the rest of the team agreed.

The first night in Lima, the church was packed, with aisles and platform jammed with people. It would have been a fire marshal's nightmare, but in those days there were few seating regulations, and everyone crammed happily together. One lady on the front row was holding a baby that started crying as Dad was preaching. The louder Dad preached, the shriller the baby screamed. Finally Dad paused, smiled at the woman and said, "Don't worry, because Jesus said: 'Let the little ones come unto me, for theirs is the kingdom of heaven'."

The lady smiled, comforted, but still wanted to get her child out back. There was no way to get out through the aisles. As Dad continued to preach, and the babe continued to scream, the lady stood up and looked towards the back of the auditorium. There she spotted a friend, who gestured enthusiastically, indicating she'd take care of the little one. With that, the lady passed the infant to the person in the row behind her, who in turn passed it over her head to the person in row three. The congregation began to laugh, and Dad stopped, grinned broadly and said, "Now that looks like an intelligent plan." While the tot was passed over people's heads, from row to row, Dad led the congregation in a quick chorus of "Hallelujah." When the baby finally reached the comforting arms of the helpful matron in the back of the church, he continued his sermon.

One bystander reported: "People were packed so closely that when the crowd laughed three or four people were pushed out into the street."

The second night they moved to the Methodist Church. It held twice as many people, but was not large enough. The crowds were still jam-full.

The third and fourth nights they switched to the Methodist High School auditorium but thirty minutes before the service began, the place was full and people were standing. They made a quick decision and opened up the gymnasium in back of the platform. Soon there were as many people behind as in front.

Dad had never been farther south than on this trip to Lima, Perú, but he was not even half way to his destination. Chile beckoned and the team traveled on, southward to Chile, the long, narrow country that snakes down the western coast of South America. The towering Andes Mountains form Chile's eastern boundary, dividing it from Argentina. The Panagra DC-4 rumbled on, hour after hour, compelling Dad to gaze out the window as South America's Pacific shoreline etched the horn-like shape he had studied so often in the map on his office wall.

When they reached Valdivia, Dad was fascinated to discover he was now as far south of Quito as New York City was north. Even though this was the southernmost destination of their campaign, he shook his head in wonder as he realized he was still 1,200 miles from Chile's southern tip.

"I wonder if this is the most distant point from Jerusalem that Youth for Christ has reached," mused Dad.

"I can't think of any place farther," said Jim.

"Well, Jesus said we should be witnesses in Jerusalem, Samaria, and unto the uttermost parts of the world. I think we may be the most 'uttermost' for Youth for Christ so far."

"Amen!" rejoiced Jim, chipper, enthusiastic, and eager as Dad to win South America for Christ. Then the conversation turned from missionary enterprise to Chile's geography .

"This country reminds me of a shoestring," remarked Dad.

"It's 2,650 miles long," added Jim.

"Imagine. It's ten times longer than it is wide." Statistics always pleased Dad, and his mind often calculated tallies such as the number of people in a meeting, the aggregate watts of transmitting power for HCJB, or the odd measures that defined a country's limits.

Dad then asked the local missionaries: "Well, brothers, it's great to be here, and we know the Lord is going to give us some marvelous victories over the next few weeks. What time is our meeting?"

"9:00 p.m."

"Nine at night?" Dad was incredulous.

"Chileans don't consider that late at all. They often eat dinner at 11 p.m. and retire at 2 a.m." Dad made a mental adjustment, thought about some of his blessed late-night campfire meetings at Maranatha and decided the Lord would work wonders at that midnight hour.

From Valdivia, the team headed north to Temuco, a town of 50,000 people. 3,000 attended each of the six nights at the spacious municipal theater. Many could not find a seat.

Dad asserted, "It would be an outstanding event in the U.S. to assemble a crowd of 3,000 people in a town of 50,000. To accomplish this in Catholic South America is nothing short of miraculous. Praise the Lord!"

After six days in Temuco, the team boarded the train for Concepción. As they left, a crowd of 100 enthusiastic gospel believers gathered in the station to sing farewell gospel choruses and shower them with Chilean souvenirs as tokens of appreciation.

Among the mementos were some delicious apples and muskmelons that Dad pronounced as "better than any I have ever tasted in my life." But his biggest joy was the gift of a Chilean onion, a perfect, white, eight-inch diameter beauty. That evening, before the meeting, Dad said, "OK, fellows, I'm going to show you what real good eatin' is all about. You're about to eat an onion sandwich!"

"Onion sandwich!" they exclaimed in unison. "How about an apple instead?"

"Fine. Fine. Fine. If you don't want an onion sandwich, that suits me, because I'm going to enjoy every bite of this phenomenal onion. Have you ever seen such a stunner?"

Dad sliced the onion, chortling with glee as he carved. He buttered two slices of bread and lay the onion between the halves. With a huge grin he bit into it, chomping with one massive bite a third of the sandwich.

"Aaaaah," he moaned, "food in heaven won't be any better than this."

"Thank goodness you're going to be on the platform, 30 feet from the audience," groaned Bill Gillam, "because if they could smell your breath, we'd lose the whole crowd."

Dad roared with laughter.

Shortly after Dad returned from Chile, on April 30, 1951, we celebrated his 37th birthday. His second four-year term as a missionary was almost complete and he could look back on twelve years as minister of the gospel with a sense of fulfillment. He had founded three churches and pastored six. He had conducted scores of evangelistic meetings all over the Western Hemisphere leading thousands of people to believe in Christ from Canada to Chile. He had authored two books and produced six gospel chorus books. He had discovered scores of indigenous Latin American melodies with gospel words, and had put them in chorus books and sung them on radio. He had served as Program Director, Field Director, and Trustee of HCJB. Hundreds of young people had dedicated their lives to missionary service as a result of Dad's encouragement. Dozens of young men in Latin America were attending Bible institutes or seminaries after he had told them, "you should do it—you can do it."

As a ten-year-old child, I was only vaguely aware of his accomplishments, but keenly mindful of his presence in my life. Although his schedule at HCJB was hectic, and his travel schedule intense, I never remember any feeling of neglect. Each day we had lunch together, and in Ecuador that was the main meal of the day. We called it dinner. The dinner hour was fun, and Dad always asked us many questions about our lives. "Who's your best friend? What's your favorite color? How many stamps do you have in your collection now? What's your favorite subject?" His eyes fixed on me with concentrated gaze and he took great delight in my answers.

Often we had guests, missionaries from Perú and Chile on their way to the States, traveling evangelists, or friends from the United States who were contributing to the financial support of the mission. We children were always included in conversations, and Dad made sure we were polite and paid attention to what was going on. He had a list of jokes he had typed on a sheet of 4" x 4" paper, folded into his wallet, stained from years of use. About half way through dinner, he pulled out the ragged page and regaled his guests with his jokes. No one laughed harder than Dad. He never tired of them. We heard the jokes a thousand times, but the contagious energy of his laughter usually made us laugh as well.

Monday night was "family night" and Dad steadfastly refused to take any radio programs or other assignments on this special night. We knew this would always be a joyful time and looked forward to popping corn around the fireplace, creating puffed rice balls or playing Parcheesi, Monopoly, or Clue.

We often talked politics. Dad took a keen interest in the Korean War, and when President Truman fired General Douglas MacArthur, Dad was indignant. "President Truman was nice to us when we met him in Washington four years ago, but I think this action stinks." I followed with great interest Time magazine's coverage of MacArthur's 13-year-old son Arthur and was impressed when I learned he had never been in the United States. I said to Mom, "Army kids and missionary kids sure get to go lots of places, don't they?

Our family also went many places together. Mostly, we went to church, but Quito offered many cultural events, and we also attended concerts by such famous groups as the Vienna Boy's Choir and pianist Arturo Rubinstein. And when the Harlem Globetrotters came to town, we never missed them. Sometimes we went to professional soccer games, but that was rare as most of them were played on Sundays. The only sports event we never attended was the bullfight, for Dad found the bloody spectacle altogether distasteful and could not bring himself to watch even one.

As we prepared to leave for our second furlough in the United States, HCJB made a commitment to major expansion of its capacity for shortwave broadcasting. They purchased a 45-acre plot in Pifo, an Indian village twenty miles east of Quito, with plenty of space to create a network of towers and antennas that could beam programs around the world. There was no electric power in the little village of Pifo, so Clarence Jones bought an Army surplus diesel generator with sufficient power to operate transmitters as well as homes of families of missionary technicians who would live there.

Inspired, Dad prepared himself to spend a big chunk of his year of furlough traveling around the United States to help HCJB raise money to pay for land and generator. One day at noonday meal he announced, "What do you think of this for a theme? $300 will buy an acre of land. Stake your claim for Christ in Ecuador." He loved slogans and no one was better at crafting a catchy phrase.

We were never able to leave Ecuador quietly. An animated crowd of Ecuadorian evangelicals and North American missionaries gathered at the airport to sing and hug and weep. Little hunch backed Conchita grasped each of us tightly, asking us to promise her that we would return for sure. Other international travelers looked askance at our group, slightly amused by the singing, slightly annoyed by the noise. As we climbed the staircase to the Ecuatoriana Airlines DC-6, the company of believers burst into an exuberant rendition of *"Alabaré"* ("I Will Praise!"). The sounds of Ecuador, the voices of our friends, the music of Latin America, rang in our ears as we took our seats, fastened our seat belts, and departed our adopted home.

When we arrived in the States, our first order of business was to participate in the wedding of my Aunt Helen to Dick Broach, an affable Texan whose easy-going congeniality charmed all the Savages, but who had two strikes against him: He was a Methodist and a Democrat. Like Mom, who was also raised a Methodist, Dick soon joined the Baptist church after baptism by immersion. As to his politics, Dad joked with him that he was not a "new deal" but an "old deal" Democrat. It was obvious that "new deal" made Dad gag, whereas "old deal" was at least tolerable. Best of all, Dick had received the call to the mission field, and the newlyweds made plans to join the Savage brothers as missionaries in South America. The circle was complete. The three children of Henry and Bess Savage were all missionaries.

After the huge Baptist wedding, we settled into summer life at Maranatha Bible Conference. Dad was one of the featured speakers on the summer conference schedule, but took many trips all over the United States to spread the word of HCJB. While doing so, however, he never let up in his vigor to get people saved. Each service he conducted was not only a missionary rally but a revival meeting. He always issued two invitations, first to accept Christ and second to dedicate your life to the Christian ministry.

When he traveled to a church, he was tireless. Not content merely to show up in a city and preach a few sermons, he put in 12 to 14-hour days wherever he went. And no task was beneath his dignity. He was as happy to stand on a street corner passing out tracts as he was to preach before a thousand people.

His travels for HCJB took him to a variety of denominations. He was fascinated with their different forms of worship and attitudes about behavior appropriate for a Christian. One Sunday he was asked to speak at a Mennonite Church in Indiana. Before the service, he asked the pastor if there was anything he should know about Mennonites before he got up and preached. The pastor said, "Brother Savage, just preach the Bible and we'll all be happy. But there is one thing I want to ask of you."

"What's that?" asked Dad.

"Would you mind removing your wedding ring? I think a few of our people might be offended because we don't wear jewelry."

"I'll be happy to take it off," said Dad, as he twisted it off his finger and slipped it into his pocket. "You know, this is interesting. I didn't have a wedding ring when I got married, but when Wilda and I went to Colombia as missionaries, one of the senior missionaries advised me to buy a wedding ring. He told me it might look bad if I as a married man did not wear a wedding band. So I bought this ring in Colombia. I put it on to be a good testimony for the Lord. Tonight I'm taking it off for the same reason. Whatever I can do to serve my Lord is fine with me."

It seemed like each group of Christians had its own set of rules. For us, jewelry was no problem, nor was lipstick. Our crowd worried about drinking, smoking, dancing, card playing, and movies. Most of the world considered us pretty conservative with all those taboos. But for folks like the Mennonites, we were rather liberal, and our lipsticked women, even saints like my mother, were considered a little "worldly."

Every time a missionary family had to enroll their children in a new school, there was fear in the hearts of the little ones. One-year furloughs meant a change of school every four years, and even though it was just two semesters, it seemed like a lifetime to a child who felt ill at ease in a huge, bold, secular culture. By the time September rolled around, I was feeling forlorn, missing Ecuador greatly. I dreaded going to school in the States, and my stomach knotted up as I thought of the sophisticated kids with whom I would attend classes. Maranatha was a safe environment, but public school was an alien land.

We decided to live in my grandparents' home at Maranatha for the entire year, so Carol and I attended Churchill School, two miles from home. Despite my nervousness, I quickly made friends and settled into the sixth grade class. I found school work easy and told Mom, "It's a lot easier here than at the Alliance Academy in Quito." I had never associated with children who were not part of the evangelical Christian world. True, some of the "embassy kids" in Quito were not Christians, but they had to fit in to the environment of the Alliance Academy, so even with them I did not experience so-called "worldly" youngsters. Now, for the first time in my life, I heard a lot of my friends cussing, and it made me nervous. The boys were friendly to me, but it got to the point where someone would cuss and another boy would quickly say, "Shut up! Stevie's here." When Great Grandpa Steele heard about it he wrote and congratulated me for having high standards. He was dean of Cedarville College, at that time a Presbyterian school. In his Calvinist strictness, he was delighted with his great-grandson. He wrote and encouraged me to maintain my "separateness from the world." That was exactly how I felt—separate. The last thing a sixth-grader wants is to be different from others, and several things made me feel odd: I was from Ecuador, had a strange set of taboos, not very athletic, a good scholar, and my clothes were stodgy. Like most missionaries, our wardrobe consisted largely of "hand-me-downs" and we were not exactly stylish.

Dad visited scores of churches across the land, promoting the Pifo project. Again, he found an appropriate slogan, dubbing that 45-acre Ecuadorian plot as "Maranatha Acres" to honor the many contributions that poured in from the conference-goers. But there was more than land to talk about and raise money for. A major item was the power plant, and Dad began to talk enthusiastically about the generator the mission wanted to buy. A lowly diesel generator should have made for rather dull fund raising. How does one get people excited about a diesel generator? No problem. Dad got people entranced with the vision by describing how the generator's mission had changed: "It was used by the United States Department of Defense in Panama to manipulate the biggest guns in the army. Now, instead of hurling armaments of DEATH, it will churn our transmitters to spread the message of LIFE. The power of HCJB's transmitters will be increased TWENTY times, and we will be able to seriously challenge the diabolical intentions of Communism to dominate shortwave bands. Missionary radio is able to get behind 'closed doors' that have swung shut to flesh-and-blood missionaries during the past two years."

When Dad conducted meetings in churches, he was usually entertained at the home of one of the church members. One lady told him, "I want to cook something special for you tonight. What's your favorite meal?"

"Do you want to know what I'd really like more than anything else?" asked Dad.

"Absolutely," replied the lady. "Nothing but the best."

"Oh my," said Dad, "I'm afraid what I want might be asking too much."

"You name it, you've got it!" she said.

"Well, what I'd really like more than anything else is

something I can't get down in South America. I'd like a can of Franco-American spaghetti."

"Franco-American spaghetti!" sputtered the woman. "I want to cook you something special!"

"Well, you asked me what my first choice was, and that's it, but I'm sure I'll enjoy anything you cook," smiled Dad.

He got his Franco-American spaghetti, and once the good-hearted woman got used to the idea, she and her husband laughed and enjoyed the platter of spaghetti right along with Dad.

Whenever Dad returned to Michigan from his frequent trips, he found his family excited. Little two-year-old Jimmy had begun to point to airplanes and say "Daddy" for he had seen his daddy come and go so often during that furlough. Mom carried on as head of household during these absences, and we thought of her as our source of strength.

Mom, however, did not always feel strong, and worried a great deal about her children, her husband, and herself. She developed an ulcer, and when she announced it to us, I felt anguished: "Are you going to die?"

"I don't think so," she replied, "but people do sometimes die of bleeding ulcers."

That information frightened me, and Mom hastened to assure me she would be following a strict diet, and all would be OK. But that wasn't enough. I wanted certainty and insisted, "Are you sure you're going to get better?"

Comforting me with a hug, she persuaded me she would indeed get better, but from that point forward we prayed earnestly at every meal and bedtime prayer that God would heal Mommy's ulcer. Her diet did not make her unhappy, for doctors told her to eat a lot of ice cream. We all helped her with this part of her regimen, and within a few months she reported with joy that "God has healed my ulcer. X-Rays show it is completely gone." Dad immediately thanked the Lord, while Carol and I breathed easier, our fears for our mother's life allayed.

As soon as school let out for summer vacation, we wasted no time in heading back to the land where we felt at ease. The family traveled by car to New York to get our visas, and even though we were driving east, we felt we were heading south, en route back home—home to South America. I was eager to get back to Ecuador, and Mom said: "We've gotten used to life in South America. I feel like I'm going home. I think Ecuadorians are generally more polite than Americans and life is less frantic." To which Dad added: "Yup. Around here people have a conniption fit if they miss one section of a revolving door."

And Mom continued, "I can't get over the waste. It still kills me to throw away a plastic spoon at Dairy Queen."

"Yes, I love Latin America," said Dad, "and we have a good life there. I guess there's only one thing I'll never get used to."

"What's that?" I asked.

"The sense of sanitation. There just isn't the same concept of cleanliness we have in the United States."

Always one to defend whomever was being criticized, Mom jumped in, "But some of the cleanest, most well-kept houses are those of our friends in Ecuador."

"Yes, that's true," said Dad. "They are impeccable in that sense. I'm talking about hygiene. I think what I like best about the U.S. is being able to walk into almost any public restroom and have it be clean and sparkling. Most Latin American communities have a long way to go on that."

Even Mom had to agree.

We did not go directly to Quito. We flew from New York (the international airport was called Idlewild in those days) on Viasa, the Venezuelan airline. Our first stop on the way back home to Ecuador was San Cristóbal, Venezuela, where we visited our Savage relatives, Jim, June, and baby Joy—the "3 J's."

Jim and June had a few mango trees in their backyard and Jimmy took to them immediately, slurping mango juice all over his clothes as he sucked on the succulent and stringy fruit. The mango strings got stuck in his teeth, and he spent his time alternately eating mangos and pulling out the strings.

Jim and June raised a few chickens and selected the two choicest and fattest to celebrate our visit. As we watched with admiration and horror, Uncle Jim killed them with his machete. He was about to hang them up on a line when the doorbell rang and we all followed him into the house as he answered the door and chatted with the caller.

Suddenly June shouted, "Come quickly! Buzzards! They're everywhere!"

We dashed out to the backyard and drew back in revulsion as we saw what looked like a black-feathered blanket—scores of big, black, ugly vultures, called *gallinasos* in Spanish.

June quickly untied their dog, and within seconds the creepy monsters were gone, out of sight, but the chickens were picked clean. All that remained were stripped bones and forlorn feathers.

"What a shame!" cried June. "We were so excited about eating our own chickens."

"Don't worry," reassured Jim. "I'll buy some more at the market." Two more chickens were bought, beheaded, and taken directly into the kitchen before the loathsome vultures could outwit us again.

When we arrived in Quito this time, the crowd that met us was many times larger than the small group of missionaries that had welcomed us five years earlier. This time there were not only dozens of missionaries but scores of Ecuadorians, and the lusty singing was in Spanish: *"Bienvenidos, bienvenidos."* ("Welcome, welcome.")

Dad stopped at the bottom of the airplane's steps and hollered back at the crowd: "Amen. Amen. Amen. We are home, brothers and sisters, we are home." As we passed through customs, Dad said to us, "No other band of friends is quite as charged with energy, excitement, and enthusiasm as the HCJB crowd."

I was immediately relieved to be back in familiar surroundings and a few weeks after we arrived, Mom wrote to her folks, "Steve acts much differently than he did in the States. Seems to be so much more independent and confident; more nonchalant and effervescent. Carol is delighted to be with her playmates, Lois VanDerPuy, Ruth Ann Howard, and Betsy Poole. They are all about the same age, same grade in school, and form quite a quartet of playmates."

I continued with my trumpet lessons and chose 7 a.m. each day to practice. The neighbors accepted the blaring without complaint, but mother worried that they were secretly suffering in silence.

I worked for Dad in his office every afternoon from 4 to 5 p.m. and earned 2 *sucres* an hour, equivalent in those days of 12 cents US. He gave me odd jobs, addressing envelopes, running errands, and filing.

About 60 per cent of the students at the Alliance Academy were children of missionary parents, but the other 40 per cent were sons and daughters of people at the United States embassy, businesspeople, and a few Ecuadorians who sent their children to our school to learn English and get an American-style education. One of Carol's best friends was the daughter of the U.S. ambassador, and she spent many afternoons playing in their exquisite mansion.

Carol became enthralled with HCJB's missionary medical work, and assisted Marjorie Jones, one of the HCJB nurses, when she gave vaccinations. Carol decided then and there she was going to be a nurse when she grew up.

Dad quickly got back into his 14-hour a day schedule, a task he was able to accomplish by his enthusiastic participation in one of Ecuador's time-honored traditions: the afternoon siesta. After lunch each day, Dad went to the bedroom, removed his shoes and pants, loosened his tie, put a pillow over his eyes, and fell fast asleep almost instantly. Twenty minutes later he awoke, refreshed, and departed for his office at the radio station across the street.

The diesel generator that Dad had campaigned for arrived

from Panama, first by boat to Guayaquil, then by train to Quito. Then the monstrous generator was transferred to a flat-bed truck, where it was driven, slowly, ponderously, and at great risk, over the narrow, winding cobblestone road to the antenna site at Pifo. Dad joined in with a team of 40 missionaries and nationals, each holding ropes and straps to assist the crane as it unloaded the generator and placed it on the cement pad that had been prepared for it. After they finished, he led the group in a prayer of Thanksgiving, "Oh God, our Father in Heaven, we thank Thee for giving us the money to buy this generator, and for keeping it safe in the long and perilous journey by water, rail, and truck. Now we dedicate this generator to Thy honor and glory. We thank Thee for changing it from an instrument of destruction to a vehicle for the advancement of Thy kingdom. May millions hear Thy word. In Jesus' name, we pray. Amen."

As Christmas 1952 approached Carol and I decorated the tree, and Jimmy undecorated it, pulling ornaments off and unscrewing light bulbs. No one dared put any presents under the tree ahead of time, for we knew he would unwrap them.

When Christmas Day arrived, we opened all our presents with glee, and Jimmy squealed with delight for every present everyone opened. We settled down to enjoy our new toys when Dad said, "There's one more present."

"Where?" Carol and I asked in unison.

"Look on that branch," pointed Dad.

There was an envelope on the tree and I tore it open eagerly. I shouted as I read the message then reread it for all to hear:

A BABY BROTHER OR SISTER IN JULY

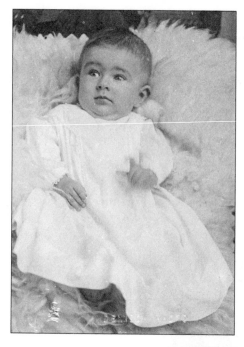

Robert Carlton Savage was born on April 30, 1914 in Barron, Wisconsin.

Bessie Savage holds Bobby, age six months.

Bobby Savage is held by
his great grandmother,
Carrie Jenson.

Henry Savage began his
ministry at the First
Baptist Church in Barron,
Wisconsin.

Jamie and Bobby Savage, River Falls, Wisconsin, 1917.

Parsonage in Almond, Wisconsin. The Savage family lived there in 1919. Those were war days; they seldom had meat. Farmers gave them vegetables. Bob always had fond memories of creamed carrots and potatoes—and it was always a favorite meal.

Bobby Savage, Baraboo, Wisconsin.

The Evangel Male Quartet: Howard Schoof, Russ Case, Clyde Taylor, Bob Savage.

Bob Savage was smitten by the beautiful sophomore coed, Wilda Johnson. They were married in 1938.

Bob and Wilda Savage, 1942.

The missionaries of the Scandinavian Alliance Mission in Colombia, 1942.
Front: Wilf and Elizabeth Watson, Dorothy Hayes, Minnie Waage, Wilda
Savage, Mrs. Ecland, Irene Garrett, Hazel Nilson.
Back: Gilly Davis, Elof and Isabel Anderson, Bob Savage with Steve on
shoulders, Cora Soderquist, Mr. Eckland, Mr. Christensen.

Missionary radio station HCJB, Quito, Ecuador, 1944. Mount Pichincha rises
in the background.

The brothers Bob and Jim Savage sing with Bill Gillam on missionary radio station HCJB.

Wilda Savage became well known all over Latin America for her soft touch at the piano, heard daily on the morning radio program, "Hymns of the Christian Life."

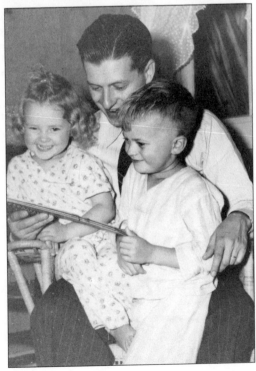

The 1948 campaign in Quito's Teatro Sucre was a major breakthrough for the preaching of the gospel in Ecuador. It was the first time the evangelicals had been able to secure an arena of such prestige and to attract such large and enthusiastic crowds.

Monday nights were "family night." Bob insisted on keeping that night open, avoiding meetings and radio programs. Carol and Steve enjoy a bedtime story.

Their first furlough was in 1948. Jim and June Savage were also on furlough from Venezuela. The Savage tribe gathered at Maranatha Bible Conference.
Front row: *Carol, Steve.*
Back row: *Helen, Bob, Wilda, Henry, Bess, Jim, June.*

Wilda Savage, 1948.

Bob Savage, 1948, preacher, singer, pastor, missionary.

Wilda's parents, Colonel Lawrence and Ruby Johnson, Kyoto, Japan, 1950.

During their second furlough in 1952, Bob and Wilda spent part of the summer at Maranatha Bible Conference with Carol, Jimmy, and Steve.

Dr. and Mrs. H.H. Savage. Henry Savage was founder of Maranatha Bible Conference and pastor of the First Baptist Church in Pontiac, Michigan for 40 years. He became well known as a radio preacher, author, Bible conference speaker, and leader in the conservative evangelical movement, serving as president of the National Association of Evangelicals.

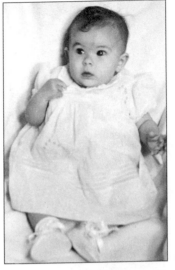

Judi Savage was on the edge of life and death many times during her first year. Bob considered her healing a miracle.

Bob and Jimmy Savage, presenting "Father and Son Time," one of the features of the children's program, "Gospel Bells."

Helen and Dick Broach were married in 1952 and went to South America as missionaries.

Bob Savage baptized with assurance, full of gusto and feeling. This was during Bob's 9-month ministry in St. Croix, U.S. Virgin Islands, when he baptized in the Caribbean Sea.

Bob's daughter Carol married Jim Plueddemann. They were missionaries in Nigeria for 12 years, where Dan and Shari were born.

Bob and Wilda attend the high school graduation of their two granddaughters, Cynthia and Allison in Danville, California, 1983.
Seated: Cynthia, John Thomas (Barrie's father), Wilda, Bob, Louise Thomas (Barrie's mother), Allison.
Standing: Steve, Barrie, Bill.

— Rejoicing in Christ —

Bob Savage presided over his last family reunion, Maranatha, July 1986.
Back row: Lance, Matt, Peggy Weller, Tim Broach, Jimbo, Shari Pluedemann, Carol Pluedemann, Jim Pluedemann, Dan Pluedemann. Second row: Allison, Steve, Barrie, Ricki Broach, Dick Broach, Bob, Jim, Alexito Castillo, Alex Castillo, Judi Castillo, Jon Savage, Whitney, Lisa, Lesley. Front row adults: Carol Broach, Paul Broach, Helen Broach, Wilda Savage, June Savage, Joy Sherwood, Bryce Sherwood. Front row kids: Nathan and Loren Broach, Alisha Broach, Elaine Castillo, Christy Sherwood, Elizabeth (Lisa) Sherwood, J.J. Sherwood.

Bob's youngest son Jimbo married Nina Jaramillo one year before Bob died. The family was now complete; Bob could rest easily. (Barrie and Steve Savage joined Jimbo and Nina at the courthouse.)

Just four months before he died, Bob met son Steve as he taxied his airplane into the Muskegon airport. His arms were thin, his body feeble, but he welcomed his family with boisterous hugs, all the while singing loudly, "There's a welcome here, there's a welcome here...."

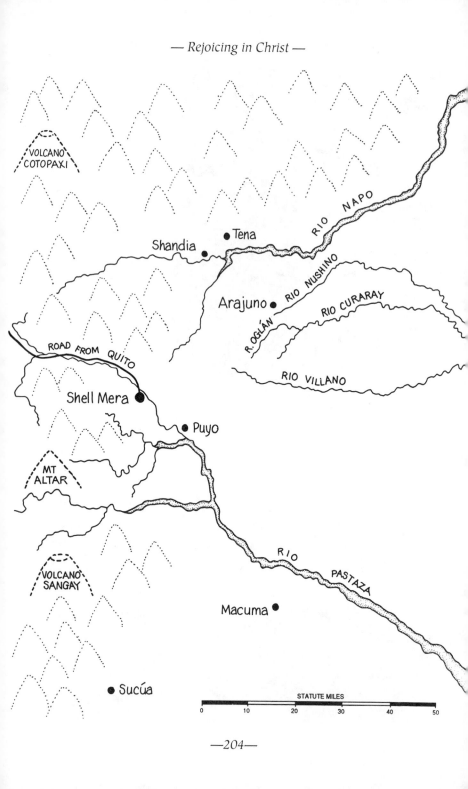

11

Judi's miraculous healing

"Is any sick among you? Let him call for the elders of the church; and let them pray over him, anointing him with oil in the name of the Lord. And the prayer of faith shall save the sick, and the Lord shall raise him up."   —James 5:14

A brooding tension hovered over the missionaries in Ecuador, for there was an ominous mood that threatened religious liberties. Velasco Ibarra, whom Grandpa Savage had met in 1946, was elected again in 1952 as a Liberal, defeating the Conservative (Catholic clergy-supported) candidate. The Army, traditionally liberal, had supported Ibarra. But by 1953, Ibarra had changed his colors, surrounding himself with Arnistas, the fanatical young men who had organized a political party that was violently anti-foreigner, pro-Catholic, rabidly nationalist, pro-fascist, and determined to gain their ends by revolutionary methods. Ibarra maintained the Army's support by cleverly giving military personnel liberal increases in pay.

Ibarra admired Juan Perón of Argentina. Modeling himself after the dictator to the South, Ibarra closed newspapers that gave him trouble, including a major paper, "La Prensa," in Guayaquil. Although Ibarra denied it, the common consensus was that the Ecuadorian constitution had been set aside and that Velasco Ibarra was now dictator.

The effect on gospel missionary work was immediate: for the first time in 50 years, open air meetings were prohibited. Ecuadorian Protestant Christians began to lose their jobs because of their faith. Articles in Roman Catholic papers were more insulting than they had ever been since we arrived in Ecuador. And most of all there was "something in the air"—a sense of opposition that reminded Mom and Dad of the tension they had felt in Colombia.

Petitions were circulated demanding that all foreign Protestant missionaries be deported, but Dad was confident they would be able to stay. Moreover, he felt no danger for his personal safety. His main concern was that missionaries' liberties and privileges would be curtailed, and gospel work would become more difficult.

To address the crisis, HCJB called for a day of prayer and fasting. Carol and I came home from school that day for our noonday meal. We were served our usual nourishing food, but Mom and Dad each had a glass of water. When I asked why, they explained, "We are fasting today, praying that the Lord will help the gospel to go forth with greater power than ever before."

"But why aren't you eating?" I asked.

"The Bible commands us to fast and pray," they replied.

"But what good does it do not to eat anything," I pleaded, puzzled.

"It cleans out our bodies, clears our minds, and forces us to think more intensely about God."

"Oh," I answered, impressed but not exactly convinced.

The furor abated, slowly, almost unnoticeably. Missionaries held their breath as the intensity of speeches subsided and the frequency of demands for deportation of the missionaries gradually diminished. It was not a dramatic change, but within a few months the missionary group began to breathe easier as it became apparent that the gospel message would not be thwarted. Dad brought it up one day at family devotions. "We fasted and prayed and asked God to preserve our liberty to preach the gospel. Six months have passed and we are preaching freely. Let's give thanks for God's answer to prayer." Then he embarked into one of his "doxologies of praise overflow from our hearts" prayers. Dad never hesitated to ask for God's help but never forgot to thank God when help had been given.

Dad had never been to the east coast of South America, and was excited about his planned campaign in Brazil. There was a non-stop flight on the Brazilian airline, Varig, from Lima to Río de Janeiro, and Dad was scheduled to take it. When he arrived in Lima, however, the plane was delayed for maintenance, and the only way to get to Río was through a southern loop which took him to Santiago, Chile; Buenos Aires, Argentina; Montevideo, Uruguay; and finally on to Río de Janeiro. Although the trip was long, Dad was delighted to set his eyes on Argentina and Uruguay, and as he flew over these countries he thought about the hundreds of HCJB listeners who had written letters from these lovely southern countries whose distance from Quito was greater than New York.

In Brazil, Dad preached in Spanish and a Brazilian preacher translated into Portuguese. As he preached in Brazilian churches, he was amazed to find very few foreign missionaries. He quickly discovered the reason: local churches were thriving. Churches in Brazil were growing faster than anyplace else in the world, and the work was being done mostly by Brazilians themselves. Brazilian pastors were excellently prepared in Brazilian seminaries. Most church activities in the cities were entirely independent of foreign funds. The Brazilian Christians sponsored their own hospitals, orphanages, and TB sanitariums. Their churches were beautifully constructed and maintained. They ran well-organized Sunday Schools, young people's societies, and ministerial councils. One Presbyterian church in São Paulo was completing a beautiful new Gothic-style edifice capable of seating 4000.

As usual in his campaigns, Dad was preaching evangelistic sermons, directing his message to those who had not yet accepted

Christ, but as he grew to appreciate the level of maturity in the Brazilian churches, he began to add a missionary challenge as well. He asserted to his Brazilian audiences: "There is no reason why Brazil can't become one of the great missionary-*sending* nations of the world, along with the United States, England, and Canada. Brazil has the Christian young people to send, and also has the needed funds. All it needs is to have a missionary vision stirred up."

He presented the missionary challenge in the same way he had preached it back in the States. At the Central Methodist Church of São Paulo 21 young people consecrated their lives for missionary service, including a young doctor. At the Presbyterian Church in Campinas, another group responded in similar fashion.

Dad had only gradually grown aware of the need to challenge Christians, so as he summarized the results of the campaign, he vowed to give greater emphasis to the growth of young Christians in his next Brazilian trip. He wrote: "If I were to return to Brazil I would emphasize the missionary challenge much more. Altogether God gave us 672 decisions during the four weeks. 203 of these were first time decisions for salvation. The others were decisions among Christians coming for full surrender, fullness of the Spirit, victory over sin, and similar reasons. I gave very few invitations to Christians, but at every such instance the altar would immediately and spontaneously be filled with 40, 50, or 60 individuals with contrite hearts crying out to God in their need."

Although there were few foreign missionaries needed in the major Brazilian cities, there were scores of missionaries working in the jungles of Brazil. The Amazon River basin was bigger than twenty Mississippi River deltas, and there was a large effort to reach Brazilian Amazon Indian tribes for Christ.

It was a difficult month for Mom, for she was now five months pregnant, and she had many bouts of nausea and trouble with pain in her legs. Our biggest topic of conversation during Dad's absence was the baby coming in July, and when Dad arrived, his first concern was Mom's health and the progress of her pregnancy.

Now that I was 12 years old I began to call him Dad instead of Daddy. I remember Dad mostly as a laughing, happy, interested friend. Another memory I have of him, however, is a stern disciplinarian. By this time, I no longer got spanked, for his strict admonitions were usually enough to keep me in line. If he got angry, his eyes narrowed and turned from hazel to grey. The rejoicing Daddy became the fierce father, and I hastened to step into line.

My most vivid memory of Dad is his laugh. I could hear him laugh from several hundred yards away. Often I'd be coming home from school, a block from the HCJB radio station compound, and could hear his voice roaring with glee. His laugh was from the belly, but as he continued to guffaw, it became more and more of a yelp, higher and higher, buoyed up, a 30-second laugh sustained by one huge lungful of air. His voice had the power, though not the quality, of an operatic baritone.

Some of his favorite exclamations were spiritual outcries such as "Praise the Lord!" "Amen!" and "Hallelujah!" These cannonaded from his mouth with naturalness and ease. And if something sounded good to him, he'd say it again, and again, and even once again: "Fine, fine, fine" or "My, my, my." Sometimes, when normal declarations of exuberance fell short, he bellowed out, "Whoop-dee-doo-den-doo!"

His laugh was indeed from the belly and by the mid-1950's, his tummy had grown quite large. Every time he went to the United States, he gained 20 pounds as he feasted in people's homes during his travels around the country. He usually lost most of his weight when he returned to Ecuador, with the high altitude, fast-paced living, and weekly tennis; however, as time went on, he found most of those pounds stayed with him and even the frenzied velocity of his work did not take away his bulk.

It was a full generation before the health-conscious 70's and Dad did not fret over his paunch. His father had one also, so he figured it was inevitable. He joked about it often, and seemed to enjoy it. One day he met fellow-missionary Vern VanHovel in the middle of the HCJB compound. Vern's middle was also expanding and Dad took note of it by proclaiming, "Vern, let's get our heads together." Their two "breadbaskets" met, leaving their heads two feet apart. Vern's high tenor laugh joined Dad's huge baritone to reverberate merry laughter throughout the mission station.

He loved sugar, and anything that contained sugar. One day, after noonday meal, just before devotions, Dad picked up his spoon, licked it off, then dipped it into the sugar bowl. He licked off all the sugar that clung to the spoon and said, "Aaah. This is great."

Mom was horrified. "Bob, how unsanitary!"

"Unsanitary?" Dad's eyebrows furrowed into deep, pretended thought. "The only sugar touched by my spit is the stuff that stuck to the spoon. Everything left in the bowl is untouched and pure."

Mom was unconvinced. It sounded like a great theory to me.

As I went into my early teenage years, there was little or no sense of conflict with my dad, and I participated enthusiastically in most church activities, especially young peoples' meetings. I was assigned the task of preparing a weekly Bible quiz in Spanish, and took the job with enthusiasm. Dad helped me prepare the questions and helped me turn them from impossible to interesting. For example, I thought it would be great sport to ask some obscure question like: "Who was the son of Buzi the priest?" (answer: Ezekiel).

Dad would say, "Now, Steve, that will definitely stump 'em, but don't you think it might be more fun if they have a chance to get it?"

"But it sounds so funny," I insisted, reluctant to relent.

"True. How about something that will make them think? How do you like this one: 'What is the Biblical plan for salvation?'" He never lost a chance to get in a word for the gospel message.

"OK. I'll put some of those questions in, too," I agreed.

Another important event took place at age 12, for Dad had promised to tell me how babies were born when I reached this mature age. Although my school friends had told me the nitty-gritty when I was 8 or 9 years old, I never quite believed it, and wanted Dad to confirm that what they said was true. I reminded him, "Well, Dad, you told me that when I was 12 you'd tell me how babies were born, and I'm 12 now."

"OK, sit down," said Dad. "First, I want you to know that God has given us a wonderful gift. It is a beautiful and lovely event between the father and the mother. It is wonderful when it takes place within the sacred vows of marriage, but it is sinful when it takes place outside of God's holy plan for one man and one woman."

With that introduction, he proceeded to tell me, calmly and factually, exactly how the mysterious and glorious act of love took place, and although I felt smug for already knowing the facts, I was pleased to hear it told authoritatively. The schoolboys who had told me about sex had made it sound "dirty" whereas Dad painted delicate word pictures that colored a rainbow of beauty in my mind.

He could not have told it more perfectly; his only mistake was that he did not tell it several years earlier, the first time I asked.

On July 2, Mom played the piano for an afternoon program at HCJB. She had another program at 6:45 p.m. As she came out of the studio at 7:00, she stopped Dad, who was on his way to prayer meeting, for this was Wednesday night and Dad never missed a meeting.

"Bob, dear," she said, "I believe it might be a good idea for you to stay close by tonight."

Dad quickly arranged for someone else to look after the prayer meeting, then called Dr. Paul Roberts, who arrived at our house a few minutes later. It was now 7:25 p.m. It took Dr. Roberts only a minute to examine Mom before he ordered, "Let's get going to the Clinic, fast."

Things happened so quickly that everyone was dazzled. One hour later, at 8:28 p.m., Judith Lynn Savage was born.

"Hallelujah!" shouted Dad when nurse Marj Jones announced the good news. "Fine, fine, fine. We have a perfect family: boy, girl, boy, girl. Praise the Lord! This is good; this is swell. Amen!"

An hour later, Mom was wheeled into her room, where Dad kissed her and said, "Wilda, you've had a tough pregnancy, a miserable nine months. You've been brave. Praise God the delivery went so swiftly."

"I feel fine," said Mom, "and now I want to see my little baby."

Marj Jones brought tiny Judi and placed her in Mom's arms. Both Mom and Dad touched the baby's cheeks, hands, arms, and feet, and kissed her fondly. Then Dad said, "Let's pray. Father in heaven, we thank Thee for Judith Lynn Savage. We thank Thee for a speedy delivery. We pray that Wilda will make a quick recovery and that little Judi will grow up to be a faithful servant of Thine. Grant her good health and strength, and give Wilda and me wisdom as we bring her up in the nurture and admonition of the Lord, in Whose blessed name we pray. Amen."

Dad left at 11:00 p.m. Mom was still wide-awake, cuddling and cooing over Judi.

In September, Mom and Dad had their fifteenth wedding anniversary, and Mom wrote her mother, "Just think, fifteen years have gone by; it hardly seems possible. What a fortunate gal I was to get such a wonderful husband! He surely is the tops of the tops and that's putting it mildly."

Dad was just as fond of Mom, and always praised her in public and private. Often he said to us, "You kids are sure blessed to have the most wonderful mother in the world, and I am doubly blessed to have the best wife."

I never remember Mom and Dad quarreling. They rarely had a difference of opinion, and if they did, it was discussed calmly, with civility and tenderness. Mom was utterly devoted to Dad and basked in the glow of his limelight. Dad honored Mom and held her in high esteem. Whenever I try to think of an example of a good and lovely marriage, theirs is the first that comes to mind.

As Jimmy's fourth birthday approached, his requests for presents reflected the influence of the radio station: a marimba like Gene Jordan's and a microphone like Daddy's. He spent most of his time on his tricycle, even driving it right up to the table at mealtime, and climbing from tricycle directly into his chair. At the end of the meal, he clambered right back onto his trike, so that his feet never had to touch the floor.

But before Jimmy's birthday could be celebrated, we spent many days of anguish hovering over little eight-month-old Judi, who had become very, very sick. She suffered intense pain in her ear, and cried day and night. She developed high fever, bad cough, and head cold. Dr. Paul Roberts treated her but she did not respond to any medicine.

Most Quito children had rosy cheeks because of the sun and high altitude, but Judi's coloring was sallow. Mom wondered if Judi was simply taking after Dad, whose olive complexion contrasted with the ruddy cheeks of the rest of the family. However, Dr. Roberts said she was anemic and prescribed iron and calcium.

After some improvement, Judi took a turn for the worse. She developed a high fever and diarrhea. At midnight Mom took her temperature and was shaken to see it register 106°. Dr. Roberts rushed over to our house, where he gave Judi a shot of penicillin and showed Mom how to give her a cool sponge bath to bring down the fever.

We were all alarmed, although Mom and Dad did not tell us just how bad her situation was. Mom wrote to her mother, "Her little body was so hot, we couldn't help but wonder whether she could live through it or not."

D. S. Clark called a special prayer meeting and the HCJB staff knelt together and asked God to put His healing hand on Judi Savage.

She showed some improvement and Mom said, "God saw fit to spare her and our hearts are filled with gratitude."

But the joy was temporary. Judi was not well by any means.

Her blood tests showed an abnormal quantity of white blood cells and she was still a very sick baby. Despite the excruciating pain of her ear infections, the sharp stinging of the penicillin shots, and the constant tests, Mom wrote, "She is a precious little bundle, and through it all will invariably give us a big smile that almost breaks our hearts."

Dr. Roberts ran tests to check for intestinal infection or parasites but found nothing. The matter of most concern was the abnormally high white corpuscle count and Dr. Roberts told Mom and Dad, "I must prepare you for some hard news, because this type of white corpuscle count is often indicative of leukemia."

"Oh, Lord, please!" prayed Mother aloud as she gasped at the sound of the dreadful word "leukemia."

A few days later another white corpuscle test showed an encouraging trend: the count had dropped from 35,000 to 16,000, still very high, but good enough so that Dr. Roberts was able to console Mom and Dad: "Well, I still don't know what it is, but I think we can rule out leukemia."

"Praise the Lord!" whooped Dad, while Mom sobbed in gratitude.

As the weeks went by, Judi continued to have periods of improvement when everyone rejoiced, followed by setbacks which gave us great anxiety. Dr. Roberts suggested that her tonsils should come out, but did not want to perform the operation himself. He asked the splendid Ecuadorian childcare specialist, Dr. Carlos Andrade Marín, if he would perform the operation, but he demurred, because she was so tiny and so sick. They considered flying to Panama to the U.S. Army medical center, but the specialists there were also reluctant to remove the tonsils of a nine-month-old baby who was in such debilitated condition.

Dad had an Easter conference scheduled at the Bible Institute in Shell Mera, and considered calling it off because of Judi's precarious health. However, during the week before Easter she was in good spirits, with no fever, so Dad took Carol and me on the four-day trip.

Young Ecuadorians from all over the country came to Shell Mera for the three-year course, and it was in these young people that missionaries placed their fondest hopes for the future of evangelical work in Ecuador.

A trip to Shell Mera was an adventure that began at 5 a.m. in Quito, where we boarded a bus to Ambato. The buses were built in Ecuador on imported Ford and Chevrolet truck frames. The shell of the bus was made of wood, and was designed in a curve that made each bus look like a bloated whale. The curved design made it structurally sound, but also provided extra space into which the bus owner could cram more people.

Most buses were individually owned, and the driver hired a *conductor* to collect fares and load baggage. Dozens of buses were parked in the early dawn, waiting to depart to destinations across the little country.

The trip from Quito to Ambato took us up to 12,000 feet, across the *páramo* region of treeless, wind-swept stubble grass, then down to the graceful and lovely town of Ambato, about 1,000 feet lower than Quito with a population of about 60,000.

The trip from Quito to Ambato was the easy part. It was now 10:00 a.m. and it was our task to find a bus going to Puyo, the frontier town at the end of the road. Shell Mera was the last stop before Puyo, so we wandered around the open plaza where dozens of buses and trucks were loading up to depart for various parts of Ecuador.

"*Puyo! Puyo!*" We heard a young boy's shrill hollering out the words we sought, and asked him where the bus was. He pointed over at a beat-up vehicle, covered with mud. The boy told us his uncle was the driver. We paid our fare, and were ushered onto the bus through one of the 12 small doors that extended along each side. Each door opened to the end of a long bench that went all the way across the bus—no aisle. The bench had a small amount of padding and was covered in leather. The beam that went across the ceiling went right over the bench and there were numbers every 16 inches designating a seat number. Nine people were expected to squeeze together tightly from one end of the bench to the other. Half of the passengers entered through the left door and half through the right. If you were lucky, you were the last one in and got to sit by a window. But you were more likely to sit between two Indian women, each with a child on her back and a basket in her lap. Under her poncho she might carry a chicken, tucked in another small basket. She took up a great deal of space, and there was barely enough room to wiggle.

Baggage was loaded on top of the bus and an oilcloth cover was tied over the top to keep it dry. When Dad looked at my tight fit and considered the journey ahead, he asked the *conductor* if we might sit up on top of the baggage. "Yes, as soon as we pass the control point," said the *conductor*. The "control" was the checkpoint where all buses had to stop and pass inspection.

After we left Ambato, we passed through the "control" where a police officer dutifully noted the license number of the bus and time of day, then waved us through. At the next stop, about ten kilometers down the road, we squeezed out of our seats and clambered up on top of the baggage. Carol giggled with delight, I grinned broadly, and Dad said, "Amen! Amen! Amen! This is the way to travel."

As we descended from 9,000 feet, the vegetation changed every hour, from eucalyptus and cactus of the highlands, to ever more lush and thick verdure. Trees grew taller, in greater variety. Orchids popped out on the cliffs on each side of the road, dazzling in their lovely pinks, violets, and yellows.

Travel from Ambato to Shell Mera took six to twelve hours, depending on road conditions. It was almost impossible to keep a roadway properly graded, for frequent rains and landslides often carried away entire sections of the throughway. Many engineers had been brought in from Europe and North America for consultation on the best way to build a road through the steep valley formed by the Pastaza River, and as they considered the nearly perpendicular walls, soft shale geology, and constant rainfall, most of them shook their heads and simply said, "It can't be done."

The plucky Ecuadorians, however, kept at it, and the road was always in the process of being built, rebuilt, and rebuilt again. Seldom could one travel to Shell Mera without waiting in a queue of trucks and buses while a bulldozer cleared rocks and mud out of the highway.

On this trip to Shell Mera, we were confronted with more than a mere landslide, for an entire bridge had been washed out by heavy rains. We came to the deep gorge formed by the Pastaza, got off the bus and walked gingerly to the edge. There we gazed down at the great river roaring 2,000 feet below and considered the method by which we would cross it.

We waded in mud to a place on the cliff overlooking the river where there was a *tarabita*, a cable stretched across the chasm with a little platform hung on two pulleys. The *tarabita* was the size of the top of a small desk, and held four people. No side walls, but each passenger could hold on to the iron rod that affixed platform to pulley. We three took our places along with a fourth Ecuadorian passenger, waited for a few tense seconds, then "whoosh"—they pushed us off the edge of the cliff, and our little table went rolling down the cable. I gazed down at the river roaring below and pictured the frail contraption breaking off and taking us to our death below. Carol giggled nervously and refused to look down. Dad chattered happily: "This is great. This is swell. Fine, fine, fine. Amen!"

The cart swooped down by force of gravity until it was half way across where it reached the bottom of the arc formed by the drooping cable. We came to a stop. There we were, suspended in space, with nothing but a raging torrent below. We sat, motionless, for a few minutes while the work crew on the other side of the abyss untangled their ropes. Then, lurch, we went forward a few feet, stopped, then groaned forward again as the fellows pulled us a few more feet. Our ears were right next to the pulleys, and they creaked along the steel cable. One tug at a time, and little by little our decrepit craft jerked to the other side. They pulled us up to the muddy bank and we crawled off.

Another bus awaited us on the other side so we climbed in and continued our trip, but not for long. A few minutes later we came to another landslide. A truck had tried to get around the muck, edging close to the side of the road. He got too close, his back wheels slipped off, but fortunately one front wheel clung precariously to the road. Various buses arrived on the scene, passengers piled out, and 70 volunteers quickly gathered to help extract the truck. Dad and I joined the throng, and grabbed onto one of the ropes that had been tied to the truck. *"Dále! Dále duro!"* (Pull! Pull hard!) The shouts animated the crowd and we pulled with all our might. Inch by inch the truck began to move out, and slowly we got it back on the road. Cheers went up, then everyone settled back to wait while workers cleared the landslide with bulldozers and shovels until we could continue.

Despite the delays, we arrived in Shell Mera at 6:30 p.m., only three hours later than the ideal time. The missionaries greeted us with great enthusiasm, telling us, "a trip to the jungles wouldn't be complete without a ride on the *tarabita.*"

The four days at the Bible Institute were fruitful as Dad preached evangelistic sermons for the Shell Mera citizens who were not believers in Christ, and teaching sermons for the institute students. Eldon Yoder was one of the missionary-professors at the institute and noted how Dad would spice his sermons by occasionally bursting into song. Right in the middle of a message, he would start singing, *"Bellas Palabras de Vida"* ("Wonderful Words of Life") and anyone in the audience whose attention had wandered was immediately brought back to attention. Dad's habit of singing had sometimes embarrassed me, but when I heard Eldon talk about it admiringly, it gave me a different point of view.

While Dad was at the institute, I spent most of my time hanging around the hangar at Missionary Aviation Fellowship, watching Nate Saint and Bob Wittig as they worked on their airplanes, asking a million questions, which the two pilots were kind enough to patiently answer. Whenever they took off or landed I raced to the runway to watch. I also enjoyed watching the Noorduyn Norseman, built in Canada, owned by *"Transportes Aéreos Orientales"* (Oriental Air Transport). The little airline was referred to as *"TAO."*

It was the most exhausting year of Mom's life. Judi's health continued to worry her, as the little tyke had continued bouts of fever, earaches, and throat inflammation. Dad was traveling a lot, so she often carried on alone. That summer I added a huge load to her already heavy burden. One day I wandered over to the vacant playground at the Alliance Academy. All the missionary kids had gone home for the summer, and the school was quiet. Doug Clark and I began to work out on the gymnastics bars. As I lifted myself upside down to go up and over the high bar, a speck of dirt fell from my pants into my eye. I shook my head, lost my grip, plummeted to the ground, and rolled over with pain. Doug looked at me, grimaced, and said, "Your shoulder is all bunched up. Looks like you disconnected it."

It was worse than that, much worse, for the humerus bone broke cleanly just below the shoulder joint. My shoulder muscles contracted and pulled the little piece upward, so the small broken part pointed up, while the rest of my arm lay dangling below.

There was no way to set it in a cast and Dr. Roberts said he'd have to put it in traction. There were no modern traction devices in any of the Quito hospitals, so the ingenious Dr. Roberts scurried around Quito, visiting hardware stores and carpenter shops until he had rigged a contraption that firmly held my arm in place. It consisted of a wooden frame, two pulleys, several weights, and a clothesline.

I spent four weeks on my back that summer, and Mom visited me for several hours every day. She bought me dozens of books and I read every book in the Black Stallion series, the Hardy Boys collection, and the Koko in Alaska books. I also read dozens of aviation magazines and every issue of *Boy's Life* magazine Mom could obtain.

While I was in the hospital, Dad and Gene Jordan were away on an evangelistic campaign in Colombia. Judi had another setback. Mom was up most of each night with Judi, while running back and forth to the hospital to see me. She was exhausted, but when Dad offered to cancel his meetings and come back she insisted, "God wants you in Colombia. We will be OK here."

When Dad returned, Judi was still sick. She had spells of relative relief, but was by no means in good health. At family devotions, he told us, "Judi is only fourteen months old and has spent six of those months seriously ill. We have tried every medicine known to man, and have prayed earnestly, but there's one thing we have not done."

"What's that?" asked Mom.

"We have not literally followed the instructions in the book of James," said Dad.

"What instructions?" I asked.

"Let me read them to you." He pulled out his Bible, turned to the fifth chapter of James, and intoned: "Is any sick among you? Let him call for the elders of the church; and let them pray over him, anointing him with oil in the name of the Lord. And the prayer of faith shall save the sick, and the Lord shall raise him up."

"How do you anoint someone with oil?" asked Carol.

"You dab a little oil on their forehead," said Dad.

"Why do you need oil?" I questioned.

"Well, the Lord tells us to use it. Oil is a symbol of our faith in His healing power," answered Dad.

"I think it's also an act of obedience," added Mom, "and we must do it."

They called together the senior members of the HCJB missionary staff, and those splendid veterans of pioneer gospel work came over to our house. D. S. Clark took Judi in his arms and asked Dad to hand him the bottle of olive oil. He poured a few drops on her forehead, then rubbed it gently as he prayed,

"Our dear Father in heaven, we anoint this child in Thy name, and ask Thy healing hand to be laid on her sweet little body. Above all we ask that Thy will be done. In Jesus' name. Amen." Mom and Dad softly added their own choked "amen," thanked the missionaries, and took Judi back in their arms.

Dr. Roberts was among those who joined in the prayer service and after it was over he said, "Let's take her off sulfa; in fact, let's take her off all medications."

A month later, Mom wrote, "For four weeks now Judi has been well, without any of those spells she has had. As you know, four weeks is a long time for her to be well, so we are very grateful."

A few weeks later, Dad said cautiously, "I believe the Lord has worked a miracle in little Judi's body. She is definitely healed."

"Why didn't you anoint her right at the beginning?" I asked.

"We should have," said Dad. "In our Baptist tradition, we've always been a little skeptical of faith healing, and we've shied away from the ceremony of anointing a person with oil. I think that's not good, and I intend to follow this Biblical imperative a lot more in the future."

"What if she hadn't gotten better?" I asked. "What would you think of praying for healing?"

"Well, whenever we've prayed for God to heal her, we've always added 'Thy will be done.' D. S. Clark also used that phrase when he anointed her with oil."

"What's the point of praying at all?" I insisted.

"Prayer is communion with God, and we need to pray just to put ourselves in touch with Him. God chooses to use the prayers of His faithful followers as part of His grand plan for the universe," he replied.

"Does prayer change His mind?" I pressed.

"Good question. Probably not, because He knows all things before they're going to happen anyway."

"If we can't change God's mind, why do we pray for healing?" I was puzzled.

Dad was patient. "We are the ones that need prayer, not God."

Mom added, "Prayer reminds us that God is the one who directs our lives, and when He heals someone like Judi, we give Him thanks."

"But what do you do if He doesn't heal?" I asked.

"You still give Him thanks, because His will was done," replied Mom.

Judi's appetite grew, her cheeks became rosy, and she began to gain weight.

"Is it a miracle?" I asked Dad.

"Of course it's a miracle," he responded. "I think every person who gets healed is a miracle. If penicillin heals them, I praise God for the miracle of penicillin. If Jesus heals a person in a split second, without any medicine, that's also a miracle."

Dad believed that life itself was a miracle. The daily rotation of the earth, the annual harvest of crops, each breath he breathed, were all the result of a meticulous and miraculous creation by the Creator, to whom Dad constantly gave thanks for every minute he lived.

"Is he for real?" Often I was asked this question about Dad, and sometimes pondered it myself. Dad was extraordinarily cheerful. He believed that a Christian should always rejoice, and he tried to internalize the qualities he preached about. Still, the question nagged, "How can a person be so constantly radiant? Doesn't he get depressed or melancholy?"

Mom shared Dad's conviction that one should "rejoice in the Lord always". But it was not as easy for her. Dad could wear the joy on his sleeve, whereas Mom often felt she was coming up short. Somewhere, somehow, she knew the Lord was in overall control, but often despaired, as she did not always feel on top of things, which is human enough. Mom was 5 feet, 4 inches, with brown hair and hazel eyes. Her complexion was fair, her face smooth. People looked at her and saw a pretty, personable, and talented woman, but she did not have the same view of herself.

Dad would consider her enormous talent, lovely spirit, and fine intellect—and would shake his head, wondering how she could possibly be tormented with such a lack of self-confidence. He set himself on a life-long crusade to cheer and buck her up. She would worry; he would tell her not to worry. She would develop a minor ailment; he would tell her to overcome it with a positive attitude.

It was ironic that this man of splendid health was ultimately struck down at age 73 with cancer. His doctor told me that Dad's positive attitude probably gave him three or four more years of life than anyone would have predicted given the magnitude of his cancer. Until cancer got him, he never understood nor accepted disease, and even as he was dying, he had little interest in talking about his illness. Yes, he was sympathetic, but only to a degree. Way down deep, he had little patience for disease, depression, worry, and self-doubt. After all, he reasoned, a Christian is commanded to rejoice, and that's certainly not a hard commandment to keep, because in Christ we have everything to rejoice about. He simply did not understand those Christians who failed to rejoice with his own degree of gusto.

However, his attitude towards lesser mortals softened around 1960 when Dad took an evangelistic trip to Perú with missionary chalk artist John Mosiman. They discovered a little book that described the "four temperaments." Dad had never paid much attention to psychology, but became fascinated with the four basic "types" portrayed in the book: choleric, phlegmatic, sanguine, and melancholic.

Two of the types were considered extroverted: choleric and sanguine. The choleric was the person of action, quick in decision making, touchy, restless, aggressive, excitable, changeable, impulsive, optimistic, and active. The sanguine was the personality person, a natural leader, warm, full of good intentions, sociable, outgoing, talkative, responsive, easygoing, lively, and carefree.

The other two types were introverted: phlegmatic and

melancholic. The phlegmatic was easy going, a bit philosophical, calm and cool, friendly, not exerting himself too much, passive, careful, thoughtful, peaceful, controlled, reliable, and even-tempered. And finally, the melancholic: the brooding thinker, the worrier, creative, moody, anxious, rigid, sober, pessimistic, and reserved.

By the end of the trip, Dad had concluded that he was part sanguine and part choleric, which to his mind were the best types. Likewise, John declared himself a melancholic and proud of it.

When Dad returned home, he was animated as he described to us how the four temperaments worked. What made him most euphoric was that he had suddenly come to understand Mom. She was—a melancholic! That was it! That explained everything. No longer did he need to change her; she was an authentic melancholic, and that was just fine. The Lord created her a melancholic and He needed her to remain a melancholic. After all, if she were anything else, she wouldn't be such a great pianist, nor such a sensitive wife and mother.

Mom was also pleased. She rather enjoyed thinking of herself as a certified melancholic—and was enormously relieved that the heat was off and she no longer had to change.

No matter what happened in our lives, Dad was a constant force. A time-aware man, he had a graceful way of closing any conversation. With great enthusiasm, he'd announce, "Let's have a word of prayer!"

It worked like magic. When visitors would come for dinner, we would eat, then retire to the living room to visit. After about five or ten minutes, Dad would begin to get fidgety, and we knew this visit was about to come to a gracious close.

As soon as there was a pause, Dad slapped his knee and said, "Well, let's have a word of prayer." He stood, and automatically everyone rose with him. He gathered them into a circle and immediately launched into spirited praise: "Our Father in Heaven, doxologies of praise pour forth from our hearts. We thank Thee for this wonderful time we've had together. We pray that Thou wilt bless Brother and Sister Johnson as they go their way. Flood them with journeying mercies and may Thy gracious blessings be heaped upon them. May each of us live our lives, every minute, every second, to the honor and glory of Thy name. In Christ's name. Amen."

There was no question about it—the visit was over. The benediction had been pronounced. No one felt dismissed, but they knew it was time to go. They left with a glow, uplifted by the prayer that had launched them into a glorious departure from the Savage home.

Late in 1954, Dad's sixth chorus book was published, and the *Adelante Juventud* series continued to meet a need in Latin American churches. In order to help people back in the States understand the significance of what Dad was doing, Mom wrote to the supporting churches: "Picture yourself singing nothing but translations of South American songs with their minor tunes. That is what these people have been doing for years, only in reverse. They have been singing our music, not their own. They enjoy much of our music, most assuredly, but it is logical they should respond even more to music which comes from their hearts."

Mom and Dad both came to love the Latin American music, and became increasingly enthusiastic about it. Dad told us, "I used to think the minor key always meant sadness, but often these Latin melodies express happiness and joy in the minor. Sometimes even marching music is minor."

Mom added, "And the music really varies from country to country. Ecuadorian music is absolutely different from music in other countries."

Dr. Bob Cook, president of Youth for Christ, flew to Colombia to join Dad and Bill Gillam for another series of meetings. When Cook arrived he asked Dad, "How are you doing?"

"*Profundo e inefable!*" exclaimed Dad.

"Sounds good, but I don't know Spanish," grinned Cook. "What does it mean?"

"Profound, ineffable, full of joy, indescribable." rejoiced Dad.

"Amen, brother! I'm glad my first two words of Spanish were so splendid. I'll never forget them," said Cook and from that point onward whenever the two greeted each other it was always *"profundo e inefable."*

Cook learned Spanish quickly and usually gave a two or three minute testimony in Spanish at each meeting. Then he preached in English while Dad translated. They got a rhythm going between them in which Cook would say three or four words and Dad would translate instantly. The teamwork was so smooth and quick that the audience almost forgot that one of the speakers was preaching in a foreign tongue.

They took a break one afternoon and went swimming in the harbor. The water was shallow, and it seemed a safe place to swim. Farther out, however, unbeknownst to the team of evangelists, there was an undertow. Bob Cook got far out, became tired, frightened, and called to Dad to help him. Dad thought he was joking. Cook called with more urgency. Dad immediately came over, swimming strongly, put an arm around Cook's shoulders and towed him in.

As they reached shore, and Cook found his footing, he stopped, took a few deep breaths, then gasped, "Thanks, brother, I believe you saved my life."

"Amen, Amen, Amen," and this time Dad did not say those words with his usual exuberance, but quietly, reverently. Then he looked his friend in the eye and told him, "The Lord has a huge life in store for you, and it wasn't time for you to go home." Standing there in the waves, the two men, still panting, bowed their heads and thanked God for saving his servant, Bob Cook.

Dr. Robert A. Cook did have a full life in store, for the ministry of Youth for Christ flourished into a worldwide major evangelistic organization under his leadership. Later he became president of The Kings College in Briarcliff Manor, New York.

12

"Himnos de la vida Cristiana"
(Hymns of the Christian life)

In November, 1955, a new era began for Bob and Wilda Savage. They began a daily radio program, *"Himnos de la Vida Cristiana"* ("Hymns of the Christian Life"). It was destined to become HCJB's most popular broadcast and would serve as the vehicle for making known hundreds of gospel choruses and songs born in the hearts of Latin American believers. After the first month, Dad wrote about this program, still rather modest in his expectations of what it would accomplish:

> For many years I didn't do much speaking in Spanish over the radio programs, felt it was better to use Nationals. However, since November 1st, Wilda and I have been presenting a daily program at 8:00 a.m. in Spanish in which we do singing, playing, and speaking. Well, we've never had such a good response to any of our programs. We've been getting letters from all over Latin America that cause the cockles of our hearts to rejoice.

Within a few months, *"Himnos"* was drawing over 10,000 letters per year. One key to its success was the bubbling enthusiasm of Don Roberto Savage as he began the program with his inimitable, *"Muuuuuuuuy buenos días."* ("A Veeeeeerrrrry good morning"). The second key was the idea of dedicating songs to people with birthdays and anniversaries. At first they dedicated one song to each person with a request, but eventually, because of the sheer volume of requests, they had to dedicate one song to dozens of listeners. The third key was the selection of songs. Instead of hymns translated from English, most songs were authentic Latin melodies, and it was through this program they became known throughout Latin America. The final key was the use of local talent. Dad sang many solos. He also sang countless duets with Mom. But he usually had a guest musician on the program each morning, either an HCJB missionary, an Ecuadorian musician, or a traveling singer or instrumentalist.

One day he asked Enrique Romero, who had been HCJB's chauffeur for many years, to sing a duet with him on the program. Enrique was stunned. "Me, sing on the radio? Oh, no, Don Roberto, I couldn't do that."

"Sure you can," encouraged Dad.

Enrique sang with Dad. His voice was smooth and plaintive, and he especially captured the feeling of minor melodies as he slurred fervently from one note to the next. He was a huge hit, and many people wrote asking for more songs by Don Enrique. He soon became a daily fixture, and became one of Dad's closest friends and associates. Within a few years, he was not only singing on *"Himnos"* but was pastor of the Church of the Divine Redeemer. Dad was always on the lookout for untapped talent that could be used for the Lord.

Dad worked closely with the talented missionary musicians on HCJB's staff, encouraging them to rise early and work with him on the daily program. He was jolly in his invitation but strict in his instructions: they had to be at rehearsal at precisely 7:15 a.m. Gene Jordan played his marimba and violin while his wife Ruth sang. Dixie Dean put on virtuoso accordian numbers. Dolores VanDerPuy sang with her magnificent coloratura soprano and Jeanne O'Dell blended her mellow contralto. The sisters Lois and Dolores Baklenko often sang duets. Vern VanHovel sang high tenor solos with purity and clarity.

Joe and Betty Springer were frequent participants. Betty played piano and organ; Joe sang bass solos. One of Dad's favorite motifs was to have Joe sing a solo—one octave lower. Joe could go all the way down to a low E-flat, but even though he was scraping bottom, his melodious rich bass would come over the airways with feeling and distinctness.

Joe Springer also had a ready wit and kept the participants relaxed with his frequent wry remarks. Dad, now in his forties, was beginning to squint and had to move his hymn book back and forth to get it in focus. Joe commented, "When you play the trombone with your song book it's time to get bifocals."

Lois Hatt Vásconez was often the organist. Sometimes she would replace Mom at the piano, giving her an occasional break. Often they would join together in a piano-organ duet. When Dad sang a solo, he roared, but when he moved over and sat on the piano stool beside Mom, his voice softened and they blended together. Lois said, "Bob, in spite of your big, bellowing voice and Wilda's sweet, soft voice, you sing a beautiful duet!"

Dad grinned. "It sure would be too bad if I drowned Wilda out. Isn't she somethin'?" He never hesitated to show his pride and affection publicly.

Dave Cliff often helped with the program. Dave was a musical perfectionist, and it often galled him when Dad would rehearse a number only once, then broadcast it all over the Western Hemisphere. Several other musicians commiserated with each other over the same issue. In the end, they generally agreed: one of the things that made the program popular was its spontaneity and freshness, errors and all.

As Dad crisscrossed the Latin American continent in evangelistic campaigns, he heard new hymns being sung—written by local Christian believers, with plaintive, minor, Latin melodies, and soulful, passionate poetry. He would listen to the hymn, record the words and melody on scraps of paper, return home, sit down at our piano, and work out a harmonic structure.

Most Latin Americans could not afford to buy hymn books,

and many could not read, so there were not many ready buyers for his chorus books. However, Christians in every Latin American country listened to HCJB via shortwave radio. When Mom and Dad began to sing these songs on their daily radio program, the hymns became popular throughout the continent—almost overnight.

When Dad traveled on evangelistic campaigns, he not only learned new songs from the local believers, but taught them songs he had heard in other countries. Once he held a campaign in Neiva, Colombia, at the church where Betty Knopp of the Christian and Missionary Alliance worked.

At the close of each service, after the invitation, Dad would go back to one of the Sunday School rooms and pray with those who had come forward to receive Christ.

Betty told him, "You know, Bob, most preachers leave it up to others to counsel with those who come forward. I admire you for your personal interest in these new converts."

Dad replied with a merry twinkle, "Any good fisherman wants to care for his own catch."

Before Dad had arrived in Neiva, Betty had told the congregation, "When Don Roberto comes, you may make requests for him to sing here just like people do on his radio program." She was startled at the response—over 50 requests—and Dad was scheduled for only two nights in Neiva. Betty told Dad what she had done, fearing she had placed a huge burden on him. "No problem," said Dad, "we'll invite everyone to stay after the service and have a good old fashioned singspiration."

The service ended and Dad attended immediately to his first priority: instruction of the new believers. He took time to pray with them, then reemerged on the platform, where the crowd awaited his return. Hardly a person had left, and Dad could not bring himself to overlook anyone, so he sang all 50 songs that had been requested. He sang the way he preached, getting as close to the audience at possible, standing right on the edge of the platform, often rocking his heels right on the edge, with the toes of his shoes suspended out in front. It seemed precarious, but he never fell off, and his vibrating presence reached people even in the back row.

Dad and Mom's theme song for their daily radio program was *"Brighten Up Your Pathway with a Song."* The opening lines were:

When you are discouraged
And your road seems dark and long,
Brighten up your pathway with a song.

Betty Knopp recalls, "During the years of the violent persecution in Colombia, many times as I walked down the street I heard the words 'Brighten up your pathway with a song' sounding out from someone's radio. I knew it was not a Christian home, and rejoiced that the gospel was reaching Colombia even though many of our churches had been destroyed or shut down."

When Betty talked about a home "not being a Christian home" she was almost surely referring to a home that was Roman Catholic, for in Colombia more than 95% of the people called themselves Catholic. In those days, the hostility between Catholics and Protestants was intense, and neither considered the other as "Christian." The "days of violence" that Betty recalled were the dreadful years of political and religious violence which lasted for about a decade from 1948-1958. Many evangelical believers were killed for their faith.

Dad always had a special place in his heart for the humble people. Conchita was 65, hunch backed, and cursed with a grotesque pockmark in the middle of her forehead. For two years, she had come to the Church of the Divine Redeemer in Quito, Ecuador, and every Sunday she had received an exuberant greeting from her pastor, "Don" Roberto Savage.

She loved his warm words of praise, and looked forward to the moment each Sunday when she would be uplifted with his cheer. From time to time she dreamed of inviting him to her home, but whenever the thought flitted through her mind, she shoved it away, scolding herself, "Oh no, Conchita, don't bother Don

Roberto. He is a very busy man and wouldn't be able to come."

When she was greeted by Don Roberto with his hearty "Conchita!" she told him the whole story of her week, of her painful arthritis, every detail. As other church members waited restlessly to talk with their pastor, he looked at her intently, patiently, focusing on her and no one else. His eyes were hazel, but often when he looked closely at a person, they looked bright blue-grey. At 5 feet, 9 inches, with olive complexion and black hair, he looked more Latin than many North American missionaries. He parted his hair high, almost in the middle, and combed it back, using mineral oil to keep it neatly in place.

At last Conchita asked the question for which she'd been trying to summon the courage, "Don Roberto, would you and your family like to come to my house for dinner?"

"Why Conchita," he replied, "I'd be honored. What a wonderful idea. When can we come?"

Conchita beamed—but I groaned. I was 16 years old in 1956 and the thought of dinner at Conchita's filled me with glumness. I cast a sidelong glance at my brother Jimmy, age 6. Our foreheads twisted into a pained furrow and our lips pressed tightly. Dinner at Conchita's. Yucch.

Later, back home, we pleaded, "Dad, do we *have* to go to Conchita's?"

Dad drew his eyebrows together in bewilderment, trying to understand. "Why don't you want to go?"

"She's funny looking," blurted out Jimmy.

"Well, that's no reason not to go," countered Dad.

"But she's boring," I protested.

"And it will take all afternoon," chimed in Carol, age 12.

"Now wait a minute," declared Dad. "Enough of this. Let's be good sports and show Conchita a good time. And I'll bet you'll have a good time too."

When Dad told Conchita he felt honored, there was no question about it. He *did* feel honored to dine at her home, and wanted his family to feel the same way. Our mother, Wilda, shared his feelings. She was not only willing but happy to go. And she would brook no discussion about Conchita's pitiful face, as Mom allowed no one to be criticized.

"Aw c'mon, Mom," I argued, "What's there to talk about if we can't say anything funny about anyone?"

"There's too much sadness in the world already," she declared. "Let's not add any more."

We all went to Conchita's, including Judi, now age 4. Conchita prepared a magnificent feast, highlighted by her specialty, *arroz con pollo* (chicken with rice). I found myself enjoying the food, but more surprising yet—I was enjoying Conchita. Her eyes sparkled with delight as she scurried from kitchen to dining room, loading our plates, pampering us, and insisting we eat more, and more, and more. Her smile beamed so brightly that her pathetic face became almost beautiful.

Conchita, appropriately, means "little shell" in Spanish, and that's where she spent her life until Don Roberto Savage gave her the courage to crawl out and bask in his warm glow. In his presence, she felt noble—indeed, became noble. His patented phrase, "Let me shake your noble hand," was one he offered with sincerity and gusto as he stretched out his hand to everyone he met. It was a clever phrase, for it always made people feel good and generally made them laugh, but Dad meant it, for he felt that every creature was noble in the sight of God.

Dad was called to be a missionary and to him that meant bringing the joy of Christ to everyone he met. He never felt that his task was a burden. He thrilled in being a missionary and enjoyed showering the light of Christ on every person, including those—*especially* those—who were often overlooked as insignificant.

Yes, he was a missionary—a total exhilarated missionary from the top of his head to the bottom of his toes. He loved to preach, teach, and sing.

He loved the masses of people; he loved the individuals even more. When he walked into a room he did not seek out the most important person, but would start with the very first, greet him warmly, and focus on that individual. He did not use his peripheral vision to see who was next in line, because when Dad talked to someone, that was the only person in the world, and received his full attention.

He made people feel worthwhile, especially those who considered themselves worthless. Once he preached a sermon on "using your talents for the Lord" and declared that everyone had some kind of talent: "Juan has a talent for preaching, Olga has a talent for singing, Horacio has a talent for witnessing, and César has a talent for handling the financial affairs of the church." True, but these people's talents were obvious to everyone in the congregation, so Dad's point was open to question. However, Dad was not finished, and he pressed home his theme: "*Everyone* has a talent. Alfonso has a great talent for passing out gospel tracts."

I suppressed a chuckle and glanced over at Alfonso, toothless, dressed in the same patched suit he had worn every Sunday for 30 years. Alfonso was grinning. A simple old fellow, he had never pictured himself as having any talent at all. But now he had been recognized in public, and beamed with surprised delight.

About the same time Dad and Mom were beginning their new daily radio program, Grandpa Henry Savage was elected President of the National Association of Evangelicals. Dad wrote his father: "I think it is a transcendental milestone in the rich, Spirit-filled ministry that has been yours. May God use you in a most unusual way and cause NAE under your leadership to bring into reality forward strides that will have a glorious impact in all parts of the world."

Shortly after, Grandpa and Grandma Savage came again to Ecuador. This time they got their first look at jungle missionary work. They had seen Ecuador's mountain and coastal region in their previous visit, but were eager to observe first-hand the work in the "Oriente"—the steaming jungle lowlands on the eastern slopes of the Andes. My grandparents and parents traveled overland to Shell Mera. Dad decided to give them an authentic Ecuadorian adventure and crowded them into one of the rickety buses that made the trek from Quito to Ambato.

The bus station consisted of several open blocks of cobblestone, with hundreds of colorful buses parked around the area. Each one had a sign showing its destination. As we walked around, looking for a bus to Ambato, we stepped on orange peels, squishy rotten bananas, trash, cigarettes, broken glass, and paper. The stench of putrid garbage lay heavy in the air. Missionaries got used to most of Ecuador's sights and smells, but few adjusted to the disgusting miasma of odious dumps like the bus stations.

Grandpa and Grandma were not used to even the mildest smells of Ecuador. They shuddered at the reek of the markets where pigs were slaughtered and hung up for display. They could not help but notice the mud walls where men urinated, leaving a dark stain on the lower two feet, emanating a stale scent. But the worst smell of all was in the bus stations, and the worst part of the bus stations was their public restrooms, where floors were usually wet and sloppy, leaking water mixed with human excrement, where toilets rarely worked, and used toilet paper was left in boxes rather than flushed.

Most of the city of Quito, like other Ecuadorian towns, was clean and fragrant with the soothing smell of the eucalyptus trees that flourished in the Andean highlands. In residential areas, streets were tidy, and most homes were impeccable. As they drove out of the bus station, out the southern end of the long capital city, their last images were pleasant, with the *"cabuya"* cactuses lining the cobblestoned road, a foreground of quiet bluish-green pastel to frame the dramatic spectacle of Andean mountains rising on the horizon.

As they drove along, Grandma mentioned she would like to use the ladies' room. Dad said, "Don't worry, Mother, there's a fine bathroom at the bus station in Ambato."

He looked at Mom and winked. Mom looked worried. She

knew all about the bathroom in Ambato.

The Ambato bus station was filthy, and the entire area smelled with the putrid reek of decaying garbage. But that was nothing compared to the municipal bathroom. The wretched stench was smothering, a sickening choke that gagged and stifled.

When Grandma emerged, pale and shaken, Dad laughed, "Well, Mother, didn't I tell you? That's a great bathroom. isn't it?"

Grandma was not amused. Normally fun-loving and gracious, she was livid. "Why, Bob Savage," she sputtered, "how could you do such an awful thing to your mother."

Dad was stunned. He thought his mother would see the humor and was not prepared for her wrath. He apologized and tried to calm her down, but she crackled on. "Bob, that is horrible. I don't ever want you to do something like that to me again."

The 41-year-old Bob got a tongue-lashing worse than anything he had received since he was a child.

Grandma eventually settled down and the rest of the journey was pleasant, although scary, for the bus would often careen within a few inches of the ragged gorge formed by the powerful Pastaza. Grandma's spirits softened as she took in the orchids that splashed all over the wet cliffs, erupting from the road.

When they arrived in Shell Mera, they enjoyed the warm hospitality of Nate and Marj Saint. The next day, Nate flew all four Savages on two flights in his Piper Cruiser, and took them to the mission station in Shandia, where Ed and Marilou McCully worked among the jungle Quechua Indians. Marilou had grown up as a member of Grandpa's church in Pontiac, Michigan, so he was particularly interested in visiting her. Grandpa and Grandma were impressed to see the bamboo house which Marilou now called home. Mom and Grandma stayed there for several days while Grandpa and Dad flew with Nate Saint to other mission stations to conduct a series of meetings.

Ed and Marilou were deeply involved in language study, teaching, and basic medical assistance. Grandma Savage was fascinated with all aspects of missionary work in the jungle, but she never got used to the way the Indians stood around the McCully house all day long, peering in through the screens, watching the strange North Americans chat and work. She commented, "They thought nothing of standing and watching, standing and watching, all day long."

Jungle missionaries got used to the Indians staring through the screens, and were able to relax and go about their business. The Indians were not rude; it was just plain interesting to watch these odd white creatures. In their open-house environment it was not considered bad manners to watch others.

A few months after my parents and grandparents visited the jungle, Ed McCully came to Quito for a few days. While there, he offered me a job. He asked if I would make a weekly run into downtown Quito to pick up the mail for the jungle missionaries with his mission, the Plymouth Brethren. My job would involve clearing packages through customs and arranging to have everything hand-delivered by traveling missionaries to the Missionary Aviation Fellowship in Shell Mera. Ed offered me the astounding fee of 10 *sucres* per week (60 cents U.S.) plus bus fare. I was thrilled, for that was a lot of money for a missionary kid in those days. The job also made me feel important. The responsibility of making sure missionaries in the jungle got their mail and packages made me quite proud of myself.

Besides Ed and Marilou McCully, there were two other Plymouth Brethren missionaries whose mail I fetched: Jim and Elizabeth Elliot; Pete and Olive Fleming. I barely knew these other couples, but within a few weeks their names would be on the front pages of newspapers all over the world.

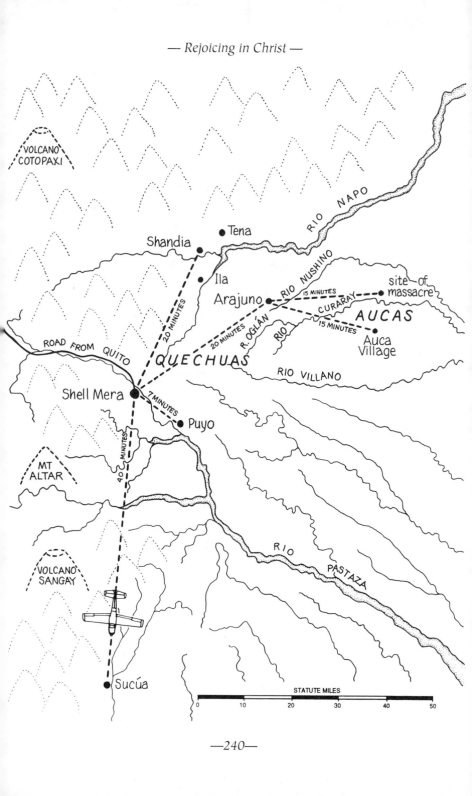

13

Mid-century Martyrs

❖

They are not dead but alive.

— Bob Savage and José Andrade
The Drama on the Curaray

On Monday, January 9, 1956, the bell rang at the Alliance Academy and we students went outdoors for recess. Usually we played touch football, but as we were walking out to the field, someone said, "Did you hear about Nate Saint?"

"What about him?" I asked.

"He's disappeared in the jungle. They think he crashed."

My heart jumped. I instantly and indignantly denied the rumor. "No! Impossible. Who told you?" Nate Saint had flown me to Sucúa, allowed me to fly his airplane, been kind to me, was my hero, and I refused to believe he was missing. I believed he was not only the greatest, but the safest, pilot in the world. He could not be lost. But then I heard more details and my spirit slumped. The rumor had foundation and was hard to deny: "They heard about it on the radio contact with the jungle this morning."

With these fragments of hearsay, several of us teenage boys huddled, not to play football, but to speculate on what had happened. Someone said, "They think he's down in Auca country."

"Auca country!" we all gasped in unison. The Auca Indians, in our minds, were the most frightening creatures we could imagine.

It was said that once a person was speared with an Auca *chonta* spear, there was no chance for survival, for the spear's ugly barbs prevented it from being extracted from the victim's flesh.

Then someone said, "I heard that Ed McCully went down with Nate Saint."

"Ed McCully!" I heaved a deep breath. He had been in our living room only a few weeks earlier, given me a job. Marilou McCully, Ed's wife, was a member of our own First Baptist Church in Pontiac. Michigan. I had always known her. Ed and Marilou had eaten dinner only recently in our home. They were almost family. Ed McCully was down in Aucaland? I shuddered.

Recess was soon over and as we took our seats we asked our teacher, Paul Prentice, if he had heard about a crash in the jungle. Yes, he replied, the teachers had been listening to the jungle radio network, a system of radio transmitters and receivers that linked all jungle missionaries in a daily morning broadcast. Usually the broadcast was over by the time breakfast ended, but today the radio was alive with worried questions and disquieting reports.

Mr. Prentice allowed us to listen to the radio, suspending the English class that followed recess. There were 16 students in our high school; I was a sophomore, 15 years old. We all hovered over the radio. We heard the voice of Marj Saint, Nate's wife, for she was the one who masterminded the daily broadcast, making sure each missionary was well, taking orders for food and supplies, and coordinating the flights Nate made to each jungle station. As we listened in grave fascination that Monday morning her voice was strained but remarkably controlled as she began to piece together the details. Nate had not crashed; that part of the rumor was false. But he was missing, and so were four of his missionary colleagues.

We listened with grim curiosity as the names of the other missing missionaries crackled over the radio. Jim Elliot was one of the five and my body felt a chill as I thought of the handsome, ruddy Elliot who had delivered a spellbinding sermon in our chapel service only a few months ago. Pete Fleming had been in Ecuador four years and I had met him on a few occasions. Roger

Youderian was with the Gospel Missionary Union. I knew who he was, but did not know him as well as the others.

We sat bolt upright when we heard the voice of Nate Saint's fellow missionary pilot, Johnny Keenan. Johnny was flying the Missionary Aviation Fellowship's Piper Pacer, and as he flew over the Curaray River, he reported chilling news. He had found Nate's Piper Cruiser on a beach of the Curaray. All the fabric was stripped off. There was no sign of any of the five missionaries.

We looked at each other in horror. The fabric was stripped off! If Auca vandals had destroyed the airplane, what could they have done to the men? Were the men alive? Were they hiding? We could not bear to leave the radio, and Mr. Prentice cancelled History, then Science, then Algebra.

Slowly, the curious story began to unfold. The five missionaries had been working on "Operation Auca" for several months. They had carefully kept all details secret, even from other missionaries, fearing that publicity would hinder their attempts to make friends with the feared Auca tribe.

The five, along with their wives, had planned each detail with precision and prayer. They believed that God was leading them to reach this lost tribe with the gospel of Jesus Christ. They were committed to reach these people, and developed ingenious ways of developing friendly contacts with the tribe of killers.

The airplane was the tool and Nate Saint's inventive genius the means by which they were able to make a friendly gesture to the Indians. Nate developed a technique whereby he dropped gifts in a bucket as he circled overhead. The bucket remained stationary like the point of a compass, and the Auca Indians eagerly retrieved the offered gifts, especially pleased with gleaming machetes, aluminum kitchen utensils, shirts, trousers, and 8x10 photos of the five missionaries.

Then, to the surprise and delight of the missionaries, the dreaded Aucas began to return gifts, inserting colorful feather headbands and a live parrot into the bucket. Encouraged by these signs of friendship, the five men decided to set up a camp at a nearby sandbar on the banks of the Curaray River, not far from the Auca settlement where they had exchanged gifts. Nate made several flights into the area, bringing the other four missionaries along with materials needed to build a treehouse. For several nights three of the five slept in the treehouse. Nate and Pete flew over the Auca settlement each day, dropping gifts, pointing the way with the airplane, inviting them over the P.A. system, in the few Auca phrases they had memorized, to come over to the Curaray River and visit. Their campsite on the beach lay about four miles north of the Auca houses.

On the fourth day, three naked Aucas, a man and two women, emerged from the dense forest. Unarmed and unafraid, the three chattered amiably with the missionaries. Nate took the young man for a flight in his airplane, circling over the Auca houses while the man whooped with delight. A few hours later, the three melted back into the jungle. It was the first friendly contact between Aucas and the outside world and the missionaries were enormously encouraged.

On Sunday, January 8, Nate once again flew over the Auca settlement, and spotted a group of ten men on their way to the beach where airplane and missionaries were camped. Nate radioed Marj with great excitement, using a prearranged code so other listeners would not know what was up: "There's a commission of ten on the way. Looks like they'll be here for the early afternoon service. Pray for us. This is the day. Will contact you next at four thirty." Those were the last words Marj heard from her husband.

On Monday afternoon radio station HCJB broadcast the news and by the next morning headlines appeared on front pages of newspapers all over the world:

"FIVE MISSIONARIES MISSING IN AUCA TERRITORY"

The United States Air Rescue Command in Panama was sent to Ecuador. A search party, led by veteran jungle missionary Frank Drown, was organized, consisting of Ecuadorian and U.S. soldiers, a few missionaries, and several Indians. A U.S. army helicopter was on the way from Panama, but the main party would tramp in by foot.

It was now 24 hours since Marj had heard Nate's transmission, and we students at the Alliance Academy continued to listen to the radio, eager for each new piece of information. The radio at our school stayed on for the next five days, and school work became purely mechanical. Teachers and students alike sat transfixed around the sturdy old metal Hallicrafter radio set. Every few hours a new piece of information arrived, and each item led to endless deliberation as we wondered among ourselves what could have happened.

On Tuesday morning we heard a stunning report. John Keenan had discovered a body floating in the river, face down, with white T-shirt and khaki pants. It could have been any of the five men, and we speculated madly about who it could be. Could the other four still be alive? Had the missionaries been armed? Had any Aucas been killed?

That afternoon Johnny Keenan found a second body, and our hopes sank. Were the other three alive? Which two were dead? The gloom that descended over our school attested to the grim feeling we all had way down deep: it was unlikely anyone was alive.

At home in the evenings, around the supper table, our family talked of nothing else. Dad gave us reports he had received from the jungle, where Abe VanDerPuy was coordinating the news. HCJB became the missionaries' link to the outside world, and both Dad and Clarence Jones served as liaisons to the press, as well as to concerned relatives and friends of the five missionary families. The phone rang every few minutes, and we thrilled to hear our father talking to United Press, Associated Press, CBS, NBC, ABC, and other news organizations. Long distance phone calls between North and South America were extremely rare, but now we were hearing from the United States all the time.

Dad also spent a lot of time with the Spanish reporters who were at the HCJB compound clamoring for details. He was continually amazed at the worldwide attention this missionary story was getting, and discovered it was front page news on every newspaper. Dad felt it was a tremendous opportunity to tell the world what missionaries were trying to accomplish, and he took pains to assure the press that these five young men were sane and sound individuals who had not gone into this venture recklessly. He talked about their witness, exemplary lives, character, and sacred mission to the Aucas. He wanted all to know that these men, like all missionaries, had been willing to lay down their lives for their Lord. He also wanted everyone to know what our attitude was towards the killers: if indeed the missionaries had been killed by the Aucas, there was no animosity among any of their evangelical friends toward these people of the rain forest, only compassion and concern for their lost souls.

We heard a report that a third body had been found, this time by a party of Quechua Indians who had boldly canoed all the way to the beach where the ruined plane sat. On their way back upriver they passed the rescue party trudging into Auca territory. One of the Indians was a Christian believer who had come to know Christ through the ministry of Ed McCully. He sadly showed the rescue party Ed's watch, and told them he had positively identified his body.

The name "Ed McCully" sputtered through the static on the radio and we drew closer to listen. Then we heard it verified: Ed's body had been found and identified. I was stunned. I did not cry, but felt wooden, and sat still in my school desk, dazed, bewildered, horrified.

There was still a chance that two were alive. Maybe even three still lived, for Ed's body might have been one of the two that Johnny Keenan had spotted from the air. Who were the survivors, if any? Where were they?

Throughout this ordeal, Marj Saint bravely continued to maintain contact on the radio, drawing strength from the work of keeping communications going with all the jungle missionaries, and dispensing information to the outside world.

By Friday, January 13, the search party reached the beach, found four bodies, and identified them. The only body they did not find was that of Ed McCully, but his was the one discovered by the Quechua Indians two days earlier. This led to more mad conjecture on the part of all us students, as we imagined Ed McCully, alone in the jungle, hiding. Fortunately, Marilou McCully was spared the agony of this useless rumination, for the Indians gave her not only his watch but his huge size 13 shoe.

Time had come to a standstill during that week of anxious waiting, and not only were the students at the Alliance Academy mesmerized by the radio accounts, but other missionaries had difficulty focusing on anything else. Mom described the feeling in a letter she wrote a week after it was all over:

It's 3:00 a.m. and I am waiting for Marilou McCully and the children to arrive. Their plane leaves for the U.S. at noon. She will have her baby in the States. They've had difficulty getting to Quito due to bad weather in Shell Mera. They couldn't fly, so started overland at 7:00 p.m. by truck. We had hoped to have Marilou and the kiddies with us much longer but with these difficulties we'll miss the privilege of a long visit.

I'm sorry not to have written sooner as I know you have wanted news, but it just seemed this was once I simply couldn't write. We were so torn up and in a daze last week that I couldn't get myself together to write.

It has surely been a time of mingled emotions, heartaches, yet blessing—grief, yet victory, and through it all such a tremendous challenge to our hearts. We'll never be the same.

My heart has ached so for Marilou and the other girls. They have been such a testimony to everyone. They have set the whole keynote of victory. But oh, how hard it must be.

Bob was on the phone almost constantly with calls from all over the U.S., cables and communications from everywhere. The world has been stirred.

I know how this has touched your own hearts and even more so having been down there in Shell Mera and the jungle and knowing these wonderful folks concerned. Surely the choice ones have made the sacrifice.

Mom finished the letter the next day:

Marilou McCully came and we had such a precious time together, even though short. They drove all that night and didn't get here until 5:00 a.m. Still, never a complaint from Marilou. She is so wonderful that it breaks my heart. She is so brave. The Pontiac church can surely be proud of her. She has been a testimony to the world. We here at HCJB love her and we'd be so happy if the Lord should lead her back here to be in the work at HCJB.

It looks like Marj Saint will be coming to HCJB and will be taking over our guest house. This is truly an answer to prayer for this ministry. She herself suggested it so we feel it is His leading. Her experience at handling a guest house is terrific as you'll remember from your visit to Shell Mera.

I've never seen Bob so broken up. He could hardly get through some of the programs. Being in constant touch with the jungle network, we were close to it all and thinking so much of Marilou and Ed and the others. It was such a week of heartache. Surely the Lord has a great plan and purpose in it all and we'll perhaps see it soon. Already we know the impact has been tremendous all over and folks have been drawn closer to the Lord.

Elizabeth Elliot, Jim's wife, wrote the best-selling account of the epic, *Through Gates of Splendor*, published by Harper & Row in 1956. Dad wanted to tell the story in Spanish. He walked into the office of his friend José Andrade, HCJB's Spanish preacher, and told him: "Don José, you will have to write a book about what has happened. But it has to be done quickly while the public's interest is still high. We want the world to get the Christian perspective before the story gets distorted. I will give you all the necessary material and photos. I'll outline it and write a rough draft, but I need your eloquent Spanish to make it right. You yourself can put in the text you think is correct."

José Andrade was frightened. "Don Roberto," he objected, "I am not a writer. I have never written a book of this type. I plead with you; don't ask me to do something impossible."

Dad looked at his colleague with a smile and answered: "Why don't you start the book out by saying what you just told me, and you will have already written the prologue. I need the first few pages the day after tomorrow."

Don José wrote the book, as Dad supplied him with the materials and helped with organization and layout. It was published as co-authored by Roberto Savage and José Andrade.

Most evangelical books were not sold in commercial bookstores, but public interest in this saga was so intense that the 60-page book, titled *El Drama del Curaray*, was sold in secular as well as missionary bookstores. Dad was thrilled that the testimony of five martyrs could reach people who would not normally read a Christian book. There were two themes he wanted all to understand: First, he wanted the world to know that the evangelicals wished no revenge against the Aucas, but longed to see them come to know Jesus. Second, he wanted the word to go forth that the Christian view of death was different, and that death was nothing to fear if one was a disciple of Christ.

Quito's newspaper, *El Comercio*, in its annual review of books published in Ecuador praised *El Drama del Curaray* for its "actuality, agility, and opportunity."

As soon as Dad was finished with the Spanish book, he began to prepare a filmstrip about the five missionaries. We were due to go soon to the United States for a year of furlough and he wanted to have a filmstrip to show in churches as he traveled around the country.

He assembled a series of slides from photographers who had

taken pictures of the missionaries and their families. He also obtained slides Nate Saint had taken of the three Aucas. The rescue party found the film in Nate's camera, smashed up and lying on the beach.

Using HCJB's sound studios, Dad dubbed in music and did the narration. As soon as he had produced it, he took a trip to Shell Mera so the widows could review it for accuracy. He invited Dr. Paul Roberts and me to accompany him to the jungle, and the three of us wound down the mountain passes in the HCJB van. Marj Saint and Barbara Youderian awaited us and watched in solemn silence as the story was replayed. The two gallant women showed singular composure as the story of their husbands' lives flashed on screen, but suddenly there appeared the dramatic picture of Roger Youderian, floating face down in the Curaray River, with a broken Auca spear sticking out of his hip. Then everyone wept, not only the two women but the two men and the teenage boy.

After the slides had been shown, everyone remained silent for a few minutes, sniffling, meditating. Finally Dad asked if there were any corrections or suggestions. Marj suggested some changes in the rendition of Nate's final transmission, to convey the urgency and excitement of the upcoming meeting with the approaching Aucas, which Nate thought was going to be a friendly time of great joy. Barbara Youderian added a small detail that fascinated Dad. "None of the jungle missionaries," said Barbara, "referred to Indian dwellings as 'huts' but as 'houses.'"

"We'll definitely change that," assured Dad.

We returned to Quito, Dad made the changes, and had the slides made into a filmstrip entitled "Mid-Century Martyrs." Two thousand copies were produced and it was shown at churches throughout the United States and Canada.

Why did the Aucas kill the missionaries? No one knew what went wrong, only that ten Aucas speared five missionaries to death. The five widows as well as other missionaries in Ecuador were unshakable in their certainty that God had a divine purpose in this human tragedy. They comforted each other with Scripture verses like Philippians 1:21: "For to me to live is Christ and to die is gain."

Gain? How could death be gain? Everyone wrestled with the question. It seemed like a horrible waste. Five of the finest missionaries in Ecuador, dead, gone forever, and this was gain? Five intelligent, healthy, vigorous, creative missionaries, the best of the best, had been slaughtered. Most non-Christians thought it was absurd and could not understand why the evangelicals were trying to describe it as some kind of "victory." Reaction ranged from "they're trying to deny reality" to "they're crazy."

Bob Savage and José Andrade attempted to answer this question for the Ecuadorian public when they wrote in *El Drama del Curaray*:

Has the death of these five heroes of the faith been a loss or a gain? We say "both."

Who can deny that the death of these beloved brothers has been a rude jolt for us? The twentieth century has not produced five young Christians more consecrated than these five who have preceded us into the Lord's presence. They were the best, and humanly speaking, they are utterly irreplaceable.

The newspapers of the world have announced in great headlines "Five Missionaries Dead" but we say to the contrary "They are not dead but alive." Why do we say this? Because for a Christian, death is merely separation of soul and body. Only the body dies. The soul is immortal. The bodies of the five are dead and buried on the banks of the Curaray River. On January 8 at 3:00 p.m., their souls entered the presence of their Savior. For Nate, Pete, Ed, Jim, and Roger, death has been incomparable gain.

There is gain in one other sense. Throughout the centuries, the blood of the martyrs has been the seed of the Christian Church. We remain convinced that the blood shed on the sands of the Curaray River will rejuvenate the Church, not only in Ecuador, but around the world.

14

The rise of Nationalism 1960s

> Knowledge is knowing the facts. Wisdom is knowing what to do with those facts. —*Pocket Quips*, p. 82

I n June, 1958, at age 17, I left Ecuador, my home, to return to the land of my birth, the nation whose passport I carried but whose personality was alien to me, much stranger than the little Andean republic in which I had grown up. The United States had always seemed a wonderful glittering place when we went there every four years on furlough, but always there was my efficient, self-confident father handling passports, tickets, phone calls. We children always tagged along, carefree, secure, wherever he took us. Now I was on my own, and it was frightening.

But there was another feeling, deeper than fright, more turbulent. It was not the pain of leaving home. Yes, of course, it tore me up to leave my family, but I was ready for that. There was something else, more compelling, more unexpected. What I did not expect was the wrenching sadness that seared through me as the Panagra DC-6 left the runway at Quito, climbed south over the long valley in which that ancient city lay, over HCJB, the Alliance Academy, our home, Dad's church, the narrow cobblestone streets, thick-walled houses, and Mount Pichincha. I stared out the window, the self-controlled teenager who never cried, whose main goal in life was to be "cool," and pressed my teeth tightly together. Then the plane began a slow lazy circle northward, and the snow caps that rimmed Quito's valley passed by my window, one by one: the twin-peaked Ilinizas, the cone-shaped Cotopaxi, the cragged Antisana, and the equator-straddling Cayambe, each with a shape and personality I knew well. As we continued climbing we once again passed over the gracious city, much higher now, the valley receded, the city became smaller, and I was no longer the cool teenager. Tears splashed in abundance over the airplane window and I huddled tightly against the pane so no other passengers would see me.

A week later I got a letter from Dad telling me how he had watched that huge four-engine airliner lift off, carrying his eldest son away, and he too, had cried profusely, unabashedly, as he leaned against the railing at Quito's terminal building. He was proud, he told me, exulting that I would be studying at Wheaton College, glorying in my spiritual devotion and love for Christ. But he missed me, he said, and when I left he felt a huge part of his life had been extracted from him.

Dad was right about my spiritual devotion. I was "on fire for the Lord." During my senior year in high school I had gone out every weekend with a group of Ecuadorian Christians, to hold services in outlying villages around Quito. I played my trumpet, crowds gathered, and my Ecuadorian friends witnessed and preached. Dad was thrilled with my zeal and earnest desire to plunge into the work of the church.

Wheaton College. There had never been any question of going anywhere else. Dad and Mom had gone there. Uncle Jim and Aunt Helen had followed. We considered it a sound evangelical college, yet academically rigorous. It was the perfect place for me to prepare for a ministry of Christian service, and as I left Ecuador, it was with with the clear expectation that I would be back in four years.

My childhood ambition to be a missionary pilot still simmered in the back of my mind, but as I got into the academic life of

Wheaton, the idea of being a flying missionary was gradually replaced by that of a preaching and teaching missionary. I never lost my fascination with flying, but it seemed I was destined to "preach, sing, and toot," just like Dad. Well, not quite like Dad. I was not as flamboyant as he, more studious, quieter, a little more like Grandpa Savage.

During my college years I got better acquainted with Grandpa. My Savage grandparents lived in Pontiac, Michigan, a five-hour drive from Wheaton. Grandpa was pastor of First Baptist Church in Pontiac and president of Maranatha Bible Conference in Muskegon, Michigan. I visited them during Christmas vacation, and during the two summers I worked at Maranatha Bible Conference. As I got to know Grandpa better, I decided I wanted to model myself after him more than Dad. Dad, I thought in my sophomoric mentality, was too giddy, too loud, too boisterous, too superficial. Grandpa, on the other hand, was a scholar, a thinker. I looked forward to coming "home" to Pontiac to get Grandpa's views on theological issues I was studying at Wheaton. He always impressed me with his unambiguous sense of certainty on each problem. He had already carefully thought through every topic I brought up, and had an arresting, authoritative, and original way of looking at it. Although his answers always fit into the prescribed fundamentalist structure, he seemed to have an interesting twist on each point, reflecting his own thought. He did not parrot others and I found him fascinating.

Although he considered himself a fundamentalist, there were Christians even more ultra-conservative. It is odd they considered the old-fashioned H.H. Savage a "liberal," but a few super-right fundamentalists parted ways with their brethren over such unfathomable issues as support of Billy Graham. Some of these fellows didn't "approve" of Billy Graham because he invited all local pastors to share the platform during his crusades. What was wrong with that? Well, said the far-right fundamentalists, a lot of those pastors were "modernists." It was wrong, they insisted, for Billy Graham to associate with these modernists, and sharing the platform implied acceptance of their "watered-down theology." Grandpa was an old friend and enthusiastic supporter of Billy Graham. He had invited Billy to preach at Maranatha Bible Conference when the young evangelist was just starting to become famous. Grandpa was happy to sit on the same platform with other ministers, even those from modernist churches. They were no threat to him. The inner-directed H. H. Savage never "gave a hoot" what others said about him and certainly did not worry that his proximity to them on stage would imply approval of their doctrines. To the contrary, he saw each crusade as a golden opportunity to witness to them, and he worked on them both before and after the meetings, trying to "straighten out their thinking." I admired his boldness in the face of criticism from other pastors.

Often when I came home from college, Grandpa regaled me with stories of his boyhood years. One day I got caught up in the romance of his childhood on the Colorado range and exclaimed, "Grandpa, what a wonderful childhood! Don't you ever wish you could go back?"

"Nope!" replied Grandpa. End of discussion. He went back to working his crossword puzzle.

He was a real "yup" and "nope" kind of guy. His views on theology were as unequivocal as his opinions of the Colorado ranges. Was there are a real heaven and a real hell? "Yup." Could a Buddhist possibly be saved? "Nope." Was every word in the Bible inspired and correct? "Yup." Was it OK to go to movies? "Nope."

One answer Grandpa never gave me: "Well, there are two sides to that issue, and both have equal merit."

On the other hand, when I asked him, "Grandpa, do you think it's possible that the biblical account of Jonah and the whale may have been a symbolic story rather than an historical event?" my question elicited an abrupt "nope."

I knew he was against Sunday professional football for it took people away from church and was a violation of the sanctity of the

Lord's Day. However, I hoped he might take a kinder view of football on TV. One Sunday afternoon, satisfied I had done my duty as a Christian by attending Sunday School and church, I asked if I might watch the Detroit Lions on TV.

"Nope," was his unyielding reply.

He claimed his "life verse" as Acts 20:24: "None of these things moves me." That described his resolute conviction. I thought there was an even better biblical description of Grandpa's style and secretly picked another life verse for him: "Let your yea be yea and your nay be nay." The self-assured H. H. Savage never had any trouble distinguishing which was which.

During Christmas of my sophomore year, I flew to Quito. It was not only a great family event, but significant in the crystallization of my post-college plans. I spent most of my two-week vacation with my Ecuadorian friends, and was deeply overcome with a renewed interest in Latin American. I liked the way my Latin pals looked at things, with more poetry, passion, and color than my American friends. I was more determined than ever to return to Ecuador, or at least Latin America, to spend my life as a missionary.

I was in the choir at Wheaton College and told Dad and Mom about one of the ancient classics we were learning: "Methinks I See an Heavenly Host." Dad was not too keen on ancient music but lightened up when I sang him one of the lines:

"..ungen'rous soul of savage mold and destitute of grace."

He whooped with glee. Any joke on savages, preachers, or missionaries always delighted him. He chimed in, "That reminds me of the Thanksgiving prayer—'Oh Lord, we thank Thee for saving us from the ravages of the savages.'" More unrestrained laughter.

While in Quito Dad asked if I had decided on my college major and I told him "philosophy."

"Philosophy!" he exclaimed, frowning with bewilderment and disapproval. "What for?"

"I'm thinking more and more about working with Inter-Varsity

Christian Fellowship, with a ministry among university students, and thought philosophy would help me understand them better."

"Hmmm. Well, I guess that makes sense," pondered Dad, "but philosophy sounds pretty tedious. How about Bible as a major?" After all, that was his major when he went to Wheaton.

"Everyone at Wheaton has to take 16 hours of Bible so I'll get a lot of Bible anyway. But I don't feel the least bit ready to cope with skeptical college students, and I think philosophy might give me what I need."

"Well, if you're going to take philosophy, I'm glad you're taking it at Wheaton, and not from some atheistic college professor at a state university."

Then I realized Dad was genuinely worried about a philosophy major, for he knew I would be studying other philosophies and religions. My life had been insulated and I did not know much about the "outside" world—the world outside our evangelical community. We were often reminded of Christ's words in John 17: "Ye are in the world but not of the world." Dad was happy to keep it that way. He was broad-minded in many ways, and kept his curious, probing mind alert. He read a lot of books, but mostly by evangelical authors. He rarely read books written by authors of other philosophies, other faiths. If he read a book on Catholicism, for example, it was not usually a book written by a Catholic. Instead, it was a book by an evangelical, picking apart the weaknesses in the Catholic faith. Thus, he honed his skills and perfected his arguments against Catholicism, modernism, atheism, and every other "ism." He never took a hard, sympathetic look at any of those views, and I don't think it ever occurred to him that there was even the remotest possibility they might be true. He knew in advance they were false. His reading was designed to buttress his faith, strengthen his arguments in favor of evangelical Christianity, and give him sermon material that would make him more incisive, colorful, and convincing as he proclaimed the kingdom of heaven.

He hoped I would not get caught up in the writings of non-

Christians. Therein lay the danger of a philosophy major. He knew Wheaton College encouraged its students to read broadly, and as philosophy majors we read original writings of all leading philosophers. It was Wheaton's objective that its students should come to a clear understanding of non-Christian viewpoints, but at the same time learn well-reasoned Christian rebuttals, presented with intelligence and sophistication by its fine philosophy professors. They hoped our faith would be strengthened, not weakened. It was a calculated risk. Some students did, indeed, lose their faith. Most emerged stronger.

I did not lose my faith, but a few cracks developed in my structure of belief. These chinks in my armor of trust were not, as Dad had feared, a result of my philosophy classes. Strangely, the fissures developed as I worried through those very courses Dad had thought were "safe": the Bible classes. The Bible course most troublesome for me was one designed to give us a "sure-fire answer" to each charge leveled against Christianity. It was called "Apologetics," a curriculum designed to give us an "apologetic" or argument for our faith. Some arguments struck me as strained. The most memorable was one in which our professor belabored the issue of whether Moses had been born in 1400 B.C. or 1300 B.C. Liberals and conservatives fought over the date, because some of the arguments for the inerrancy of the Bible depended on the dating of ancient scrolls that had been discovered in archeological diggings. It seemed terribly important to the earnest teacher, and he spent hours battering away at the issue. I found it not only boring but troubling. Why, I wondered, did it matter, and was our faith in the inerrancy of Scripture built on such a thin eggshell of reasoning? I shoved these worries into the back recesses of my mind, but they gnawed away at me.

What was wrong with having doubts? After all, wasn't that what a college education was supposed to be all about? Didn't all colleges encourage students to develop a healthy skepticism about everything, to go on a wide-ranging search for truth? Most secular colleges declared that they wanted their students to let the quest for truth take them wherever it may. Wheaton did not want the pursuit to go that far. They hoped everyone would search while retaining and fortifying their Christian beliefs. At Wheaton, we were encouraged to ask questions, to search, struggle, learn, and grow. The college administration had faith in the power and truth of Christian doctrine and felt confident that its students would emerge from their pursuit by selecting the Christian path.

But doubts were dangerous. Some Christian colleges were far more restrictive than Wheaton, and did not expose their students to non-Christian writings. Wheaton was sometimes criticized as being "too liberal," because it permitted such wide-ranging explorations.

Many evangelical pastors did not encourage questioning and doubting. Indeed, we often heard sermons about "doubting Thomas" who refused to believe in Christ's resurrection until he had seen and felt Christ's wounds. How much better, we were told, to believe Christ based on his word alone. I sincerely wanted to believe, but as I approached my senior year, I felt more and more like Thomas.

There were safe doubts and dangerous doubts. Once I went to Pontiac to visit my grandparents and asked Grandma Savage, "Don't you ever have any doubts about your faith?"

"Oh, yes," she replied, "I have doubts all the time."

Amazed, I pressed for more details, "What kinds of things do you doubt?"

"Sometimes I just wonder how God can love us at all, considering how sinful we are," she sighed.

I smiled to myself. Bless her heart, those were hardly the kinds of doubts afflicting me.

And Grandpa, did he ever have any doubts? None, so far as I could tell. He had wrestled with the basic truth of Christianity back in his college days, and once confronted by the power of the Holy Spirit, accepted the gospel story without question. He was an intellectual, highly curious about many things, always reading, expanding his mind, but never questioning the basic validity of the

Christian claims. His splendid mind was always searching—but not for truth—for he had found it. His search had a more specific focus: a quest for ways to explain that truth better, to transcend past efforts to organize the church, to bring more people into the kingdom. His was not a mind that wandered all over the range, seeing all views, absorbing winds from all directions. Grandpa's was a mind, instead, that had found a mountain to climb and the top of his mountain was clearly visible. His only objective was to reach that peak as fast as possible, bringing as many people in trail as he could persuade to join him.

Both my parents and grandparents had a clear idea of how they wanted me to "turn out." They painted a picture of their idea, over time, as they described what qualities they admired in other people. Nothing impressed and pleased them more than a young person, full of talent, who was using those gifts for the Lord. Often I'd hear Dad make comments like, "He has oodles of talent. He can play the trombone, sing, and preach. He's good at sports. He's great with young people. And he's on fire for the Lord." That pretty well summed up the type of person Dad approved of, and I tried to be like that.

I wanted to marry someone who met their approval. Grandma would describe an ideal young lady like this: "My, what a fine Christian she is. She can play the piano and sing. She's a nurse, good-looking, full of personality, and she wants to go to the mission field."

When I met Marilyn Johnson, she perfectly fit Grandma's description of the model Christian woman: nurse, singer, pianist, missionary-minded, personable, and pretty. Marilyn grew up attending a church in Kansas City pastored by Walter Wilson, one of the fundamentalist warriors who fought, side-by-side with Grandpa Savage, against the evils of modernism in churches. Marilyn's parents were outstanding and devout Christians, successful in business, leaders in their church.

After graduating from Wheaton College, I went on to Michigan State University to get my master's in business administration.

Marilyn was finishing her senior year at Wheaton. I drove from Michigan State to Wheaton many times that year. We made elaborate plans for our wedding the following June.

Our wedding was huge, attended by hundreds of friends and relatives, many traveling long distances. It was a joyous affair, for not only were two "sharp" and "keen" Christian young people getting married, but they were going to the mission field. Both Dad and Grandpa participated in the wedding ceremony and rejoiced that a third generation Savage was on the threshold of a lifetime of Christian service.

Marilyn and I left for Ecuador only three weeks after I graduated from Michigan State University. Our missionary organization was the American Bible Society. I was asked to take over the job of Paul Young, veteran missionary in Ecuador who had been in charge of Bible Society operations in that country. He was retiring, and personally recommended me for the job. I liked the Bible Society, for they did not require their missionaries to sign a statement of faith, nor did they inquire much into the details of our theology. I was relieved, for I was having serious doubts about such fundamentalist issues as the inerrancy of Scriptures and had worried that the Bible Society might want me to declare myself on that point. They did not, for they felt their task was to distribute Bibles, not take theological positions on its origins or nature. They wanted us to have good relationships with all churches, not only the fundamentalist, for they needed the cooperation of all missionaries to get Bibles into the hands of the maximum number of people. They would be happy with me if I did an efficient job of getting Scriptures distributed through churches, bookstores, and missions in Ecuador. They would be even happier if I could increase the number of Bibles distributed in the country, and that was one thing I was absolutely confident I could do.

With a Master's in Business Administration, plus the experience of four summers working my way through college selling Bibles door-to-door, I thought I could dazzle missionaries and national pastors all over Ecuador with a business-like, marketing approach to Bible sales. The job was tailor-made for me, as it gave me a chance to return to the land I loved, participate in the missionary endeavor, with enough intellectual space so I was never forced to preach something I didn't believe. As far as Dad and the other missionaries were concerned, I was completely one of them. I did not let anyone know my doubts.

Although I often wondred how Dad's faith could be so sure and single-minded, and wished I could see things just as clearly, I seldom doubted his genuineness. But at times I asked myself: Was he superficial? Did he gloss over deeper feelings of hurt and sadness? I felt that way once. A few months after we arrived in Ecuador, our first daughter, Heidi, died two days after birth. My grief was overpowering. I could barely talk; I was not only sad but angry, terribly upset when well-meaning Christians told me how wonderful it was that my daughter was happy in heaven. Although I believed that Heidi was in heaven, I did not feel wonderful, and the remarks struck me as glib and superficial. I tried to be polite, but got so irritated that I closed myself off at home. My dear melancholic Mom knew how I felt, and did nothing more than put her arms around me and weep. That was precisely what I needed.

Dad was undoubtedly sympathetic but it did not feel that way to me. His mind immediately leaped to organizational details. He wanted to have a big funeral service preceded by a major announcement on radio station HCJB, inviting all listeners to attend. His idea was to let everyone know that Christians rejoiced in the face of death, and that in Christ we had defeated the final enemy. He viewed this as a great opportunity to testify for Christ.

I would have none of it. I wanted to grieve in peace, without a huge crowd milling around trying to pump me up. I insisted on a small family service. Marilyn shared my desire for privacy. She grieved all alone, for she had to remain in the hospital while the rest of us went to the cemetary for the service and burial.

He did not press it, and quickly accommodated my request. Although he was gracious, he looked disappointed, and through my sadness I detected in his eyes a look of hurt bewilderment.

The funeral service was lovely, and Dad conducted it with tenderness and dignity. Once he realized how strongly I felt about having a small family affair, he bent over backwards to make the sad occasion as comforting as possible. He carried the tiny white casket with delicacy, and after it was lowered into the grave, he gently threw in a handful of dirt as he thanked God for the two days He had blessed us with the life of his little granddaughter Heidi. Then, as I looked at my dad, barely able to see him through my tears, I saw that he too was crying and I was consoled.

Although I did not discuss with Dad my doubts about the fundamentals of the evangelical faith, we did talk about a wide range of issues. A major theme was of great concern to both of us: the rise of nationalism in Ecuadorian churches. Many Ecuadorian Christian believers, like those all over the world, were simmering with discontent. Nationalism in the church reflected the broader problem of nationalism throughout the world. A wave of resentment against the United States swept through all third world countries. Although the Latin American countries had freed themselves from their colonial shackles in their wars against Spain in the mid-nineteenth century, in the 1960s, they all felt, in varying degrees, economically enslaved and beholden to the United States. This created great frustration and resentment. Therefore, American companies with overseas subsidiaries were looking for ways to turn their operations over to nationals.

American missionaries, who had once been revered as heroes and saints, were now increasingly denounced. Among some of the younger Ecuadorians, the censure began to grow bitter. They complained that North American missionaries had created an empire for themselves, surrounding themselves with gullible followers who toadied to their whims while remaining mired in servile peonage. The nationals, it was said, were not being given a voice in the direction of the church, only perfunctory jobs and minor pastorates. Missionaries were powerful, rich, and domineering, said the more vocal of the nationals, and it was about time they stepped aside and let Ecuadorians take over.

The American Bible Society had only recently become attuned to these forces of nationalism. It was now its stated policy to actively seek nationals to take over the direction of Bible Societies in each nation of the world. When they hired me, they told me to find a competent Ecuadorian to take over my position. My job was a two- or three-year assignment, and I was on the lookout for the Ecuadorian who would eventually replace me.

The idea of turning over my work did not trouble me, for I knew something else would turn up once I worked my way out of a job. I was young, and a short-term assignment appealed to me. However, it was not that easy for older and more established missionaries. Many of them had, indeed, set themselves up in secure positions, pastoring churches, running missions, or departments within missions. They were called to be missionaries for a lifetime of service, and many had never considered moving on.

Dad's original idea, back in Colombia, was to found a church every year or two, turn it over to a local pastor, and move on. Indeed, he had done that very thing in Colombia, and had repeated the process several times in Quito. The Church of the Divine Redeemer was flourishing under a national pastor, while other churches and missions Dad had founded were thriving in other parts of the city, each with its own national pastor.

On the church level, then, Dad was accomplishing his own goals and was in step with the times. As far as I know, no national criticized him for his church work. When it came to major administrative positions at HCJB, however, Ecuadorian nationals had cause to wonder whether they would ever be allowed to take over. All top positions were held by North American missionaries, and there was little talk of having a national take over any major department, to say nothing of the entire mission. HCJB ran a printing department, for example, with two missionaries, and several nationals wondered why it couldn't be run just as well by Ecuadorians. The hospital, with its American staff, was another object of criticism, for there were many outstanding and brilliant Ecuadorian doctors. Were Americans, it was asked, simply taking jobs away from Ecuadorians?

Dad felt something had to be done. He encouraged several talented young Ecuadorian Christians to get more education, and helped make financial arrangements to send several of them to Bible institutes or seminaries. He personally gave between 20 per cent and 30 per cent of his meager missionary salary in order to support the local church, help several poor people, and send nationals to seminary. Some of the outstanding young Ecuadorians were the brothers Washington and René Padilla who went to the United States to study. Washington returned to take over key roles with HCJB's Bible Institute of the Air, while René became one of the top leaders at Inter Varsity Christian Fellowship. The multi-talented Lenín de Janón, artist, dramatist, preacher, and singer, went to Biola College and returned to assume major responsibilities in both news and religious programming departments at HCJB. Vicente Vieira, converted priest, dynamic and bubbling radio announcer, became one of HCJB's first Christian television preachers when the TV era began.

Dad was also ahead of his time in advancing the cause of women. Carmen Montesdeorca was a good friend of Carol's and Dad decided she should get advanced training. His first thought was that Carmen should do something typical for a woman, like being a nurse, and he urged her to get into nurse's training. He offered her a scholarship. Carmen, however, had other thoughts. She wanted to go to seminary. At first Dad resisted, but once he became convinced that Carmen's call was genuine, and that her determination was firm, he encouraged her, convinced that in people like Carmen lay the future of Christian ministry in Ecuador. While in seminary in Costa Rica, she met the witty and vivacious Chema Reinoso from the Dominican Republic. They were married and returned to Ecuador where they serve HCJB as full-fledged missionaries to this day.

These were shining examples, but there were not enough

young people of their caliber. Thus missionaries still retained most top technical and administrative positions.

I was in synch with the nationalistic movement, for I spoke fluent Spanish, my friends were Ecuadorian, I understood their passions, and my own job was destined to accommodate growing sentiments for "gringos to go home." Dad also understood their feelings although he was alarmed at the bitterness displayed by some Ecuadorian Christians. He agonized over the issue, and worried that the church might be rent asunder as Ecuadorians became more and more estranged from missionaries.

He began to feel a little less at home in this beloved land he had adopted as his own. Even I, who was young and close to the Ecuadorians, felt ill at ease. There was something going on, and it didn't feel as cozy as it used to. Dad began to talk about his longing to be "a pastor in the homeland." I was surprised when he first brought it up, for I thought he would always be a missionary. But he was serious. "I have a pastor's heart," he said, "and there's nothing I like better than to pastor a church. I'm not sure I belong in Ecuador much longer, and besides I don't like all these administrative details here at HCJB. I'd rather be preaching than shuffling papers."

The idea of Dad gone from Ecuador was disheartening, for he seemed so much a part of the land. In my mind, missionary, musician, composer, preacher, Spanish, Ecuador, and HCJB all blended to define who Bob Savage was. How could he even consider leaving? At that point it was still an abstract discussion, very tentative, and we let the question dangle. Neither of us wanted to face the possibility of leaving South America for good. I knew I'd soon give up my job with the Bible Society, but figured I'd stay in South America in some other capacity. Meanwhile, Dad continued with his usual vigor, working on many things simultaneously: daily radio programs, field director, mission trustee, earnest pastor, new church founder, music compiler, and traveling evangelist.

The rumbling of discontent among Ecuadorian Christians broke into the open—suddenly, dramatically, viciously. I was intrigued when I arrived at my office at the American Bible Society and found a strange-looking newspaper on my desk. I picked it up and was startled to see my picture on the front page. With a rush of excitement I examined the title: *"¡Despertar!"* (Awake!) I had never seen this publication before. What was my picture doing on the front page? Then I looked at the caption under my picture:

Stephen Savage, one of the new wave of missionaries
Ecuador so desperately needs.

I felt a flush of pleasure, a surge of pride. Then I read the lead story and my joy vanished. It was a nasty article, highly critical of Abe Dyck, missionary with the Gospel Missionary Union, veteran of nearly three decades of work in Ecuador. It was with Abe Dyck that Dad had taken his memorable boat trip up the River Guayas, evangelizing towns along the way. Abe had been director of the Bible Institute in Guayaquil for many years. Now, this mean-minded article lit into Abe Dyck, describing him as a tyrant who oppressed his truckling students at the Bible Institute, who lorded it over his fawning converts, who made them grovel in shame when they failed to achieve his impossibly rigid standards of perfection. The article went on and on, vicious, bitter, demanding that Abe Dyck leave Ecuador. I was sick. My picture on the front page made it look as if I were part of this witch-hunt and I was mortified.

Worse, the newspaper, eight pages long, went on to dissect many other missionaries, exposing their foibles, claiming they were obstructions to the gospel rather than assets to the advancement of the kingdom.

I immediately called Abe Dyck, in Guayaquil, from Quito. The scandal sheet had been distributed throughout all evangelical churches in Ecuador, so he had just seen the paper himself. The poor man was reeling with shock over the attack. I assured him I had nothing to do with it, did not share its sentiments, and was confounded and angry over its publication. I went on to compliment him on his lifetime of fruitful and successful ministry. He appreciated my call, but remained utterly devastated.

Although the newspaper horrified me, I knew the writers and understood the depth of their feelings. I told them I objected to the ugly tone of the publication and the use of my picture, but agreed they had several valid points, for American missionaries had often failed to appreciate Ecuadorian culture. Many of us had been guilty of the "ugly American" syndrome, often acting lordly and superior, insensitive, unfeeling. It was unfortunate the young Ecuadorians had chosen to broadcast their complaints in such a forum, but there it was, in black and white, and no one could retrieve it.

All missionaries in Ecuador were thunderstruck. To have such a paper in print, with the church's dirty linen laid out for all to see, was terribly embarrassing. Dad was nearly as chagrined as I that my picture, with such a seemingly nice compliment printed beneath it, was associated with such a low-grade rag. I went to his office at HCJB, two miles from my office at the American Bible Society, plopped the paper on his desk, and said, "It's awful to see this stuff in print, but all the missionaries ought to realize one thing. This is what many young Ecuadorians have been saying in private, and it's about time the missionaries were aware of what's going on. We've got serious problems on our hands."

Dad agreed. He was thankful he had not been singled out for any venomous articles, but still each story hurt him as though he himself had been the target. He respected Abe Dyck and admired his ministry. He thought it the meanest cut that anyone could so shamelessly denounce a man of his dedication after thirty years of sacrificial service. As usual, Dad's solution was to pray. The two of us bowed our heads there in his office as he cried out to the Lord, "Oh, Lord, forgive us missionaries where we have failed to treat our national brethren with love and respect. Forgive also those who wrote this evil paper. Cleanse their hearts of the bitterness that fomented this scurrilous sheet, and may we all work together in harmony to further the advance of Thy kingdom."

Although the paper had declared me as "one of the new wave of missionaries that Ecuador needed," it served only to disillusion me. I was nearing the end of my two year assignment and had found an Ecuadorian businessman to replace me. I did not want to continue in missionary work, and the newspaper had made me feel even more eager to move on. I began to send my resume to United States corporations with offices in Latin America, hoping I could stay in some South American country without being involved in missionary work. It was distressing to find that virtually every American company had caught on to the furor of nationalism and was no longer interested in hiring Americans for overseas assignments. They all seemed to be looking for nationals to take over everywhere.

When I got an offer from the Southwestern Company of Nashville, Tennessee, it did not exactly fit my goals for they had no plans to operate in South America. However, their offer was lucrative, irresistible. I knew the people at Southwestern, for I had worked with them for four summers, selling their Bibles and reference books door-to-door, earning enough to pay for college, buy a car, a few stocks, and all our furniture for Ecuador. The money I had earned had gotten me off to a far better start financially than most college grads. My job now was to be a sales manager, to recruit and manage other college students to do the same thing I had done.

I was excited about my prospects and hastened the pace with which I trained Angel Cisneros, the Ecuadorian national whom I had trained to take over my job. Angel fit the profile of the type of person the Bible Society was seeking. He was young, energetic, and successful as a middle manager with the Ecuadorian national airline, TAME. He was a fervent Christian, and had married Raquel Hidalgo, daughter of one of Ecuador's most respected national "lay Christians." The Hidalgo family had been one of the first converts to evangelical Christianity back in the early days of missionary work in Ecuador.

Sales of Bibles and Scriptures had tripled during my two years. In turning over the work to Angel Cisneros, I could leave feeling my mission was accomplished.

Marilyn seemed happy to leave. She had left the United States with a vision of missionary work that somehow never quite materialized. She told me I had never been sympathetic with how difficult it was for her to learn the language and adapt to Ecuador. For me, it was a homecoming. For her, it was an alien land. She never felt at home.

Marilyn and I had shared the grief of losing our first daughter, Heidi. Ten months later, Cynthia Lorraine Savage was born, also premature, also afflicted with hyaline membrane disease, the same lung disorder that had overcome little Heidi. The first 48 hours of Cyndi's life were precarious as her little chest heaved to fill its lungs, then collapsed as she exhaled, showing all her ribs as she struggled to live. On the third day, the tiny five-pound tyke began to breathe easier in her incubator and quickly gained strength. Only eight days later she was home. Dad and Mom came with Judi and Jimbo to our home to see the new baby, whom Dad promptly dubbed, "our little miracle baby."

Cyndi was eleven months old when we left Ecuador, bound for Nashville. I was 25. This time, as the airplane left the runway at Quito's airport, I once again felt sad, but not nearly as heavy-hearted as when I had left the first time, seven years earlier, just after my high school graduation. This time I was relieved to get out of the evangelical world, unburdened from the nationalistic movement, and eager to begin a career in business. My goals were changing.

15

Oh, what love!

O what love! what wondrous love!
Love beyond all degree;
O what love! what wondrous love!
Jesus at Calvary

This song, written by Jaime Redín in Ecuador, harmonized by Dad, in a minor key, is an outstanding example of that distinctly Latin way of expressing joy in a melancholic melody.

One reason I was relieved to leave Quito was because I felt nervous about my secret doubts about the faith. I did not share them with Dad, but it was not easy to evade the issues, especially when he asked in his guileless manner, "How's your spiritual life?" I always answered, cheerfully, "Fine!" But I did not answer with the same zeal I had once given him. It was easier to keep things pleasant, even though artificial.

I had kept secrets from Dad for many years. When I was a 15-year-old sophomore at the Alliance Academy in Quito, I asked Dad how he would feel if I wanted to go to a movie. "Well, one thing's for sure," he said, "I don't want you sneaking off to a movie. If you ever want to go, please tell me."

"And what will you say if I ask you?"

"I'll give you permission to go, but I'll be extremely disappointed in you."

A week later I snuck off to my first movie. I was not about to disappoint my father.

In mid-1965, during my second year with the American Bible Society in Ecuador, Dad called me from across the street: "Steve, I want to talk with you."

"Sure," I replied, and walked briskly over.

Dad's stentorian voice hushed, and he said in a muffled tone, "Let's walk over here where no one can hear us."

Moving out of anyone's earshot, we stopped and Dad turned to me. "Steve, I'm troubled about something. Last night when we came to your house for dinner, I saw some playing cards on the coffee table."

"Yes," I replied, "we were playing Canasta."

"Well, I don't even know what Canasta is," he said, "but those cards do not belong in a Christian home."

"Look, Dad," I countered, "I don't gamble, but those cards can be used for hundreds of non-gambling card games."

"That may be true," he agreed, "but why use those kings and queens and jacks? Those cards have the look of sin smeared all over them."

I began to feel angry. I was an adult, had my own home, did not think it was any of Dad's business, but tried to keep a cordial tone. "Dad, I think Christians are too legalistic, and it's about time we began to talk about what's really good and evil. There's nothing evil about a few cards. They can be used for evil or for innocent fun. I think we ought to teach Christians how to make judgments rather than force a bunch of narrow rules down their throats."

"But think of your testimony," Dad argued. "What if someone comes into your house and sees those cards and thinks you are using them for gambling?"

"Well, I think that's a pretty lame reason not to have cards. If there's nothing inherently wrong with them, then I'm giving the wrong testimony. I'm telling somebody I think these little pieces of paper are bad, and I'll fail to tell him what's truly bad."

It was the first time Dad and I had ever seriously argued about one of these issues, because I had pretended that my beliefs were the same as his. For several years, my mind had balked at these matters that I considered peripheral. I felt they consumed too much of the attention of the missionaries: cards, movies, dancing, drinking, and smoking. Although dancing was still foreign to me, I had dabbled with the other four of the big five "no's"—but had never let Dad know.

Dad did not press the case, but made one request: "Well, we can talk about this later, but in the meantime, would you do me a favor, and not leave those cards out where Judi and Jimbo can see them?"

I agreed. My sister Judi was now 10 years old. Jimbo was 14. Carol was 20, a junior at Wheaton College. I was 24.

Then he said, "Well, Steve, I can see you're not a carbon copy of me, but that's fine. As long as you love the Lord, and follow in His footsteps, everything's going to be fine."

Although I had considered working with the Bible Society in another country, or staying in Ecuador with another mission, I knew way down deep I was not called to be a missionary. By the time I prepared to leave Ecuador, I was struggling with issues far deeper than mere card playing. The Bibles I was charged with distributing throughout Ecuador were supposed to be the inerrant Word of God, but I was not convinced. It would be dishonest to continue as a missionary when I was not convinced of the message. No one knew these inner reasons, especially my parents, and the word that went forth throughout Ecuador was, "Steve Savage has turned his work over to a national Ecuadorian Christian, and is returning to the United States to work as a Christian businessman."

That was an acceptable explanation, but not totally satisfying. There was a rumbling of questions: various missionaries and Ecuadorian Christians pleaded with me, "Steve, how can you turn your back on Latin America? You know Spanish better than 98 per cent of the missionaries, you know the culture, and you belong here."

Dad did not confront me directly with that question, but I sensed it was troubling him, so I brought it up myself: "Dad, how do you feel about my leaving Ecuador, leaving missionary work, and going into business?"

On the surface, he was supportive. "Steve, I want you to seek the Lord's perfect will for your life. If you're convinced you can serve Him best in business, then more power to you."

I did not feel called to be a missionary, but neither did I feel any "call" to be a so-called "Christian businessman." Business fascinated me, but I was not led by the Lord. The real reason I wanted to go into business was one I dared not utter: I wanted to make lots of money. If my Christian friends wanted to think the Lord was "leading me into business," I would just let them think it. No one in our world ever would have declared blatantly, "I want to make a ton of money." The word "money" was the subject of many sermons, and we were told, "You cannot serve God and Mammon" or "Money is the root of all evil" or "It is easier for a camel to get through the eye of a needle than a rich man to get into the kingdom of heaven."

On the other hand, there were Old Testament examples that told a different story. God often rewarded His faithful followers, like Abraham, Isaac, Jacob, and Joseph, with success and prosperity. He promised Joshua, "This book of the law shall not depart out of your mouth, but you shall meditate on it day and night, that you may be careful to do according to all that is written in it; for then you shall make your way prosperous, and then you shall have good success." I liked the sound of that.

For our evangelical Christians, it was OK to make lots of money, as long as that was not one's primary goal. In our fundamentalist world, missionaries depended on wealthy businessmen to support the mission, so money was appreciated, and those who gave their money were treasured and respected friends.

When I was ten years old, we were at Maranatha Bible

Conference, and Dad pointed out a man seated in the dining hall. "He's a millionaire," Dad said with an awed hush. The word "millionaire" was spoken in a tone reserved for other titles like "college president," "ambassador," or "senator." All were worthy callings, as long as one was a Christian. Yet there always seemed to be an underlying feeling that even those worthy people had chosen God's "second best plan" for their lives. The best plan was "full-time Christian service" and the best type of service was overseas missionary work.

Thus, even with Dad's verbal support, I felt uneasy, knowing I was not about to become a "Christian layman" or businessman in the sense he thought of it.

Shortly after I began my new job in the United States, Grandpa Savage was conducting a series of meetings in California. I took a two week recruiting trip, traveling to college campuses on the West Coast. While there, I joined Grandpa and Grandma for dinner, then attended church with them. Grandpa was preaching that night and paused at the beginning to introduce me to the congregation: "Here is our grandson, Steve, who has just completed two glorious years serving the Lord in Ecuador, and now is traveling all over America witnessing to college students."

I squirmed, because it was not the way Grandpa thought. My contacts with college students were 99 per cent business-oriented, and only occasionally did a theological discussion ever take place. Even those discussions could hardly be considered witnessing, for I myself was truly confused about the faith.

Grandpa's three children—Bob, Jim, and Helen—had all become missionaries, and he was so proud of them. He mentioned this feat at every opportunity. He hoped all his grandchildren would follow suit, and there would be a grand dynasty of Savage missionaries. Now, the eldest of the grandchildren had left the mission field, and the dream lost its crispness. However, as long as Grandpa could claim that all his children and grandchildren were in some kind of full-time Christian service, there would still be cause for great rejoicing.

Dad surely must have hoped his four children would follow the same missionary line his own father had begun. He never laid a heavy burden on us about it, but I always felt that down deep he really wanted it.

Was he disappointed? Perhaps, but as long as he could maintain the myth that we were in full-time Christian service, he and Grandpa could both feel everything was going according to plan.

It was not. I was not witnessing for the Lord, although I continued to wrestle, quietly, in my mind, about the faith. I wanted to distance myself from my Baptist background and so did Marilyn. We joined a Presbyterian church in Nashville. It was a safe move, for even though Grandpa and Dad would have preferred that we remain Baptists, they could be happy as long as they thought we were still zealous Christians. They were unaware of how little zeal I had, and they would not have liked the real reason I joined that Presbyterian church. What I liked best about that church was that no one asked me about my theology or the state of my spiritual life. The sermons were not very interesting, but not very demanding, either. It was an enormous relief no longer to pretend to be something I was not.

Gradually, I quit torturing myself with the intellectual turmoil over unresolved theological and spiritual issues and quit thinking much about them—sort of a spiritual vacation. No one knew, for Dad and Grandpa continued to think I was serving the Lord, telling college students of America about Christ.

In January, 1987, our first son, Lance, was born at Baptist Hospital in Nashville. Unlike our first two babies, Lance was full-term, husky, and weighed in at eight pounds. When the doctor told me he was normal and healthy, I was overjoyed. When I heard he was a boy, I whooped a Bob Savage-style "Whoop-dee-doo-den-doo!" When Marilyn's mother called and I tried to say "it's a boy" I found the words locked in my throat and I used up a minute or so of long-distance time just trying to sputter out a few words.

We seemed to be the model, happy, All-American family. Marilyn worked as a nurse at Vanderbilt Hospital and I was coming on strong as a rising young businessman. Our two children, Cyndi and Lance, were stunning, blond, beautiful, high-spirited kids. All our friends thought we were an ideal couple, completely in harmony. They were wrong. There was an ominous gap emerging, and I was just about as oblivious to it as everyone else. I was chipper and optimistic. Sure, a few little problems here and there, but we could always work them out. Think positive. This was one of Marilyn's objections to me. She saw me as too shallow, too breezy, too work-oriented, too uptight, too insensitive. She mentioned it first occasionally, then with increasing frequency. Ever confident, I'd go to work on it, and make a project out of becoming a little more profound, more relaxed, more sensitive. "That's what I mean," she'd object, "you think you can just change your technique. You have to change the way you are." I never quite got it.

In November, 1967, Dad flew from Ecuador to the United States to be at the bedside of his dying father. I had seen Grandpa Savage a few weeks earlier and said farewell as he lay dying of cancer in his hospital bed.

"See you at the wedding," said Grandpa as I shook his hand in parting.

"What wedding?" I asked.

"The wedding feast of the Lamb," he replied, referring to the Lamb of God, symbol of Christ, the bridegroom, and the Church, His bride.

Although I was impressed with Grandpa's calm humor in the face of death, I could not identify with the utter joy he was feeling as he talked about his eagerness to meet his Master face to face. He was genuine, there was no question. All his talk about heaven was not glib sweet talk. He meant it. He wanted to see his Master. He was ready. I left that hospital, choked, pensive, grateful for my grandfather, still afraid of him, wanting to please him, knowing he would feel very let down if he knew about the doubts swirling through my mind.

Grandpa died a few weeks later, December 3, 1967, age 80, surrounded by his three missionary children. All had flown up from South America to be at his side. One of Christianity's great patriarchs was gone. He had lived a life of distinguished achievement, but had always taken care to credit his accomplishments to the Lord he served. Over the next few months, I became more impressed with the scope of his ministry and influence, for wherever I traveled, to over 60 colleges and universities across the land, people often said to me: "Savage. Hmmmmmm. Are you related to Dr. H.H. Savage?" Then they would tell me how they had heard him in an evangelistic campaign, on the radio, or at Maranatha Bible Conference. Although it gave me great pride to hear these comments, it also disquieted me for I knew I was not accomplishing great things for the Lord, and felt guilty.

Meanwhile, Dad had become convinced he should spend the rest of his years as "a pastor in the homeland." He repeated, "I have a pastor's heart, and nothing is better than leading a church." A few months later, he returned to the United States to speak at some churches in the Midwest. He was a candidate for several pastorates and was now in the process of appearing before each one. He flew through Nashville to visit us. His next stop was Chicago. By coincidence, I also had to go to Chicago on a business trip and offered to take Dad with me. The two of us had been together a lot, but always with many other people around. We had never been together, alone, for a whole day and Nashville to Chicago was a ten-hour drive. Dad exclaimed, "What a great time for some good old chin-waggin'!"

It turned out to be a momentous ten hours, for Dad began to ask the inevitable questions, "How's your spiritual life?" and "How's your witnessing for the Lord on college campuses?" Up until that day, I had been able to deal with these questions smoothly, because visits with Dad were usually a swirl of activity with lots of people, energetic meetings, and other happenings, with little time for in-depth conversation. I had been happy to keep it superficial. Not today, however, for it would be pretty hard to play games for ten solid hours, cooped up in a car.

After an hour of "chin-wagging", the inevitable query came: "Well, Steve, give me a little report on your spiritual life."

I hesitated, knowing an honest answer was a big risk, and did not want to hurt him. After a moment's hesitation, I decided to open the door a crack.

"Well, Dad, I think my spiritual life is OK, but you probably wouldn't think so."

"What do you mean?" He was startled and sounded anxious.

Well, I thought, he asked for it. "Mmmm, well, things that are important to you just aren't as important to me anymore."

Dad wouldn't let up. "What kinds of things?"

"Well, for example, you believe the Bible is the inerrant, inspired Word of God. I think the Bible is God's Word, but I'm not convinced it's inerrant."

Dad was stunned. The doctrine of the inerrancy of Scriptures was the cornerstone of his entire ministry. To doubt the Scriptures was almost to doubt God Himself. When Dad preached, it was sufficient to declare, "The Bible says..." If you didn't accept his initial premise, the rest of the message was built on a shaky foundation.

It was as I had feared. I had feebly hoped we could have a calm intellectual discussion but instead I had dealt him a severe blow. He was wounded. "But Steve, how can you doubt God's Word?" he anguished.

"Look, Dad, I don't want to hurt you, and I know it means everything to you, but perhaps you can take a little comfort that at least I'm telling you what's really going on with me. I've been doubting this for years, and never told you, just because I didn't want to hurt you."

"It does hurt," replied Dad, "because there's nothing I want more than to see my son living a God-fearing life."

"Let's make a deal," I offered. "I'll tell you what's going on in my mind if you'll try your best to just hear me out. When I was a junior in high school, I asked you what would happen if I ever asked permission to go to a movie. You said you didn't want me to sneak off to a movie, and hoped I'd ask you if I ever wanted to go. You said you'd give me permission, but you'd be terribly disappointed in me. Well, Dad, I've gone to lots of movies over the years, but never told you, because I couldn't stand to disappoint you. But, worse than that, I've never confided in you about other spiritual matters because I did not want to hurt you. I'd love to discuss these issues with you, but I don't want you to feel I'm whipping you with them. I love you and have never rebelled against you or the Christian faith. It's not a matter of rebellion; it's simply a matter of not being able to make sense out of it."

Dad shuffled in the seat, and did not make a sound. I was driving, but took a quick glance over at him. He looked grim. I swallowed hard and shook my head to keep the highway in focus. We drove in silence for several minutes.

Dad cleared his throat, reached over, and put his hand over mine. "I love you, Steve, never forget that. No matter what, remember I love you, and God loves you."

He took a deep breath. "OK, let's go on. I can take it. What else?"

He wouldn't quit. I sighed. "Well, Dad, this reminds me of something you said once: pull out one brick in the wall, and the whole foundation comes crumbling down. It's like that with the Bible. You start doubting the Bible, and you start doubting everything else too."

"What else do you doubt?" he persisted.

"The doctrine of Hell. I really gag on that one."

"So do I," agreed Dad, "but you can't deny it."

"Well, you can if you deny the Bible," I retorted.

"OK, good point. Go on. What else do you doubt?"

"I'm not sure if Christianity is the only way to God," I murmured. This was getting sticky.

"But remember John 14:6—'I am the way, the truth, and the life: no man cometh unto the Father but by me'." Dad was preaching.

"Yes, Dad, the Bible says that. But remember the premise of this discussion: I'm not sure about the Bible, so how can I be sure about that verse?"

Dad became more animated. Although troubled, conversations like this stimulated him. "OK, just how far is this going to go? Do you believe that Christ was born of a virgin?"

"I believe Christ was a real person, but it doesn't worry me too much whether He was born of a virgin or not."

Dad was now fascinated. "How about Creation?"

"Sure, I think the world was created. It strains my brain to think it was an accident. However, I do think that Fundamentalists put themselves in a box when they reject evolution as a theory."

"Why's that?" asked Dad.

"Who cares how God created the world? Who cares if it took seven days or seven billion years? The issue is whether God did it or whether it just happened. What if they absolutely prove evolution someday? I'll still believe God did it, but the Church is going to look ridiculous."

"Well, at least you're telling me you believe in God, right?" queried Dad.

"Probably," I said, "but the word 'belief' is troublesome. I don't believe in God in the same sense that I believe you and I are talking right now."

"I'm not sure I follow you," said Dad.

"Well, I can see you and hear you. I can't see or hear God."

"Don't you hear God speak to you when you pray?" asked Dad.

"Yes, in a way. Sometimes I think I hear the voice of God, but then I wonder if it's just my imagination."

"Whew!" rapped out Dad. "I told you I could take it, but this is a lot more than I had ever imagined."

I took a deep breath. "I'm sure it must be terribly hard for you to hear me say all this, but I'm enormously relieved to have it all off my chest."

"Yes, Steve," he sighed, "I'm relieved too, because I could tell you didn't have the same old zeal, and it's better to have it out in the open than simply to wonder. But I have faith, as Abraham of old, that the Lord will bring you back into His fold."

I gulped and said, "I hope so."

Dad was offered the pastorate of the Dalton Baptist Church in Muskegon, Michigan. He returned to Ecuador to finish up his work and make plans to leave. For several years my parents had discussed the idea of returning to the United States, but now that departure from Ecuador was imminent they began to wonder. Missionaries and Ecuadorians alike were shocked that Don Roberto and Doña Wilda were actually leaving, and pleaded with them to reconsider. The couple had become an institution throughout Latin America, particularly through their daily radio program on HCJB. Dad's name was on hundreds of hymns and choruses sung throughout the continent. "How can you leave us?" was the anguished lament they heard several times a day.

The question gave them pause. They loved Ecuador and had often called it "home" in the very deepest sense that word conveys. But Mom's health was not good, and Dad felt clear about his call. Just as God had called him to South American 26 years earlier, He was now calling him back to the United States.

Hundreds of people gathered at the airport in Quito, Ecuadorians who loved my parents, from the wealthiest people in the upper strata of Quito's elegant society, to the humblest Indians whom Dad had befriended. Little hunchbacked Conchita was there, sobbing, as were members of several churches Dad had founded around the city. The missionary staff of HCJB was there, as well as missionaries from other mission boards in Quito. They joined in a gigantic chorus and began to sing the songs they had learned from Don Roberto and Doña Wilda Savage. Song after song, spontaneous, richly sung in harmony by some, off-key by others, joining in love. For once in his life Dad could not sing. He and Mom stood there, weeping, trying to smile, waving, hugging, choking, until finally the airline attendants announced the final boarding call, and they struggled up the stairway, to leave the land where 26 years of their lives had been joyfully and productively spent.

Dad began his new ministry in the United States with the troubling thought that the very message he was preaching wasn't taking hold with his first-born son. Further, the two youngest, Jimbo and Judi, weren't showing much enthusiasm for "things of the Lord." Both were disinclined to sing and participate in gospel services, and Dad constantly looked for ways to get them "on fire for God." They participated from time to time, reluctantly. For Dad, a person's zeal was almost as important as his faith, and if one was a "lukewarm" or "halfhearted" Christian, that was cause for deep worry and fervent prayer. Therefore, Jimbo and Judi's lack of spiritual ardor became one of the main items on his daily prayer agenda.

Carol was the only one of the four children carrying on the family tradition. After graduating from Wheaton College, she married her college sweetheart, Jim Plueddemann, in 1966. Jim was from Midland, Michigan, a Christian Education major who felt the call to the mission field with the same earnest intensity that Carol sensed. They left shortly after their wedding for Nigeria as missionaries with the Sudan Interior Mission.

Even this happy event had a strange sidelight, for Grandma Savage commented acerbicly about the waste of Carol's talent. She sniped, "Carol knows perfect Spanish and now she's starting all over again in Africa. Imagine!" Grandma was nothing if not opinionated. She was convinced the Lord wanted Carol back in Latin America. Dad, however, had no such troublesome thoughts, and joyfully enthused over their call to Africa. He also rejoiced when two more grandchildren, Shari and Dan, were born in Nigeria.

In June, 1969, Marilyn gave birth to Matthew Morgan Savage. Like Heidi and Cyndi, he was born prematurely and struggled with hyaline membrane disease. It had become predictable: if the child could survive the first 48 hours, he could usually live. By the end of the second day, during which I was teaching a sales school, managing 200 salesmen, and making frequent visits to the hospital, I was exhausted. Just before leaving the office for the hospital one of my business associates invited me to stop for a glass of beer.

I had never drunk one single drop of alcohol until I was in graduate school at Michigan State University. I had my first beer in an East Lansing pub and thereafter sipped it occasionally and sparingly. One glass was enough to make me dizzy. I had not drunk any during my two years in Ecuador, but in Nashville, I had begun to enjoy an occasional drink with my friends. The invitation to drink a beer sounded perfect on that hot summer afternoon in Tennessee.

I stayed an hour, letting my weariness seep into the bar stool. I drank more than I had ever drunk in my life: three beers. Relaxed, I went to the hospital and wandered into Marilyn's room. "Quick!" she exclaimed, "the doctor needs your blood for a transfusion for Matt."

"Oh no!" I hung my head. "I just had three beers."

"You should be ashamed!" she snapped. "Here your son is, dying in the incubator, and you're out drinking beer."

I had not quite come to terms with drinking beer under the most ordinary circumstances, and this accusation made me reel with guilt. I shuffled down the hospital hallway to the doctor, and he quickly said, "Great. You're here at last. We need your blood."

"Wait, doc," I mumbled, unable to look him in the eye. "I'm afraid I can't give any blood. I just finished drinking three beers."

"Wonderful!" said the doctor, "it'll make the kid feel super. Roll up your sleeve."

After I had my blood drawn, I sashayed back into Marilyn's

hospital room with an enormous smirk: "Guess what! The doctor said the beer would make Matt feel great." We both laughed. We could do that. It was funny how much we had in common. We could enjoy a good laugh together, share the excitement of a new baby, talk about family and friends. But even in the midst of our happiness over Matt's quick recovery, and the rounding out of our family with three adorable, vivacious children, the marriage was beginning to fray.

Dad knew nothing about the strains on the marriage. He worried only about my spiritual doubts. Despite his worries, however, our family always had jolly fun together. We often arranged family get-togethers at Maranatha Bible Conference. Dad was effervescent in his pride for his grandkids, and when we visited in Muskegon in 1969 he took us to an amusement park. Dad slipped away with Cyndi and Lance to buy Kentucky Fried Chicken, leaving baby Matt in the care of the adults. On the way back to the picnic grounds, he winked at his two grandchildren and with a furtive look whispered, "Hey, let's sneak a piece." The two kids and Grandpa each snuck a piece, then another, and another. Cyndi and Lance had no appetite left when they arrived back at the fairgrounds, but Grandpa still managed to down a few more pieces, and every few minutes all afternoon, Grandpa would confide, "We've got a secret! Hooray, hooray, hooray!" A few amused smirks around the picnic table showed that everyone knew precisely what the secret was, for Grandpa had at one time or another played the game with each of us.

My brother Jimbo was now a student at Wheaton College, Judi was in high school in Muskegon, still living at home with my parents. Carol was in Nigeria with her husband Jim. I was finishing my fifth year as sales manager with Southwestern Company. Dad continued to hope and pray that I would see the light, and would occasionally check me with the inevitable "How's your spiritual life?"

I answered, "Dad, I'd love to turn on the old fervor, because I know it would please you so much. I know I'm letting you down, and it pains me, but I can't drum it up just to make you happy."

He and Mom prayed for me daily, pleading with God to open my eyes and help me see the Light. These prayers began to include Jimbo as well, for Dad had the uneasy feeling that Jimbo was not in close touch with the Lord. Jimbo did not feel any compulsion to spill everything on his mind, and maintained a breezy, friendly joviality with everyone in Dad's church. Jimbo knew how to "speak the language" and used the evangelical lingo with gusto, dropping "Hallelujahs" and "Praise the Lords" at appropriate times, always with a bemused smile.

Dad suspected that Jimbo was not completely sincere, but Jimbo's good humor and jolly manner gave him a good defense against penetrating questions like, "How's your relationship with the Lord?" Patented evangelical phrases like "I'm waiting on the Lord's Will" or "I feel that God is leading me in this direction" bothered Jimbo, but he had a way of cleverly deflecting his feeling. He had a matchless style that let him make humor out of the sacred, always bordering on the edge of irreverence.

Jimbo kept the family in stitches despite their concern about his spiritual state. He usually did something in the middle of all the festivities to make Mom laugh. He had an uncanny knack for getting her to giggle, especially during prayers. He'd sigh, say "Amen, Amen," in the most sincere-sounding voice, and Mom, knowing he was only partially serious, would start to giggle. Devotions often disintegrated with the entire family convulsing with hysterical laughter. Dad would stop the prayer, look at Jimbo, half disgusted, half amused, then say "You crazy galloop!" As soon as everyone was settled down, he'd continue with the prayer.

Dad, who had a ready laugh in most circumstances, resisted during these moments of solemnity. He desperately wanted to keep family devotions on a serious plane, and continued to read the Scriptures or pray while everyone else was snickering and trying to restrain their laughter. Eventually Dad, too, would give in, helplessly shrug his shoulders, shake his head, chuckle, and conclude, "Well, I know the Lord loves laughter, so this madness must be OK."

It was OK, yes, but Dad was disturbed. He didn't mind an occasional breakup of devotions, but wished Jimbo would not be quite so frivolous about the solemnity of Scripture reading and prayer. He felt that Jimbo's humor masked a lack of fervency and devotion to Christ and yearned for his son to "get more serious."

Dad continued praying for us, longing for and believing in the day his kids would "get on fire for the Lord." But then the most shattering, devastating blow of all came. It was a sudden and unexpected jolt for Dad—the end of a long struggle for me. After eight years of marriage, Marilyn and I split up. She took the three children, Cyndi, Lance, and Matt, to Princeton, New Jersey, and I moved to Atlanta, Georgia.

Dad was frantic and flew to Atlanta to counsel and encourage me. He stood in my little kitchen, erect and fervent. "Steve, Steve, my son Steve," he lamented like an Old Testament prophet. "What is happening? What can we do to save the marriage? Why can't you get right with the Lord?" He continued, "I know the breakup of your marriage is linked, intricately, with the deterioration of both your faith and Marilyn's. Get right with the Lord and your marriage will get right again, too."

I felt a rush of anger, and recalled the day Heidi had died in Quito. Back then, he wanted the show of a big funeral; now he wanted the show of a good marriage. I said hotly, "I wish you wouldn't be so concerned about outward appearances. You just want it to look good to everyone. Dad, I'm hurting."

His posture softened immediately and he reached over to hug me. Then I said, "Dad, I'm embarrassed and I know I've embarrassed you. I don't care much about the marriage any more, but I care desperately about my three kids and care very much about you and Mom."

He was right about the link between the deterioration of Christian faith and the marriage. There were inherent problems in our marriage from the beginning, but we were able to overlook them to some extent as we put Christ first. As the marriage became more strained, we sought marriage counseling but the prevailing vogue of the day was not to "save the marriage" but to "find yourself." We talked to psychologists and associated with friends who found divorce "liberating" and encouraged us to free ourselves of the "inhibiting bonds of marriage." As devout Christians, divorce had been unthinkable, but now the freedom we took to explore other ways of behavior and thinking made the idea not only thinkable but palatable, then interesting, then attractive, and finally irresistible.

It became obvious to me, after a few months of living apart, that the rift was irreparable, and we were not going to get back together. I still felt very ashamed, and the idea of myself as a divorced man was hideous. I would have endured the marriage for the sake of the kids, my parents, and my public image. Marilyn, however, was determined and eager to get a divorce. I reluctantly agreed, but in the end was glad she had taken the initiative, as it unleashed me for a whole new era in my life. Had I not gotten divorced, I would never have gone into business for myself, nor would I have met Barrie.

I met Barrie one evening in Atlanta as she was returning from a Bible study at All Saints Episcopal Church, and we were introduced by a mutual friend. We dated a few nights later. We had a great deal in common, for we had each been through an eight-year marriage and divorce. She had two children, Bill and Allison, ages 7 and 5, and was their sole support. She worked for an insurance company in Atlanta.

I had never met anyone remotely like Barrie. She was a devout Christian, but unlike any of the Christians I had ever known. Theological issues that tormented my mind didn't seem to distress her at all. She was interested in my intellectual thrashings-about, and heard me out on each one, patiently, with intense interest, never disagreeing, never correcting. I'd ramble on and on about an issue like life after death and conclude, "Well, I give up. I can't make an airtight case for it, but I want to believe in it, so I'm just going to. After all, the Bible says 'faith is the evidence of things hoped for.' Well, I hope there's life after death, so I guess that's faith, right?" She'd nod her head.

"Tell me what you think!" I'd insist.

She'd smile, shake her head, and say, "That's a pretty way to look at it."

"Pretty!" I'd exclaim.

"Yes, pretty," she'd say.

"Not right. Not wrong. Just pretty. Is that what you're saying?"

"I guess."

It really didn't bother her one way or the other.

She accepted the Christian faith in the same way she accepted me: easily, gently, happily. She didn't have to make a case for it, or for me.

Barrie was soft, quiet, mellow. She had a ready smile that glowed over her smooth face. Her hazel eyes were intelligent and alive, but they also had a tranquil, almost sleepy look about them. She told me her biggest goal in life was to find calm.

"Calm!" I exclaimed, "then why do you like me? I'm hardly the calmest thing around."

"Oh yes, I feel very calm around you," she offered. I had a hard time believing she could be tranquil with me, but I was beginning to realize that Barrie always said exactly what she meant, and there was never any double edge to her meaning.

We both knew the pitfalls of marriage and treated each other with delicacy. She gave me lots of room to be myself, and I tried to do the same for her. We both sensed we were on the edge of something very good and were careful not to tamper with our success.

I was selling men's suits in Atlanta, biding my time until I could figure out something really interesting and lucrative. I earned enough to pay my bills and send money each month to Marilyn to take care of the three kids in New Jersey, but was eager to get into business for myself. After a few months in Atlanta, I got a call from two Southwestern Company salesmen whom I had managed while they were in college, Mike Rippey and Bill Siemann. They had graduated from Notre Dame and were selling silk-screened T-Shirts out in California, selling them to high schools, who in turn sold them to raise money for their bands, choirs, classes, clubs, and teams. It sounded perfect. The only thing that was holding me to Atlanta was Barrie, but our relationship still had a temporary feeling to it. I wanted to join those guys more than anything. Barrie and I spent a weekend together on Jekyll Island, off the coast of Southern Georgia. The whole time I talked about Mike and Bill and working with them. They were the most creative and interesting people I had ever known, and I could not imagine doing anything more exciting. To my amazement, Barrie encouraged me to go. Again, she behaved differently from anyone I had ever known. She wanted me in many ways, but knew I should follow my instincts. She showed her wisdom.

After I had gotten settled in California, I asked Barrie if she would consider moving out. With almost no hesitation she said she'd like to. She was a brave woman, for she took off from the city where she had lived all her life, with her two kids, in her old '62 Chevy, and struck out across the country. When she first arrived, we lived in two separate homes, but after three months, we began living together.

Thus a new troublesome note was introduced for my long-suffering folks. I did not want to trouble them, and just wanted to mind my own business, but everything was a disappointment to them. Divorce had been intolerable, but Dad's view was, "If everything goes down the tubes, there are provisions in the Bible for a divorce. However, once you are divorced, you are not allowed to remarry, for that would be adultery."

One day I said to Barrie, "Do you realize my parents think we are living in sin?" She was stunned. That idea had never occurred to her, and she replied with bewilderment, "This is the most beautiful thing I've ever known. Our relationship seems holy. How could it be sin?" Barrie, although raised a Southern Baptist, had never been troubled with all the fine points of doctrine that had been my daily fare, and although I often vacillated between guilt and joy, she felt nothing but joy in our life together. She joked, "I come from a whole line of backslidden Baptists!" I was amused by her use of the phrase, for "backslidden" to me had terrible connotations of great spiritual agony, whereas for her it was simply jolly family legend. I said, "You know, I'm sure all my family, as well as my missionary friends in South America, think I'm backslidden. But I haven't rejected the faith, and I'm still trying to make sense out of it."

Dad and Mom came to California to visit us. They felt extremely nervous about entering our home, feeling there was something improper about it, and took pains to let us know they would stay in a motel, not with us. Once they had established a careful distance by getting settled in a nearby motel, our time together became cordial and even festive. Dad took a special interest in Barrie's children: Bill, 7, and Allison, 5.

We lived in a beautiful house in Benicia by the Suisun Bay, along the Sacramento River, where ocean-going freighters passed on their way to the San Francisco Bay and the Orient. Interesting rock formations jutted out of the water along the shore and Dad invited Allison to go on a walk. They took a loaf of bread to feed the ducks. Allison's enormous blue eyes melted my Dad's heart, and the two hit it off like a couple of buddies. They were gone over an hour.

Dad was also charmed by Barrie, and set aside his preconceived image of a worldly and evil woman who had led his son into sin. Before he had met her he referred to her coolly as "that gal." Now, whenever we talked on the phone, he asked warmly, "How is Barrie?" Although the situation was intolerable to him, he couldn't help but become fond of the easy-going and gentle Barrie. He also found consolation in that we were not totally selfish and irresponsible but were looking after her two children. He was impressed with my efforts to support and keep in close touch with my own children, and found comfort that I had not forgotten them. He could not help but be pleased to see me so deeply in love, and to sense the utter adoration this lovely woman had for his son. Shortly after that visit, he switched his line of questioning. No longer was it "Can the marriage be saved?" or "Nuts, when are you going to stop this monkey business?" Now, the question was, "When are you and Barrie going to get married?"

One day, during a visit to Muskegon, I said to Dad, "Look, let's not talk about this any more. Let's just have a pleasant relationship. I think we'll be better off if you don't ask me about my spiritual life and if you don't ask me when I'm going to get married."

He agreed, and there ensued a finely constrained period of about three years when we visited once or twice a year and talked about everything but the two things Dad cared about the most: how is your spiritual life and when are you going to get married?

Dad kept his bargain, let up on me, and did not ask me those questions. But Barrie had never bargained with him. One day she and I visited my folks in Muskegon, careful to show up and leave the same day, so there would be no uneasiness about where we were to sleep. After eating lunch at a restaurant, Dad said, "Wilda, you drive home with Steve in his car, and I'll take Barrie in mine."

Dad and Barrie did not go directly home but drove for over an hour. He quickly got to the point: "Barrie, do you love Steve?"

"Oh, yes," she replied, "very much."

"Well, then," he probed, "why don't you get married?"

"Well, you know, Bob, Stephen and I have been married before, and we don't think we like marriage too much. We haven't quite figured that out yet. We're getting along so well that we're thinking marriage isn't right for us."

Later, Barrie told me, "That really distressed him, but he was real sweet about it. We weren't even tense; it was a very loving conversation. It helped me to get to know him a little better. I really felt his love and concern for you."

Dad always wanted to tie up loose ends—and this one was way too loose for him. I tried to explain. There was a song out by Kris Kristoffersen called "Lovin' Her Was Easier than Anything I'll Ever Do Again" and I repeated those words to Dad.

"That's what it's like with Barrie, Dad."

The father was happy for his son. The man understood the other man. The preacher couldn't fit it into his theology. It's the only time I've ever seen Dad unable to sum something up, to weave it into a clear definition.

While we lived in Benicia, I invited Grandpa Johnson to fly out and visit us. Grandma Johnson had Altzheimer's disease and spent her days giggling as she played with her Raggedy Ann doll. Grandpa read the newspapers, looking for the latest scores of the Chicago Cubs, Northwestern University, and the Republican Party. It was not a happy time for Grandpa; his wife was in another world, and all the teams he rooted for were losing. Even his beloved Republican Party was losing, for this was the time when Nixon's Watergate problems were front page news. A trip to California sounded like a welcome break, and he agreed to come.

The airlines had a parent-child special going that summer, with two for the price of one, so we arranged for my sister, 17-year-old Judi, to fly out with Grandpa, as his daughter. Judi was a senior in high school, and I had not seen much of her over the years, with 12 years age difference separating us. I prepaid the ticket and arranged for it to be picked up at the Muskegon ticket counter.

When Dad arrived at the airport with Judi and Grandpa, he went to the ticket counter to get their ticket. The agent cheerfully said, "Here it is, the parent-child special!"

Dad looked it over, then replied, in that unabashed honesty that marked his character, "Now wait a minute. This gentleman is

Judi's grandfather, not her father."

The ticket agent reassured him, saying, "No problem. That's fine."

But Dad pressed on. "Now, we want to make sure we aren't cheating. I'll be glad to pay the difference."

It was only when the ticket agent assured him this was a legitimate combination that Dad felt satisfied. He raised me to be honest, but when I heard Judi tell that story I shook my head and said, "Well, I believe in being fair and square, even with a huge and faceless corporation, but that's taking honesty to a fault, don't you think?" Judi not only thought it crazy but was disgusted: "That's ridiculous!" Grandpa Johnson, who often over the years had been bemused by his earnest son-in-law, could only chuckle and mutter: "He has no guile."

Although Dad had worried about Jimbo's lack of zealousness for the faith, good news came when Jimbo graduated from Wheaton College in 1972 and left for Ecuador soon after as an independent missionary. Jimbo's mission was to help organize sports teams and musical groups. Combining his athletic skills and musical talent with his winsome and engaging good humor, Jimbo attracted many young people to play at the games - and his music group performed at churches around Ecuador.

Dad raved about Jimbo to everyone, estatic that his second son had chosen to be a missionary. He and Mom helped contribute towards Jimbo's personal support, and encouraged others to do the same.

Jimbo may have been the most happy-go-lucky missionary in Ecuador. Missionaries and Ecuadorians alike enjoyed his relaxed good humor and mischievous pranks. Always, however, there was the question, "When is Jimbo going to settle down?"

Jimbo did not feel settled by any means, either in geography or career. Although Dad had labeled him a missionary, Jimbo did not feel like one. "I felt like a chump," he told me, "taking money from friends in the United States, just so I could live a great life in

Ecuador." He returned to the States a few months later, and began to find ways of earning enough money in six months so he could spend the remaining six months of each year in Ecuador.

Dad was disappointed with Jimbo's decision but as always found a way to cast the best possible light on it. He figured that Jimbo had merely quit calling himself a missionary, but was still in Christian service. "Jimbo has now become a self-supporting missionary" was the way Dad rationalized it. "He's earning his own way, just like the Apostle Paul did when he made tents to support his missionary work."

Dad was fascinated with Jimbo's carefree lifestyle, but it made him uneasy. He would ask me from time to time, "When do you think Jimbo's going to settle down?"

"Dad," I counseled, "don't ask Jimbo that question. It just makes him nervous."

A far more troubling note came out of Mexico, where Judi had gone to the Central University of Mexico, after a freshman year at Wheaton and sophomore year at Bethel College in St. Paul, Minnesota.

While in Mexico she met and fell in love with Alejandro Castillo, a brilliant and fascinating young Mexican businessman. Alex had been a bullfighter, drove extravagant sports cars, wore expensive clothes, flashed gold Rolex watches, and swept Judi off her feet.

They decided to get married—but Alex was a Roman Catholic. Dad flew to Mexico City.

In his years in Ecuador, Dad had counseled many American missionary women about the tremendous hurdles they would have to overcome if they married Ecuadorians. Almost all ignored his advice and followed their hearts. Juanita Kilgore, Dad's secretary, married Doctor César Cabascango, head surgeon at the Vozandes Hospital in Quito. Dad had given them his blessing after considerable counseling.

But their case had been quite different. César Cabascango was an evangelical Christian so Dad had counseled Juanita only about potential cross-cultural conflicts. Now, however, his own daughter was not only proposing to marry a Mexican, but a Mexican Catholic! It was unthinkable. Dad had spent his missionary career persuading Roman Catholics to leave the church that had abandoned the true path to Christ, and to join the church that preached the Bible, with Christ as the only mediator and way to God.

The burden on Mom and Dad was overwhelming as they thought of their oldest son living out of wedlock in California and their youngest daughter about to marry a Roman Catholic in Mexico. Things were not working out the way they had hoped and dreamed, and they prayed fervently that God would work miracles in the lives of their children.

Dad took two plane trips to Mexico City, trying to talk Judi and Alex out of the marriage, but they were determined. Finally, he sat up, brightened, and announced to them, "OK, I've given you all my arguments and you've given me yours. You aren't persuaded, so—I give in. Now, let's make this a joyful affair."

He met the Castillo family priest, Father Rosas, who would be performing the ceremony. The two talked for many hours and became friends. Father Rosas begged Dad to participate in the ceremony, but Dad was not sure. He asked for time to think about it.

Shortly after, I saw Dad again in the States, and he told me, "You know, I believe that Catholic priest is a brother in Christ. We talked for hours about things of the Lord, and we agree on almost every issue."

On May 25, 1974, Reverend Savage, Baptist, and Reverend Rosas, Catholic, conducted a joint wedding ceremony for Judi and Alex, with Dad singing his booming *Padre Nuestro (Our Father, Who Art in Heaven)* just as he had sung it hundreds of times on radio station HCJB. Mom accompanied him on the church organ.

Before the service, Mom had entered the church to practice the organ. She had felt uneasy playing a pipe organ from a balcony in the rear of a huge Catholic church. After becoming comfortable with the organ, she descended into what she thought was an empty church, only to find Father Rosas, who said, "I've been sitting down here listening, and that's the loveliest music I've ever heard played on our organ." Mom couldn't help but like a guy that would talk to her like that, and found herself contrasting his warmth with the hostility they had experienced 27 years earlier from Catholic priests in fanatical small-town Colombia.

My sister's wedding was not the only one that summer. Although I had wanted to marry Barrie for quite some time, I had to be sure it was right for us, and not merely to make Dad and Mom happy. Our relationship had seemed lifelong and eternal for almost the entire three years we had been together. We were unbelievably happy, and could not imagine ever wanting out of this relationship. Way down deep, we were committed to each other for life. But marriage? Well, we were both pretty spooked, and hesitated. We didn't even talk about it. I did, however, think about it a lot. One day, out of the clear blue sky, I up and popped the question: "Barrie, let's get married."

I thought she would want to think about it for a few weeks or months, and was stunned when her reply was an instantaneous, "Oh yes, let's!"

We called Mom and Dad from Jackson, California, just after we left the courthouse. It seemed we heard Dad's voice without the telephone, 2,000 miles away, as he roared from Muskegon, Michigan: "Praise the Lord! Hallelujah. This is swell, this is great, this is marvelous. Amen, amen, amen."

The first of Dad's two concerns was answered. He wanted me married, and that I was. The second was still a blur. He continued to worry about my spiritual life, but faithful to our agreement, he did not ask. I still wished I could be a zealous Christian, to please him, if for nothing else. But answers to my doubts about the faith continued to elude me.

There was, however, the continuing drive to try to make sense out of it. I think the drive came mainly from my desire to make Dad happy. Without that, I don't think I would have felt it was worth the effort to keep seeking for the answers. I had, by this time, become a complete unbeliever. I did not reject the Christian faith. I just quit thinking about it altogether. After years of trying to make sense out of it, I felt relieved to quit the effort.

However, after I got married, I felt I ought to do something in the way of spiritual leadership for Barrie's two children, Bill and Allison. I bought *The Chronicles of Narnia* by C.S. Lewis and began to read a couple of chapters per night to the children. They were spellbound by the hair-raising adventures of the marvelous creatures inhabiting that magic land. As the kids listened in fascination, they were sometimes puzzled when my voice choked and I was unable to keep reading. "Go on," they urged. I would clear my throat and continue.

To the children, the stories were sheer adventure. To me, they were a whole new way of looking at the Christian faith. I was jolted by the magic of Narnia. Aslan the Lion (symbol of Christ) was compelling and caught me by surprise. I had answered every argument advanced in Christian Apologetics, but suddenly my mind was bombarded from another angle. This was no mere fairy tale. Aslan, the great and majestic lion, attracted to his side the good people of that land of Narnia: the honest human girl, Lucy; the chivalrous and courageous mouse, Reepicheep; the majestic unicorn, Jewel; the steadfast fawn, Mr. Tumnus; the practical and good-hearted souls, Mr. and Mrs. Beaver, and many other fascinating and varied personalities, all bound together by qualities of decency, loyalty, courage, truthfulness, compassion, and humility. On the other side were the rascals, the followers of Jadis, the White Witch. One of them was Edmund, Lucy's brother, who was drawn under the witch's spell by his craving for Turkish Delight. Other followers of the witch were the wolves and dwarves.

Throughout the six books, the conflict between good and evil was portrayed vividly, both in day-to-day relationships among Narnia's creatures, as well as in the final battle that raged between the forces of light and darkness. In a way I had never seen before, I now saw the various faces of evil. And after years of feeling dull toward all spiritual talk, I found myself charmed with the supernatural. I was touched in a very particular way by the Great Lion, Aslan himself. I was impressed with the boundless, leaping joy he conferred on his country, and the dread he elicited in those who feared and loathed him. Aslan voluntarily sacrificed his life to win back the betrayer, Edmund.

Fascinated, I went to several bookstores until I had bought every book Lewis had ever written—and devoured them all. His science fiction trilogy gave me yet another way of looking at the faith, in bright colors, vast spaces, and fantastic descriptions about the struggle between good and evil on other planets. It helped me feel the reality of the spiritual warfare here on earth.

A moment of drama came as I read *The Great Divorce* and suddenly found the idea of Hell not altogether outrageous, for Lewis depicted it as a place people *chose to go.* I had viewed it as the vendetta of an angry God who flung people into the cauldron, willy-nilly, simply because they hadn't quite figured out the story during their short journey on earth.

The doctrine of Hell had been one unpalatable point of theology for me. The idea made it difficult for me to buy the Christian story. Now I had an alternative way to think about it. Lewis drew a picture of Hell as a place of ever-increasing distance from God—because its inhabitants *preferred* it that way. They *always* had a choice to go back to Heaven, but as time went on, they became more set in their ways, and less likely to have any desire to return. Although Lewis did not set this forth as an actual doctrine of Hell, and advised his readers that his book was nothing more than a fantasy, it still gave me a way of dealing with the once-impossible topic.

In *The Great Divorce*, each person was given many oppotunities to choose. The ultimate choice was simple: "My will or Thine." Those who preferred their own way of self-seeking aggrandizement were given precisely what they wanted. Those who said, "Thy will" were ushered into an eternity of delirious joy as they joined the throngs in heaven who chose to bow before their Master and say, "Not my will but Thine."

One night I awoke at 2 a.m. Much to my great discomfiture, I found myself praying that very prayer: "Not my will, but Thine." Immediately, I questioned myself, "Hey, take it easy, Steve, don't get sucked in. This will fade away in a few days." I was deeply suspicious of any emotional conversion experience, and wanted to avoid any silliness.

Over the days and weeks ahead, however, the conviction stuck, and I found myself praying quite calmly and quite often as I went through each day, "Not my will but Thine." I became at ease with the prayer, and even got a little emotional at times.

I wanted to tell Dad about all this, but hesitated, not wanting to get him too excited. I wasn't sure how long this would last, and didn't want to arouse his expectations. For several months, I kept it to myself and to Barrie, and continued to read Lewis' books. Then finally, I visited Mom and Dad in Muskegon, and described the events of the past few months. As my story unfolded, Dad became increasingly ecstatic. Finally he could contain himself no longer. "Praise God!" he shouted. "My son has come back home!"

His outburst made me feel uneasy, for although I wanted him to be happy, I didn't want to get his hopes up too much. I thought to myself, "Whoa, Dad, it's not as good as you think. I'm getting warmer, but I'm not hot." Then I saw tears running down his cheeks and decided not to say anything to destroy his happy moment. I went over and hugged him. Then mother joined us and the three of us held onto each other for several minutes. Dad could once again rest easily. Our relationship immediately relaxed, and we began to develop a new interconnection, a close, loving link that deepened and expanded over the next thirteen years until his death in 1987. I told him, "Dad, all these years I've wandered in the spiritual wilderness, and you never wavered in your love for me. I've seen a lot of parents reject their kids when they had problems with the faith, but you have stood by me all these years."

He replied, "I've prayed for you every day. I knew the Lord would show you the light. I've always been proud of you and always loved you, but I must admit I've felt pretty low about your relationship with Christ."

"I don't think I would have bothered pursuing the faith so diligently if I didn't care about you and Mom so much. I couldn't drum up something just to please you, but it was your constant care that made me want to keep searching."

Soon after, I joined my wife's (and C.S. Lewis's) church and became an Episcopalian. If I had become an Episcopalian ten years earlier Dad would have been deeply disturbed, as he thought Episcopalians were liberal in their theology and strange in their worship. But the fact that I was *anything* was such an enormous relief that he was extremely enthusiastic.

Barrie and I moved from California to Massachusetts, so I could be closer to my three children who lived with their mother in Princeton, New Jersey. I was still in the same type of business, school fund-raising. Our original partner Bill Siemann had spun off to form his own business. Mike Rippey and I had stuck together for a few years, built a good business, hired 250 salespeople, overextended ourselves, run out of cash, and shut the business down. We then set up our own independent businesses, each working out of his own home. Mike and I remained in close contact, and often pooled our resources to buy our products and thus get better prices. After experimenting with several different products, we had begun to specialize in fashion jewelry. It was perfect. I could live anywhere I wanted, Barrie could do all the office management, and I could do the selling.

We decided we would buy a farm somewhere in New England, but while we searched for the "perfect" spot we rented a beautiful two-story home on the banks of the Annisquam River, a salt-water tidal river that divides Cape Ann from the mainland, about 30 miles northeast of Boston. We immediately joined St. John's Episcopal Church, an ancient church that had comforted Gloucester seamen and their families for many generations.

Mom and Dad came to visit us in Gloucester, Massachusetts, and we attended St. John's together. It was their first Episcopalian service and I worried about their discomfort in being served real wine during Holy Communion. Baptists always used unfermented grape juice. I told them, "You don't need to go forward when they serve the bread and the wine. No one will mind, and it will be completely acceptable."

"No, we'll do it," agreed both my parents, and good sports, participated fully in the service.

As we came out of the service Dad said, "Well, I'll have to admit one thing. You Episcopalians read a lot more Scripture during the service than we Baptists do."

He continued to talk about the service. "You know, I think every Baptist ought to go to an Episcopalian service every once in a while. It's a broadening experience. Of course, I think every Episcopalian should go to a Baptist service as well!"

I asked, "Dad, there was a time when you didn't think an Episcopalian could even be saved, wasn't there?"

"Well, I would probably have allowed that an Episcopalian might have squeaked into heaven, but it wouldn't have been easy," he laughed.

He went on, mulling over the experience, "I guess it's like taste in food. Some people like to go to Howard Johnson's, others choose McDonalds, and others prefer a gourmet meal."

I grinned and asked, "Which one do you think is the gourmet meal?"

He joked, "Well, you probably think the gourmet meal is the Episcopalian service, but I kind of like the Baptist feast we get every week."

Then he wrinkled his brow and quizzed me, "Now, what about Communion? I hear the Episcopalian service saying quite literally 'this is my body' and 'this is my blood.' Surely you don't believe that the bread and wine become the body and blood of Christ like the Roman Catholics do?"

I got a sly smirk on my face. "Well, Dad, you know we

Episcopalians believe in the literal interpretation of the Scriptures. You Baptists are pretty liberal and say the bread and wine are merely a symbol. Symbol! That's what the modernists say about the whole Bible. You are on the wide path towards the left!"

Dad roared with laughter. "OK, you've got me!" he yelped merrily, as he slapped his knee, "but seriously, what is the Episcopal view?"

"As best I can figure it's something like the Lutheran view. Roman Catholics believe in 'transubstantiation,' in which the bread and wine are transformed into the true presence of Christ. The Lutherans believe in 'consubstantiation,' in which the body and blood coexist with the elements of bread and wine. The Episcopalians don't give it a name, exactly, but believe Christ is truly present in this sacrament as He is also present in other sacraments, such as baptism, marriage, and the rest."

"But they don't call it anything?" asked Dad.

"Not that I know of," I replied. "That's one thing I like about the Episcopal Church. They don't seem to feel any urgency to put labels on everything. It seems sufficient to declare 'this is my body' and be done with it."

A year later, I became a lay reader in the Episcopal Church and when Mom and Dad visited, it was my turn to read the Scriptures. At the end of each Scripture reading, the reader declares, "The Word of the Lord." The congregation responds, "Thanks be to God."

After the service, Dad said, "Hey, I like that. It's great when you proclaim 'The Word of the Lord.'"

"Yes, I like it too," I replied.

"Do you Episcopalians believe the Bible really is the Word of the Lord?"

"Oh yes, of course," I replied, "but most Episcopalians I know don't appear to be interested in discussions about inerrancy like the Baptists do. It's just not an issue. It seems enough to declare 'The Word of the Lord' and take it at face value."

"Well," mused Dad, "I like my theology buttoned down tighter than that, but I guess I can deal with that. I'm just so happy that you are involved in Church and serving the Lord."

During the same service, it was my duty to assist in serving communion, and I tilted the cup of wine to the lips of each person who came forward to kneel at the rail. As I tipped the chalice to the mouths of my teetotaling parents, I thought it ironic that I was administering the vile liquid to them, the very substance they had preached against their entire lives. I felt uneasy, but amused.

Old-time Episcopalians generally grab the bottom of the chalice, and help the cup-bearer steer it, thus assuring the proper amount of wine to swallow. Mom, however, left her hands on the altar rail, so it was up to me to decide how much wine she should imbibe. Cautiously and gingerly, I canted the goblet to her lips, then swiftly pulled it away and moved on to the next worshiper. After the service, Mom said, "You know, I don't think I got any wine. I'm not sure if I really had communion after all."

I said, "Mom, you'd feel bad if you had drunk the wine, and now you feel bad because you didn't drink it. You can't win!"

Dad yelped merrily, but Mom was puzzled. It did confuse her, and she wanted so earnestly to be right. But that was a small matter. Way down deep she felt at peace. Her family, after years of unease, was relaxed again. We were united in a knot of affection, an attachment that had withstood severe challenges to the core of Mom and Dad's most fundamental beliefs. Despite their anguish, they had been relentless in assuring us of their love. And they still had a few years left on this earth to enjoy the fulfillment of their steadfast loyalty.

16

A pastor's heart

❖

"Well, if you're gonna have a meetin' it might as well be a good one."   —Bob Savage to Tedd Bryson
                                               at Maranatha tabernacle

In the early 1970s, when I was living with Barrie, Dad had told the Board of Deacons at Dalton Baptist Church: "I don't think I should continue in the ministry any longer. The gospel I'm preaching is not being lived by my oldest son. How can I talk about raising children in the faith when my own son has gone astray?" The broken-hearted man was in terrible anguish; unlike his own father, whose three children had all gone into missionary work, only one of his four was taking up the banner. Where had he gone wrong, he wondered. The deacons assured him of their love and support. They refused to contemplate his resignation and offered instead to join him in prayer for his son. Dad was wise and kind: he never told me about his offer to resign. I did not learn of it until preparing this biography.

Once I came to see Mom and Dad at the same time that Judi and Alex were in town, visiting from Mexico. Jimbo was also there. On Sunday, we all went to Dad's church. Jimbo, Alex, and I all had beards. None of us wore a coat and tie. We looked scraggly and disreputable, in stark contrast to the well-groomed, neatly-dressed Baptist men in the congregation. I was uneasy, not for myself, but because I knew we were embarrassing Mom and Dad. I looked at Mom, playing the organ. She rendered a quiet introductory number designed to hush the congregation into a spirit of reverence before the beginning of the morning service.

Then Dad strode onto the platform, opened with his usual vigorous prayer of praise to God, led us in the opening hymn, and asked the audience to be seated. "Before we go any farther," he said, "I want you to know how proud I am to have my kids here this morning. My daughter Judi and her husband have flown here all the way from Mexico City, my son Jimbo has come all the way from Ecuador and my son Steve has come all the way from California. Let's give them a hearty Baptist welcome." He asked us to stand. Everyone applauded. It was one of Dad's finest moments.

He asked me why I had grown a beard. It was the height of the hippie era in the mid-70's and he associated beards with hippies. For Mom and Dad, it was also associated with my loss of faith, for I had started growing it the day Marilyn left. I told my folks that I had a lot of hippie friends, but they would laugh if they knew he was worried about me becoming one of them. They thought of me as a hard-driving businessman, "establishment" all the way, whose primary virtues were that I hired a lot of hippies and didn't wear a coat and tie. I told Dad the reason I didn't wear a tie was simply because I had gotten sick of that noose around my neck during my seven years as a missionary and sales manager. One of the primary advantages of having my own business was that I could at last dress comfortably. And as for the beard, why that had nothing to do with hippie stuff. I had wanted one ever since I was nine years old, when I admired the beard sported by missionary Dave Cooper in the jungles of Ecuador. That explanation relaxed Dad somewhat, but he still looked askance at my whiskers.

One day he told Mom, "Wilda, we may not see Steve come to the feet of Christ during our lifetime, but someday he will. We have the Lord's promise. We're standing on a platform of faith."

Mom replied, "Yes, I know we're on that platform but right

now it feels pretty wobbly. I'm afraid it might collapse and we'll go down with it."

"We must believe, Wilda honey, because we raised our children in the nurture and admonition of the Lord. Let's claim the promise in Proverbs 22:6: 'Train up a child in the way he should go: and when he is old, he will not depart from it.' This is a time of trial, but we will come through it."

Although they questioned themselves, I never felt Dad and Mom had done anything wrong in the way they brought us up. No two parents could have given their children a richer feast of biblical knowledge, nor could they have exemplified it any better in their lives. They showered us with love, kindness, spiritual teaching, and moral leadership. My struggles with the faith were no reflection of any deficiency in the way they reared me. It saddened me that they felt so burdened and troubled, but I could not trump up some belief just to make them happy.

All that changed after 1975. It was a time of deep satisfaction for Dad. In his view, his elder son was once again "right with God." The "prodigal son had returned," and all was well. The ultimate fulfillment for him, I suppose, would have been for me to go into full-time Christian service. He never pressured me that way but occasionally I would get a hint of his deeper longings. For example, once he listened to a cassette tape of a rousing speech I had given to the 250 salespeople who worked for our company. I compared the salesman out in his territory with the gladiator in the arena, and Dad listened with pride to each word, especially savoring the enthusiastic applause at the end of my speech. After congratulating me, he said, "Boy, I can just see you using your talents in the pulpit."

Although I was not in the Christian ministry, there were interesting parallels in the careers of both father and son. We had both left Ecuador, the land we loved, and returned to the United States. We both had a tendency to move on, to start something new, not to do the same thing very long. During the late 1970's, both Dad and I were launching new ventures, each in his own field. Dad pastored a series of churches, in each case taking over a church that was sputtering along, split with dissension, attendance declining, and spiritual life downcast. Each time, the Bob Savage magic touch reinvigorated the church. Through much prayer and hard work, attendance soared, alienated Christians started loving each other again, and hundreds of people accepted Christ.

Meanwhile, I was launching a new business, writing a book on how to start a "mom-and-pop" business, composing a newsletter, and trying to establish myself as a genuine "back-to-the-earth" soul. Barrie and I moved with Bill and Allison to Vermont, where we bought a 54-acre farm, a cow, some chickens, and a couple of horses. We grew our own vegetables, heated our house with wood, and plunged ourselves into the life of small-town New England. I called on schools in New England, talking to them about raising money by selling our jewelry. Barrie handled the shipping and customer service. It was a mom-and-pop, out-of-the-garage venture.

Dad was fascinated. Not only was he intrigued with our way of life, but was captivated with the thought that the Savage family had come full circle. Various Savages had lived in New England dating way back to John Savage who was born in New Hampshire in 1782. One century later, Dad's grandparents, Lucy and Hubbard, had been born in New Hampshire, but had moved to Nebraska, then Colorado, to establish their homestead. Dad's uncle Hubbard had moved all the way West, to California, and I had just lived in California for four years. Now I was back in New England, and Dad felt it was quite fitting.

Mom's health was not good. She had always been afflicted with a series of minor ailments, and good "melancholic" that she was, did not mind admitting she was a genuine hypochondriac. Colds, headaches, ulcers, they came and went. But now she got smitten with two things far more severe: a stroke and Parkinson's disease. The stroke was mild, and she recovered within a few weeks, but it made her move with greater caution. The Parkinson's disease was kept under control by the wonder drug "L-dopa." Although it did not debilitate her, it slowed her motor responses, so she walked slowly. For many months she did not play the piano or organ.

Dad was supportive and sympathetic, but impatient. He wanted her to get back to her piano playing. After several months, she tried to play. It sounded good to Dad, but Mom was discouraged as her light easy touch was gone. She gradually got back into accompanying the congregation, but tried to get other pianists in the church to take over the heavier duties.

Although Mom was physically weakened, her smile was as quick as ever and her sense of humor was still light-hearted. For awhile she had a hard time smiling because of the mask-like effect of Parkinson's, but eventually her face relaxed and she was able to cope remarkably well despite the seriousness of her disease. Her life became more sedentary, and she took great pleasure in watching all the Christian television shows, including Billy Graham, the 700 Club, Robert Schuller, Jimmy Swaggart, and PTL with Jim and Tammy Bakker. Yes, she was one of those "little old ladies" who loved Jim and Tammy and sent them a check each month. Even after their tragic downfall in 1986, she never quit loving them.

In October, 1975, the Church of the Divine Redeemer in Quito celebrated its 25th anniversary and invited Dad to return as guest speaker for a two-week series of meetings. Mom did not feel she could handle the trip and stayed in Muskegon. Barrie and I flew to Quito with him to celebrate the event. My sister, Judi, also joined us. Her husband and son (big Alex and little Alex) were back in Mexico City. The great pea-green Braniff Boeing 707 four-engine jet made the trip from Miami to Quito non-stop in a mere four hours, about the same as flying from Chicago to San Francisco. Both Dad and I shook our heads in wonder as we thought back to the DC-3 days when it took fourteen long hours to hop from Quito to Cali to Panama to Miami. As the huge jet flew down the western coast of South America I was disappointed that I could not see the continent's edge, for a layer of clouds covered the land. Then we began our descent into Quito and dipped below the cloud layer at about 15,000 feet. The majestic Andes Mountains leaped into the little window and I leaned to one side so Barrie could share the view and so I could shake the tears out of my eyes.

It had been ten years since I had left Ecuador for my job in Nashville, and I was eager to introduce Barrie to this special land, and to my extended family of missionary "uncles" and "aunts."

I was apprehensive, for I had felt a great gulf grow between me and my past. Ever since Marilyn and I had separated, I had lost almost all contact with the extensive network of missionaries and Ecuadorian Christians who had been such an all-encompassing part of my childhood and early adulthood. I figured they had rejected me, and often pictured them in dreams, wagging their fingers at me, pointing, accusing, judging, disgusted, disappointed. I knew how they talked about other people who had strayed away from the Lord, and reckoned they had been saying equally harsh things about me.

I could not have been more mistaken. My brother Jimbo met us at the airport, along with my uncle and aunt, Helen and Dick Broach, and their children, Tim and Peggy. (Their oldest two children, Rickie Lou and Paul, were in college in the United States) They took us promptly to a huge welcoming party gathered at the home of Abe and Marj VanDerPuy, on the northern end of Quito, overlooking the great Llano Grande valley. It was an outdoor reception and over 200 people had gathered. Ten years earlier, when I had left, I had hugged the passionate Ecuadorians and shaken hands with the reserved missionaries. This time, something was different, for missionaries no longer hesitated to throw their arms around each other. They offered their open arms to me and I hugged them all. I had worried they might be wary of Barrie for I had left ten years earlier with Marilyn, and they all knew her. But once again they allayed my fears for they were warm and loving to Barrie and enveloped her with enthusiasm and grace.

Later I remarked to Dad, "Missionaries didn't used to hug each other, did they?"

"Nope!" he said, emphatically.

"What changed it?" I wondered.

"Marj VanDerPuy," replied Dad.

The hugging phenomenon was surely more complex than that, but Marj was indeed one of the warmest-hearted people I had ever known. I had first met her when I was ten, when her name was Marj Saint, wife of missionary pilot Nate Saint, in Shell Mera. After Nate was killed by the Aucas, and Dolores VanDerPuy died of cancer, it was a lovely event when Abe and Marj joined their lives together. Over the years, Abe had succeeded Clarence Jones as president of the World Radio Missionary Fellowship, and Marj had become its heart.

Our time in Ecuador was busy. We spent many evenings attending the special meetings at the Church of the Divine Redeemer, listening to Dad preach. His Spanish was still excellent, and only once did he flounder, looking for the right word. He wanted to describe an aerosal spray can, and described it to the audience, with his thumb pressing down on the button and his tongue hissing out the sound of the spray. In unison, the audience told him the word: "*Eh-spray.*" I laughed, for I had many Puerto Rican and Mexican friends who scattered Anglicized words into their Spanish conversation, but it was the first time I had heard such corrupted Spanish in the elegant and formal city of Quito. My old Spanish teacher, Señorita Arboleda, would have writhed in dismay.

Barrie and I left Dad and took a trip to the jungles, flying on the fine old DC-3 owned by the Wycliffe Bible Translators. We traveled to a part of the jungle I had never visited, the northern jungles, not far from Auca country. We spent two days at the lovely jungle mission station at Limoncocha, then took a four-hour canoe trip up the mile-wide Napo River, arriving at the frontier town of Coca.

Oil had been discovered in Ecuador since the time we had left, and Coca was a boom town. Streets were muddy, everything was in chaos, but there was an electric spirit of energy and enthusiasm. We got a room above the little store and bar, and tried to sleep as music played all night out in the streets. Our walls were made of thatched bamboo, so light and sound streamed through without interruption. I eventually fell asleep but Barrie lay awake all night, convinced the gruesome bug she saw on the bamboo wall would soon crawl over her body. She kept an eye on the varmint all night long.

When we returned to Quito, Dad was wrapping up his campaign, already apprehensive about saying goodbye again. He confided in us, "When these folks said goodbye to Wilda and me ten years ago, I didn't think I'd ever be able to go through something like that again. I wish I could sort of sneak out of town."

Barrie and I did not stay to share in Dad's torment, but left for the coast, riding on the train. I had shown Barrie the mountains and the jungle. Now I wanted her to see the coast. But most of all, I wanted her to have the incredible experience of riding the train down the western slopes of the Andes. Engineers from Europe and the United States had told the Ecuadorians that the grades were too steep and a railroad could not be built. The biggest trouble spot was *"La Nariz del Diablo"* (The Devil's Nose). It was almost a sheer cliff, several miles wide and three thousand feet high. The imaginative Ecuadorians had ignored the common wisdom and had designed a switchback, whereby the train went forward for a few miles, then switched rails, and went backwords, descending another thousand feet. Finally, it switched again, went forward, to the valley below.

All this time Barrie and I had the best view of all—sitting on top of the baggage. She was game, but I noticed she looked straight ahead, not down, as the train switched back and forth and inched down the steep rails.

For Barrie and me, the departure from Ecuador was quiet. We

simply boarded a plane in Guayaquil and flew back to Miami. But Dad could not get away so easily. Once again, a huge crowd gathered at the airport to sing and hug farewells. It was not as sad for Dad as their big departure nine years earlier. It was wrenching, nevertheless, and as the doors of the plane closed, he could not restrain his tears. Yes, he had a pastor's heart, and he was happy in his work in the States. But that magical land of Ecuador could never be matched by any other place in the world, and no ministry could ever again be as colorful, exciting, and passionate as those momentous 26 years of missionary service.

Back in the States, Dad was always eager for the family to get together and nothing pleased him more than when all his children and grandchildren were together under one roof. He always organized us into a choir. Barrie and I had five children between us: Bill, Cyndi, Allison, Lance, and Matt. Carol and Jim had two, born in Nigeria, Shari and Dan. Judi and Alex had Alexito and Elenita, born in Mexico City.

Jimbo, now in his late 20's, was one of the most eligible bachelors in Western Michigan. For our family, he was lead guitarist, court jester, and good buddy to all. For me, he was my best friend. Just as Dad had considered his brother Jim his closest pal, so my brother Jim was mine. I felt more relaxed with him than anyone in the world except Barrie. We understood each other without explanation, often had the same doubts, both kept searching for answers. Jimbo always made me laugh but I also saw his serious side more than many people did. Although he was ten years younger, we enjoyed the same music, games, and conversation. I often envied him for he was loose and easy whereas I was driven and tense. I told him, "All the obsessions of generations of Savages have come down on my shoulders. How would you like to have a few?" He grinned, picked up his guitar, and played a tune by Cat Stevens.

Dad gloried in his nine grandchildren. For Christmas one year we gave him a silk-screened tie with the names of all nine and he wore it like a proud peacock, strutting around, bragging to everyone. Usually he had a good sense of timing, read his audience well, and kept most conversations brief. But when it came to his grandkids, he lost perspective, and talked about them until everyone's eyes glazed over.

His belly made for great comedy when he'd entertain us by singing "Shortnin' Bread." At each family gathering, we'd always ask him to sing the old song and he was always happy to perform. Mom would play the piano. They were like an old vaudeville act, with Mom plinking the keys and Dad blustering out the words:

"Mammy's little baby loves shortnin', shortnin', Mammy's little baby loves shortnin' bread..."

As he sang he merrily rubbed his protruding abdomen with great enthusiasm and feeling.

Dad always got us up on the platform to sing. He introduced us as the "Savage tribe." But it was not restricted to us Savages. Anybody willing to open his mouth and "make a joyful noise unto the Lord" was welcome to sing in public. If other people wanted to come and sing with the Savage tribe, that was fine; they were always made to feel part of the family. When our family sang, I often wondered if we were enjoying it more than the audience, but those good long-suffering folks from Michigan always told us they liked it. We had all learned to harmonize and carry parts as we were growing up, so even an impromptu sing-along by the Savages turned out to be a hearty feast of song.

One time we had a massive family reunion to celebrate the 50th anniversary of Maranatha Bible Conference. As usual, Dad got us all up on the platform and told the audience about each of his children, grandchildren, nephews, and nieces. He told the Maranatha crowd which church each of us attended, even admitting that his daughter Carol and her family were

Presbyterians. When he got to me, however, he gulped and said, "Now, here's my son Steve and his wife Barrie. I don't think you'd even want to hear about the church they go to."

I blurted out, "He can't even pronounce Episcopalian!" And everybody laughed.

Later I wondered if Dad was genuinely embarrassed that I had become an Episcopalian and asked him. He said no, he was happy for me to be in any church as long as I was in fellowship with the Lord. I think way-down deep he would have been happier if we had all been Baptists, but was always supportive in our spiritual choices.

Dad had many little techniques for making people feel special. One was to look at you square in the eye, eyebrows raised with delight, big grin. Then he'd poke his finger in your belly and exclaim, "I know ya'!"

Whenever we ended a visit to Muskegon, the farewell was as festive as the hello. Dad would lead in prayer and then announce, "Huggin' time! Huggin' time!" and we'd all gather each other into enormous bear hugs. Then he'd look at each of us in the eye and say: "Three P's and an L. I'm proud of you, praying for you, and praising God for you. And I love you." Usually I flew away in my airplane. As my Cessna taxied out to the runway, he and Mom would stand, waving, waving, waving, until car or airplane was out of sight. Whenever I left in my plane, I always made it a point to take off, then return over the parking lot and wave my wings as they waved their arms.

During his years as pastor in Michigan, Mom and Dad often entertained their former missionary colleagues from Ecuador. One day Lois Hatt Vásconez came for a visit. When she had first arrived in Ecuador, back in the '50s, she was single. She fell in love with Oswaldo Vásconez, a control operator at HCJB. The mission policy was harsh: if a single missionary woman got married, she left the mission. Dad was field director at the time and spent many hours counselling Lois, urging her to stay with the mission, which, by default, meant not marrying Oswaldo. She chose to marry Oswaldo, and although she had to resign from the mission, she continued to help on HCJB programs with her virtuoso organ, piano, singing, composing, arranging, and choir-directing skills. Her talent was phenomenal; indeed, she had been well-known in evangelical circles in the States before she came to Ecuador, and could have had a successful career back "home."

Without her missionary support, she and Oswaldo struggled. Dad became aware of this, and raised a special fund among the missionaries to give her some financial help. They gladly gave, as they treasured Lois as a friend and valued her as a top-notch radio musician. Thus, even though she was not officially with the mission, she was able to carry on the ministry to which she had been called.

Now, many years later in Muskegon, Michigan, as Lois chatted with Mom and Dad, she was intrigued when Dad said, "Lois, please come into my office. There's something I want to talk with you about." Apprehensive, she wondered if she had done something wrong. Dad looked her in the eye and declared, "Lois, I was wrong about you and Oswaldo. You've had a strong marriage, a lovely family, a wonderful testimony for the Lord." It had been 25 years since Dad had tried to talk her out of that marriage. He was 62 years old and not above apologizing.

Nor was he above changing his attitude toward Roman Catholics. After the joint wedding with Father Rosas in Mexico City for Judi and Alex, he was willing to admit that Catholics could be saved. Mistaken in their theology, yes, but saved nevertheless, as long as they had indeed accepted Christ in their hearts.

In 1978, I witnessed an event that dramatized how far both Catholics and Protestants had come. It specifically involved my dad. Pope John Paul XXIII made his first pilgrimage to the United States. The whole country was excited by the event and it consumed a major part of the nightly news. One night I was watching television and saw a recap of his activities that day.

Madison Square Garden was packed with 40,000 people and the Pope was going around the arena in his "Popemobile." Everybody was waving, clapping, and cheering. Suddenly they burst into song, and the song was in Spanish. I sat up straight, transfixed, because it was an evangelical chorus Dad had discovered and published back in 1953. The entire crowd of English-speaking Roman Catholics was singing the chorus *"Alabaré"* ("I will Praise"). They sang it with gusto, everybody knew all the words. The entire Garden rocked with sound.

How in the world, I wondered, as I wiped a tear off my cheek, had these Roman Catholics learned this chorus, and how had it become so popular?

The very next day I made a sales call to a Roman Catholic school in New Jersey. I asked one of the nuns if she had been at Madison Square Garden the night before.

"Oh yes!" she exclaimed. "It was marvelous!"

"I was intrigued with that song you sang in Spanish," I told her. "Where did that come from, anyway?"

"I don't know. They say it's a song composed by some unknown author in South America."

She was right. The author is still unknown to this day, but it was Bob Savage who heard that song in Puerto Rico when he was there on an evangelistic campaign in 1953. He published it in his book *Adelante Juventud*, and helped it become popular on his radio programs, never imagining that one day, years later, thousands would sing it for the Pope.

Back in 1968, when Dad first took over the pastorate of Dalton Baptist Church, right after returning from Ecuador, he challenged its members to increase their attendance, invigorate the youth and get on fire for the Lord. Within a year, attendance had climbed to over 600 and by the time he finished his pastorate, crowds of over 700, sometimes 800, came every Sunday. A new youth center was built.

The Board of Deacons voted to paint the gym and Dad rolled

up his sleeves to help in the work. Although he had often used a paint brush, he was not familiar with a paint roller. Since that was the only tool available, he gamely picked one up and started rolling vigorously, splashing paint all over the gym and himself. Finally, deacon Cloyde Shirk showed him how to roll the roller in the pan to remove excess paint. Everyone laughed, and Dad laughed the loudest.

When Dad arrived in the States, he bought a pair of cowboy boots. It was the first pair he had ever owned and he liked them so much he bought a few more. For the rest of his ministry, his cowboy boots became a trademark. He wore them with his formal suits as well as casual clothes. The boots were particularily effective as he led singing, for he was a real "foot-stompin'" song leader. When he wanted the audience to belt it out real loud, he banged that cowboy heel onto the platform and commanded, "Now let's really sing!"

At the end of each year, the board of deacons offered him a raise in salary. He declined each time, saying, "I have plenty to live on. Put it where it can be better used." His salary was $1,000 a month in 1978. He gave $300 of that to missions. Finally they persuaded him to take a raise, to $1,100. He gave the extra $100 to missions. When I talked about this with Dad's sister, Helen Broach, she told me, "My parents also gave at least 30 per cent of their income to the church. Both my dad and your dad were content with what they had. They make me think of the verse 'Godliness with contentment is great gain.'" (I Timothy 6:6)

As I was preparing this biography, I came across Dad's list of monthly contributions. I had never seen it while he was alive, for he kept his generosity to himself, never bragging. His gifts included several missionaries as well as the church he was pastoring.

Dad and Mom also contributed to several radio and television ministries, not only HCJB but the Billy Graham Association and the 700 Club. At one time they had given to the PTL club, but Dad had drawn a strong and heavy line through that one. When it became apparent that Jim and Tammy Bakker had misused God's money, Dad was righteously indignant. Mom was broken-hearted.

His list also included many Latin American evangelists and preachers. He continued to contribute to the education of several young and promising Ecuadorians, encouraging them to attend seminary and return to Ecuador as pastors and missionaries. But the most touching part was his list of individuals in South America whom he had never forgotten, like Vicente Vieira, whom Dad had encouraged to go into the ministry. Sara de Colom, widow of Dad's dear friend, the Guatemalan song-writer Alfredo Colom, got a letter and a check from Dad every month. The list goes on.

During this time Dad developed a prayer list with 600 names on it. Every day he prayed for 60 individuals by name. Every ten days, he got through the entire list. The people on his list not only included his family and church members, but the missionaries at HCJB, colleagues at Maranatha, evangelical leaders like Billy Graham and Bob Cook, and politicians ranging from Ronald Reagan to Ted Kennedy. He prayed for world-famous leaders from Margaret Thatcher to Muhammar Khadafy. He prayed for my business partners, Mike Rippey and Dennis Snyder. But most of all he prayed for people that most have never heard of—folks in Ecuador whom he had known and loved: Luis Chicaiza and Marianita Morales, men and women in the States whom he had pastored, people he had bumped into at a grocery store or a gas station.

These were his daily prayers. But there were always the spontaneous prayers as well. One of his church members, Marv Richards, came to install an air conditioner in their home. As soon as the installation was complete, Dad said, "OK, Marv, let's have a word of prayer." Then he proceeded to thank the Lord for the comfort Wilda would receive from the unit. He precisely practiced the verse in Scripture that said "In everything give thanks."

At his services, he wanted everyone to capture his vision of joy in the Lord. He always gave visitors a cordial welcome and encouraged the members of the church to invite their friends. "If a visitor can receive a better welcome at the Alibi Bar than at Dalton Baptist Church then something is wrong!"

He wanted everyone else to be just as joyful as he was. He'd tell them at the end of the service, "You aren't allowed to leave until you've shaken hands with at least five people."

Most of the members loved his simple, direct sermons, but once a member criticized him, saying that his messages were not deep enough. His reply, "Put the food on the lowest shelf so the children can reach it, and you will be sure everyone gets some."

His approach to personal evangelism was simple and direct. He would often say, "To be sure of getting to heaven you must have the right ticket. Where is your train bound?"

On Friday afternoons, he met for an hour with five teen-age boys in Cloyde Shirk's home, singing songs and choruses with them. When Cloyde mentioned to Mom that he probably had more important things to do, she assured him, "Oh, he just loves to do things like that."

He loved the folks at Dalton and often said to them from the pulpit, "My oh my, anyone could be pastor here at Dalton. The people are all generous and warm-hearted and the women are the best cooks to be found anywhere."

He was always reluctant to take a vacation. A few days at a time was usually all he would take. His excuse: "Where can I find better people and better fellowship than at Dalton?" When he did slip away for a quick get-away he and Mom were content to check into a Motel 6, just 20 or 30 miles from home, where they would spend their days reading Christian books. It was a relief to be away from the telephone.

Meanwhile he continued to work on his Spanish chorus books. He still had a huge collection of unpublished hymns, and continued to produce them from his distant vantage point in the north. He maintained close contact with his former colleagues.

Missionaries came to visit Mom and Dad whenever they were in Michigan and kept them up-to-date on what was happening in the field. Dad kept up correspondence with many of the Ecuadorian pastors with whom he had worked.

After 8 years at Dalton, he received an invitation to take over the pastorate at Haslett Baptist Church in Haslett, Michigan. It was a tough decision. He could have stayed indefinitely at Dalton. The congregation was large and still growing. He and Mom were loved by the church members, who begged them to stay on.

But Dad felt he had accomplished his mission at that church, and there was a new challenge at Haslett. The church there had been split in acrimonious strife and Dad's job was to heal the wounds. The company of believers at Haslett had dwindled to only 150, a paltry band compared to the vigorous 800 at Dalton. But Dad saw a special ministry there and accepted the challenge. Within a year Haslett won the Sunday School Contest for Baptist General Conference churches in Michigan. The sense of gloom that had oppressed the membership had been transformed into an exciting atmosphere of joy and worship. Dad attracted all kinds of people to the church, from rugged blue-collar folk of Lansing to sophisticated professors at Michigan State University. All enjoyed his loving humor, incisive sermons, zest for life, and constant prodding to make sure they all rejoiced in Christ.

His life was exuberant. All was well with his family and his church. He was doing what he loved best—pastoring a church. The church was growing. The sky was bright.

Then cancer struck him.

Dad called to give us the news. "Hey, Steve, got a little problem here. No big deal, just a spot of cancer on my prostate. I don't want anyone to make a fuss about it, because the doctors think they can get rid of it with some radiation treatments."

I could not let it go that easily. I probed and quizzed him about all details: bloodcount, exact description of the cancer, treatment, and prognosis. He answered my questions but then skipped away from the issue saying, "Now look, let's just keep this in the family, so we won't worry the folks in the church. I'm sure it's going to be OK, but let's get one thing straight. If the Lord wants to take me home, that's fine. Let's not fret. I'm rejoicing and want you to rejoice as well." He was 64.

Mom called a day later while Dad was at the church. She wanted to talk about it in more detail. She didn't feel nearly as cheerful as Dad; she was heavy-hearted and deeply worried. She said, "I don't want to alarm you but don't want you to take it lightly either. It's cancer, no matter how you talk about it."

From the beginning, I appreciated the way Dad was able to say the dreaded word "cancer." It was a hush-hush word for some, but for Dad it was just a descriptive term and he didn't mind saying it out loud.

I wrote him: "Well, Dad, I don't know if you'll arrive in heaven in six months or twenty years, but one thing's for sure. It'll be a noisy, triumphant arrival. I can imagine Bob Savage at the gates of heaven greeting Peter and the apostles with your famous loud 'let me shake your noble hand!' Then the word will spread around heaven and they're going to shout 'He's here! Bob Savage is here!' Then they'll laugh and clap and shout and sing, thousands and tens of thousands, angels and archangels, saints and sinners, the redeemed from all the ages, they'll sing and sing, rejoicing as Bob joins the heavenly throng."

A few weeks later, I flew out to Michigan to visit my folks and Dad told me how much my letter had meant to him. I told him, "Well, I've had a lot of doubts about the Christian faith over the years, but that's one scene that is crystal clear in my mind. I know that's the way your arrival in heaven is going to be."

Then a more humorous thought hit me: "I can see it right now. There will be 5,000 sopranos, 5,000 altos, and 5,000 tenors. It'll be a great chorus."

"What about the basses?" asked Mom.

"Basses? No problem. Dad will sing bass!" I replied.

Dad roared, confirming once again that his single voice would be a fine match for 15,000.

Over the next few weeks, Dad took 37 linear accelerator radiation treatments, then took another test. The urologist who had diagnosed his prostate cancer reported, "There is no clinical evidence of any disease."

"Praise the Lord!" whooped Dad, as his voice reverberated down the hospital corridors. "He wants me to serve Him a little longer. Amen. Amen. Amen." Even the dour urologist could not suppress a smile.

Meanwhile, tensions arose at Haslett Baptist Church. At issue: the "Charismatics." Several folks in the church had received the "baptism of the Holy Spirit," accompanied by the "gift of tongues." These modern-day charismatics in Dad's church were bubbling over with exuberant joy, and tried to encourage others to receive the Holy Spirit's baptism and the gifts that came with it. Many traditional Baptists resisted, thinking it was merely an emotional experience. Dad wanted them all to worship together, as he considered them all brothers in the Lord. Many did not agree. Even the charms of the effervescent Bob Savage were not enough to convince some of the members. Eventually most of the Charismatics either left to join a church where the practice was common, or kept the experience quietly to themselves. Dad grieved over this, never understanding why Christians couldn't "simply get along with each other and praise the Lord together."

Dad had been dealing with the Charismatic movement for several years, both in South America and the United States. The Pentecostals were the largest "charismatic" denomination in South America. Among Protestants in South America, the dilemma had arisen in the early 1960s as the Pentecostal movement swept the continent and scored staggering successes way beyond anything to date. The Pentecostals achieved results that other missionaries had not been able to realize in over 100 years of missionary work. Within a few short years thousands of new converts were baptized into the Christian faith through efforts of Pentecostal missionaries. The exuberance and spontaneity of Pentecostal worship struck a responsive chord in the Latin soul.

Whereas one faithful "old-guard" missionary might have labored for 60 or 70 years to gain one or two converts, the Pentecostal missionary would be enjoying the gratification of leading to Christ several converts almost every day. The old-line missionaries looked at this phenomenon with mixed feelings.

Discussion about these issues had raged through the missionary community. Some missions had felt compelled to put out "position papers" describing where they stood on the issue, and several missions carefully distanced themselves from the movement. HCJB had tried to stay neutral during the time Dad was there.

Both Mom and Dad had wide open minds about the issue and had many long conversations with their Pentecostal friends. While they were still in Ecuador, they prayed at great length that they would have the right attitude about the baptism of the Holy Spirit. They agreed together they would like to receive the Holy Spirit's baptism and prayed with some Pentecostal missionaries. They asked the Lord to give them the baptism. "Oh Lord," prayed Dad, as he knelt and the Pentecostal missionaries laid their hands on his head, "fill me with Thy Holy Spirit and let me speak in other tongues, if it be Thy will, to declare Thy praise." Nothing happened. Neither Mom nor Dad received the gift of tongues. The Pentecostal missionaries were disappointed. Dad was not. He said, "The Bible says there are many gifts of the Spirit. Speaking in tongues is one, but not the only one. If the Lord chooses to give me the gift of tongues, I would love to receive that gift. But in the meantime, He has not chosen to bestow it on me, so I'm happy the way I am."

Occasionally he wondered if he had been remiss. Perhaps he hadn't "prayed hard enough." Perhaps he hadn't had enough faith. Perhaps he hadn't been willing to "let go."

I cannot imagine anyone who exemplified the gifts of the Holy Spirit more than Dad. He may not have been blessed with the gift of tongues, but if anyone was ever baptized by the Holy Spirit, it was Bob Savage. And if he never spoke in "tongues" his tongue certainly praised God with as much ecstasy as any Charismatic Christian ever had. His tongue was a vibrant instrument of constant praise, not only in his preaching and singing, but in his daily life. When I thought of Dad, I often thought of Galations 5:22: "The fruit of the Spirit is love, joy, peace, longsuffering, gentleness, goodness, faith." No words could better describe Bob Savage's qualities and no one ever lived with a more crystallized consciousness of the Holy Spirit.

In 1980, my sister Carol and her family returned from Nigeria, after 13 years of service with the Sudan Interior Mission. Her husband, Jim Plueddemann, had received his Ph.D. in education during their quadrennial furloughs, and had been offered a professorship at the Wheaton Graduate School. It was not an easy decision. They loved Nigeria, and their ministry was far reaching. Jim and Carol were both involved with Christian Education, training Nigerians to teach others about the gospel. Their two children, Shari and Dan, had been born in Jos, a city in the northern highlands of the country. Mom and Judi had visited them in 1970. Barrie and I spent two weeks with them in 1976.

Dad had never visited them in Nigeria, but had followed their ministry with avid interest. Every four years, when the Plueddemanns came to the States for their one-year furlough, Dad spent a great deal of time with his daughter, son-in-law and two grandchildren. Jim became as close to Dad as his own two sons, closer in some ways, because he and Dad were on the same wavelength on theological issues. In Jim and Carol, Dad was able to cherish the satisfaction and joy of a continuing missionary tradition in our family. Although he was enthusiastic about their ministry in Nigeria, he was equally excited about their return to the United States. He could understand it, for he too had received his own call "back to the homeland" after years of fruitful and productive missionary service.

When Barrie and I traveled to Nigeria, I told Carol: "You

know, I used to think the smelliest place on earth was the public bathroom at the bus station in Ambato, Ecuador. Now that I've smelled the streets of Jos and Kano, I think I'll have to change my mind!" She laughed. Then she frowned. "It's sad to realize that a hundred years ago, these folks lived in little tribal villages, tidy, well-swept, clean. They were part of the land. Garbage could be thrown into a ditch and would soon become absorbed by the soil. Now, they've been thrust into these huge cities in the last two generations, and they're just not ready for it." Bless her heart, I thought, she was revolted by sewage running through the streets, just like any tourist, but she was totally different in her interpretation because she loved these folks and understood them.

I found myself envying Carol and Jim. I admired their intellects and enjoyed the probing theological discussions that lasted late every evening. What I envied was their certainty about their mission, their earnestness in carrying out the Great Commission. It seemed so right, so natural, for them to be there serving the Lord. It was a fulfillment of all my father and grandfather had ever dreamed.

When I observed that Carol was the only one of the four that had "fit" the mold, she hastened to tell me she didn't want to be considered a "goodie-goodie."

"No way!" I reassured her. "After all the grief you caused me while we were growing up, no amount of goodness will ever atone!"

On a more serious note, I told her I admired her devotion to God and to His work, and wished I could be as dedicated. Rather than thinking of her as a "goody two-shoes" I respected her as someone in command of herself, profound in her faith, clear in her reasoning.

Carol and I had not seen much of each other since I had left Ecuador at age 17. These two weeks gave us a closeness we had never experienced, for instead of two fighting children, we were two seasoned adults. We discovered each other in new ways while reminiscing with merry laughter about our youth in Ecuador.

As we observed the Plueddemanns in Nigeria, we were impressed with how relaxed they were with the Hausa people, and how fluently they spoke the language. I smiled to myself when I thought of Grandma Savage's conviction that Carol belonged in South America. She had become a part of Africa. It was as hard to imagine the Plueddemanns leaving Nigeria as it had been to imagine the Savages leaving Ecuador. But the signals were clear in each case. They left home to come home.

Dad had the most profound respect for Carol and Jim, not only for their ministry but for the way they conducted their personal lives. He once remarked, "When it comes to spirituality, I believe Carol is more devoted than her parents."

In 1980, the same year the Plueddemanns returned from Nigeria, a new opportunity opened for me. Barrie and I moved back to California, as I started a new business with two long-time associates: Mike Rippey and Dennis Snyder. We formed a marketing company called Institutional Financing Services whose purpose was to help schools raise money by selling our fashion jewelry.

Barrie's son Bill was a student at Daniel Webster College in Nashua, New Hampshire. Her daughter, Allison, and my daughter, Cyndi, were both juniors in high school and came to California with us, where they enrolled in the Athenian School, a private school across the street from our home, nestled in the foothills of Mt. Diablo, 30 miles east of San Francisco. My two sons, Lance and Matt, still lived with their mother in New Jersey.

A few months after we got settled, Mom and Dad flew out to visit us. While in California, Dad announced two exciting bits of news: First, his latest book *Pocket Prayers* had just been published by Tyndale and was enjoying brisk sales. The Billy Graham Association bought 170,000 to give to people who subscribed to "Decision" magazine. Second, was his surprise plan: "After 49 years of uninterrupted Gospel ministry, I'm going to follow the Old Testament pattern and celebrate a Year of Jubilee." His idea was not to retire, exactly, but to spend a year relaxing, for spiritual refreshment and physical renewal. He was genuinely excited about the idea, and went around the house singing the old Negro spiritual, "Jubilee, jubilee, yes I'm goin' to that happy jubilee."

His "year of jubilee" lasted three months. The Sunny Isle Baptist Church in St. Croix, Virgin Islands, needed a pastor to fill in for nine months while their regular pastor took a furlough in the United States. Dad, age 68, already restless, readily agreed, and embarked with Mom on a new adventure: ministering to a congregation of 400 enthusiastic, exuberant black Baptists. Dad had spent his life trying to get people to sing louder and more joyfully. At St. Croix he found a group that did it his way, instinctively. They sang with vivacity, even before Dad asked them to turn up the volume. Their gaiety matched his. Pastor and congregation took an instant liking to each other, and enjoyed their fellowship with lighthearted buoyancy.

Within three months, Dad had visited every home and knew every name. This was made clear to all at the Thanksgiving service. He asked everyone to come forward to relate one thing they were thankful for. Everyone was impressed to note that this pastor, who had been with them only a short time, introduced each person by name as he or she came up front to talk.

The folks at Sunny Isle loved Mom and Dad. They especially enjoyed his particular brand of down-home humor. One day Dad was preaching a sermon, getting quite intense. Suddenly he paused and told the story about a preacher who took his car to the garage and, hoping to get a good price on his repairs, told the mechanic, "You know, I'm just a poor preacher."

The mechanic replied, "Yes, I know. I heard you last Sunday."

The congregation roared with laughter. They were easy, relaxed, a joy for Dad, a tonic for Mom. They loved his sermon style, especially when he preached about Naaman, captain of the host of the king of Syria, who was afflicted with leprosy. The prophet Elisha told Naaman he could be cured of his disease if he would only go and wash in the River Jordan seven times. Naaman was insulted. Wash in the Jordan seven times? Couldn't the prophet simply smite away the leprosy? Or if he had to dunk himself in a river, why did it have to be the dirty Jordan? Couldn't it be one of his rivers back home, near Damascus, clean familiar rivers like the Abana or Pharpar?

Dad went on, dramatizing the arrogance of Captain Naaman, and his refusal to accept Elisha's simple prescription. It was a vivid sermon, but it got even more colorful. At last Naaman gave in, and agreed to bathe in the River Jordan. Dad held his nose, imitating the way Naaman dunked himself, with great distaste, down into the water, then up and out, spitting out a mouthful of water. As Dad acted out the drama, the congregation split their sides with merriment. After Naaman had gone under the water once, he examined his skin. Still leprous. Disgusted, he chided the prophet, describing him as a fraud. The captain's aide, however, pressed him to go down seven times as the prophet had instructed. Dad played it out seven times, down, up, spit, down, up, spit. The congregation laughed hilariously. The more they laughed, the more they egged Dad on, and he played his role, increasingly theatrical. At the end of the seventh dunk he came up, blew out his mouthful of water, examined his skin and whooped with joy, for it was skin like a baby's. No preacher ever made the story of Naaman come more alive. The Sunny Isle congregation rollicked in their pews.

Another memorable sermon was "Let the fire fall." Dad was talking about revival, and used the blackboard to put a few key words in capital letters to support his point:

> If the lukewarm people will FIRE UP, all dishonest people will CONFESS UP, all sleeping people will WAKE UP, and all disgruntled people will SWEETEN UP. Those who aren't speaking to each other will MAKE UP, those who are in the dumps will CHEER UP. The gossipers will SHUT UP and the dry bones will SHAKE UP. Church members will PRAY UP. Then we can and will have revival. O God, let the fire fall.

Revival came to one of the Sunny Isle families who had been out of fellowship with the church. Mom and Dad went to visit them. They discussed their spiritual condition and shared the main thing on their mind: their daughter Sally was going to be married, but not at Sunny Isle Baptist Church. They had chosen a country club as the location. Dad said, in his own loving but determined way, "Sally's wedding will have to be held at Sunny Isle."

"But we've already sent out invitations to everyone, announcing the location," they replied. "Also, Pastor Shirley, a United Pentecostal minister, has been chosen and we have less than three weeks."

"Let me have a list of the guests and their telephone numbers," said Dad, "and I will call each and every one of them and let them know of the place change. And Pastor Shirley will preside." The family was astonished. Not only was this pastor willing to make a few hundred phone calls, but was happy to invite the Pentecostal minister to his church. How could they refuse?

Sally had a beautiful church wedding and the family was restored to fellowship at Sunny Isle. All the members were impressed that Dad had allowed a Pentecostal minister to share his pulpit. They were subsequently treated to ministers from the Nazarenes, Free Will Baptists, and others. Dad was a wholehearted Baptist, but enjoyed fellowship with all those who proclaimed the same gospel he preached.

One night Dad sponsored a "holiest night" at Sunny Isle. He asked all the congregation to form a huge circle, holding hands. Then he asked for "popcorn" testimonies. His idea was to give the shy people courage to testify. "You don't have to give a long-winded testimony," he declared. "Just 'pop' it out like 'popcorn'." One woman said softly, "I love Jesus" and another said, a little louder, "Praise the Lord." Then a shy girl who had never spoken said, "Thank you Jesus." That gave everyone courage and the popping continued until everyone popped with at least one short testimony.

A few days later, a lady came to see him and said, "Pastor

Savage, I'm going to divorce my husband."

Dad said, "Give me one good reason."

"I can give you a hundred," she replied.

"Just start with one," he countered.

She thought through her list of grievances and realized that none would qualify as a "good reason" in Bob Savage's book. She sat and smiled and shook her head. She is still married today.

Over the years, Dad had baptized thousands of people in rivers, lakes, ponds, and baptismal pools. Now, he had a new opportunity. On Good Friday, he conducted a unique baptismal service out in the beautiful Caribbean Sea. Thirteen were baptized on that splendid morning, bringing baptisms to a total of 45 during his months at Sunny Isle.

As it came time for Mom and Dad to leave St. Croix, in a farewell service, one of the church members reflected on the personality of the man who had brought them great joy for a short time: "He was the kind of man who made you feel comfortable in his presence. It seemed like a ray of joy penetrated your being. He could transform your emotions, change your thinking, because there was a spiritual vibration in the man which made contact with you."

Dad's year of jubilee had indeed been jubilant, but hardly a time of rest. His time in St. Croix was over, but his ministry continued. Fair Oaks Baptist Church in Concord, California, invited him to serve as associate minister. Dad saw it as a great opportunity to minister as well as to be close to me. For Barrie and me, it was a time of rich enjoyment as we lived just a few miles from my parents and had frequent meals with them. I played tennis with Dad each week. We came to know each other better than at any time in our lives. Barrie and I occasionally attended the Baptist Church, when Dad was preaching. Mom and Dad also attended St. Paul's Episcopal Church a few times with us. Dad always commented on the amount of Scripture read, amazed that the Episcopalians read so much at every service.

Dad and I had long conversations about the events in my life that had caused him such anguish. He told me, "Well, Steve, I still preach against divorce, but I must confess that nothing makes me happier than to be around your lovely wife, Barrie. My, my, my, what a splendid woman she is! I love her dearly and praise God for her daily."

"Well, even though Barrie and I were each divorced before we met, and even though we're grateful we found each other, she and I don't believe in divorce either," I told him. "It's awful, hideous, and our biggest hope is that none of our five kids will ever go through it."

Barrie had several Morgan horses, and was becoming very good at driving carts and carriages. She won several ribbons at horse shows, culminating in the National Championship in antique carriage driving. One day she took Dad for a carriage drive, up the road that led from our house around the base of Mt. Diablo. He was enthralled, jabbering constantly about the magnificent scenery, the perfect weather, Barrie's skill at handling the reins, and the power of her splendid Morgan horse. He was always enthusiastic about people's careers and interests, and was particularly fascinated with Barrie's horses, quizzing her about every detail of her operation.

Barrie had a young stallion named "Don Quixote" and Dad took a shine to the high-spirited and flashy colt. Whenever he called Barrie on the phone, he'd ask in his booming voice, "And how's my good friend Don Quixote?" I think the main reason Dad was enraptured with this specific horse was because of his Spanish name.

It was a happy time. Then came bad news. Dad's cancer returned. This time it was in the lymph system. That sounded a lot more ominous to me than a single spot like the prostate, but as before, Dad was cheerful and carefree about it. He took the prescribed medication, and insisted that he felt no pain, discomfort, or hindrance in his activities. His legs were a bit swollen, but that was the only outward evidence of anything amiss. Anytime we tried to ask him about his cancer, he waved it off with a grand gesture, saying, "Aw shucks, it's not worth talking about. Let's talk about your business." He was always curious to know how my enterprise was going.

During the three years since we had moved to California, our company had grown rapidly and dramatically. We had moved locations twice, from 5,000 square feet to 15,000 square feet. Then we leased the adjacent building so we had 30,000 square feet. It was still not enough. We had to build our own facility. I took Mom and Dad out to our site in Benicia, 40 miles northeast of San Francisco, overlooking the Suisun Bay, with Mt. Diablo off on the horizon, the city of Concord lying between water and mountain. At that point, only the walls of our new building were up; the finishing work was still under way. The shell of the structure covered 65,000 square feet. He gazed at the edifice in wonder, shaking his head with awe as I told him how our sales had risen, more than doubling each year. He looked at the *Inc. Magazine* list of the "Top 500 fastest-growing privately held businesses." We were No. 31 that year. Always fascinated by statistics, he quizzed me about each detail of the business: number of salespeople around the nation (250), number of employees in Benicia (300), dollars in sales ($40,000,000). "Fine, fine, fine," he declared, "my, this is G-R-E-A-T! Amen!"

We all piled in the car to drive back across the Martinez bridge to Concord. Dad was in the back seat, nestled between Allison and Barrie. He began to talk, louder and louder, with increasing animation and excitement, babbling about our achievement until he was almost beside himself with rapture. Finally he was shouting, right there in the close confines of our car, "My son! My son! This is wonderful! That's my boy! He did it! Hear that, folks? That's my boy!" Yes, we folks in the car could hear all right. No problem. Our ears were ringing.

I was both embarrassed and pleased. Pleased, yes, I was pleased with Dad's enthusiasm and obvious approval of what I had done. But I was also nagged with a disturbing thought. I wondered way down deep, "Is he still disappointed? Wouldn't he have been even happier if I had taken him on a tour through a 65,000 square-foot missionary hospital or a 65,000 square-foot Bible institute, or a 65,000 square-foot missionary radio station?" These thoughts afflicted me, but I think they were my own problem. He never gave any hint of disapproval and his joy in my achievements was genuine.

Dad celebrated his 70th birthday while in California and told us he had just gotten another report from his urologist. The latest test for cancer: negative. "Praise the Lord!" we all declared and this time we all shouted almost as loudly as Dad. It was the second time he had been healed. It was now six years since his first cancer diagnosis. Those six years were some of the most productive of his life, for not only was he pastoring a series of churches, but putting the final touches on his "pocket" series of books. Already, *Pocket Prayers,* with "777 ways to pray for others," was a bestseller at nearly a quarter of a million copies. But Dad was busily assembling all the files of a lifetime of "sentence sermons." *Pocket Quips* came off the press with 777 quaint and quotable definitions. One of them, defining the future, described Dad's attitude about his cancer: "The future is as bright as the promises of God. We know not what the future holds, but we know who holds the future."

A few months later, *Pocket Wisdom* came out with 777 sentence sermons. Then came *Pocket Smiles* which Mom dubbed "777 moldy oldies." Tyndale agreed with her remark and put that comment right on the cover.

While Dad was working on his pocket books in California, I mentioned to him that I would enjoy a book full of prayers of praise. Always one to take the bait, he immediately went to work on it, and *Pocket Praise* joined the other pocket books a year later.

A year later, the Spanish version of *Pocket Prayers* was published. Judi in Mexico City had assisted him on the Spanish translation and he jabbered with joy about her "special translation ministry." That was his style. Anytime he could define something as a "ministry" he felt satisfied for it fit his idea of the way a Christian should conduct his life. When he thought of Judi, far off in Mexico City, he had often worried about her, wondering how he could get her involved in the work of the kingdom. The publication of the book afforded him that opportunity.

Dad's six-month stint with Fair Oaks Baptist Church came to an end and our happy interlude came to a close. Although the church offered him a full-time position, he had always considered it a temporary assignment. He told us, "We love to be near you guys, and we're fascinated with California, but we're Michiganders, lock, stock, and barrel." He and Mom returned to Muskegon, and he took over as interim pastor of the Mona Shores Baptist Church, just a few miles from Maranatha Bible Conference.

Shortly after Mom and Dad moved away from California, back to Michigan, I adopted Bill and Allison, Barrie's two children. Bill was now 20 and Allison 18 but I had looked after them since they were seven and five. We were all pleased with the court's wording of the legal document: "...grant this adoption in order to establish in law a relationship that exists in fact." At the end of the ten-minute session, the judge looked at us, smiled, and said, "You know, my day is usually pretty sad around here. It's nice to preside over such a happy occasion."

Dad was ecstatic. He had treated Allison and Bill as his own grandkids ever since Barrie and I had gotten married. Now, however, he could claim, "They're Savages now, and I'm proud they bear that name. Fine. Fine. Fine."

A few months later, Barrie and I also left California and returned east, all the way back to our beloved Vermont. I had found a replacement for my job of managing the nationwide sales force. It was fun building the company, but I didn't enjoy administering the bureaucracy we had created. Like Dad, I did not like corporate structures. He had left Ecuador to become what he enjoyed most: a pastor. I left California and went back to being what I enjoyed most: an entrepeneur. I still kept my ties with my company in California, but operated a separate "business development center" out of my home in Vermont. I tested new products and marketing ideas. Most of the ideas did not work, but the theory shared by Mike, Dennis, and me was: "if one idea out of ten works, that's all it takes."

Dad took a keen interest in my projects, and was supportive in my failures just as he had been in my successes. When I got discouraged, he gently reminded me that he had had his share of each in his lifetime.

Dad, now age 71, accepted another full-time pastorate at Evanston Avenue Baptist Church in Muskegon. Within seven months, the church experienced a 30 per cent increase in attendance with dozens of new members. After three "interim" assignments (Sunny Isle Baptist in St. Croix, Fair Oaks Baptist in California, and Mona Shores Baptist in Muskegon) he was once again doing what he loved best: pastoring a church full-time.

He was also on the Board of Directors at Maranatha, and served as program coordinator and vice president. Maranatha was facing some major decisions, and Dad's sparkling enthusiasm helped inspire the board to move forward boldly on a major program of renovations. When Grandpa Savage had founded the Conference in 1938, it had a family campground atmosphere. Many families camped, and others stayed in the rustic houses that were named after the countries where Maranatha had missionaries: Perú, Jordan, India, Tibet, Ecuador. By the early 1980's these buildings were rickety, and most modern American families no longer enjoyed staying in those types of lodging. Many old-timers who had come to Maranatha since the early days hated to see things change, but Dad encouraged them to proceed with construction of a brand new lodge, complete with air-conditioning, carpeting, and all the other luxuries that families of the 1980's demanded.

Although he supported the modernization program, he was also eager to provide simpler, less expensive lodging. It concerned

Dad that Maranatha could be afforded only by the well-to-do. He wanted options for everyone. He proposed some very simple structures to be called "Praise Cabins" but these were never endorsed by the rest of the board.

Dad's favorite spot at Maranatha was the prayer tower. Sitting snugly atop sturdy cement pilings that were driven deep into the shifting sands, the picture windows looked out through the soft Western Michigan pines, over the quiet beaches, out onto the blue lake. As Dad prayed, he could hear the lapping of waves a few hunded feet away. It was an atmosphere designed to bring a person right into the presence of the Almighty Creator.

The prayer tower had been one of Grandpa Savage's inspirations, and was the modern replacement of the old tottering prayer tower that had been there in Grandpa's days. It had been Grandpa's vision that those who attended Maranatha would pray in the prayer tower every morning, then attend services in the tabernacle. Those who participated in prayer and services enjoyed the full Maranatha experience.

Dad went up to the prayer tower daily, climbing the winding wooden steps that rose up from beach to tower. When he met with a group of worshipers, he encouraged them all to kneel. Baptists did not often kneel in their services, and some people were reluctant, preferring to pray in the sitting position. They could not sit long with Bob Savage egging them on, for he would announce assumptively, "Let's kneel and pray." He would quickly kneel, and his movement almost always drew the others down into a kneeling position.

Dad loved the meetings at the tabernacle, a building rich in gospel history. Most of America's famous evangelists had preached there at one time or another. Billy Graham had preached there several times in the early years of his ministry. Dad considered the unpolished wooden structure a temple, its sawdust trails a path to heaven, for here thousands of young people had accepted Christ or dedicated their lives to the gospel ministry.

Tedd Bryson was director of Maranatha Bible Conference. One

day, after a rousing meeting in the tabernacle, he met Dad in the little prayer room off to the side of the platform. Dad had led the singing, the audience had been responsive, and the sermon inspiring. Tedd was full of enthusiasm and exclaimed to Dad, "Wasn't that a good meeting?"

Dad replied, "Well, if you're gonna have a meetin' it might as well be a good one!"

17

A great roar went through Heaven

One summer morning a child stood in a great cathedral watching the sunlight stream through the beautiful glass windows. The Bible characters in the windows were bathed with the brilliant colors that resulted. When she was asked, "What is a saint?" she replied, "A saint is a person who lets the light shine through."   —*Pocket Quips*, p. 125

In February, 1986, I flew my plane to Philadelphia from Vermont. Dad flew in from Muskegon. We met at his gate, checked into the hotel, then drove to Princeton, New Jersey, to pick up my youngest son, Matthew, age 16. We met Matt in front of Princeton High School, then turned right around and headed back to Philadelphia. Our destination: the famous Spectrum where the Philadelphia Flyers played hockey. On that day, my son Lance, age 18, a senior at Lawrenceville School, was playing hockey against the Philadelphia Flyers junior team. Lance was captain of the hockey team at Lawrenceville, a private prep school near Princeton, and his team was in contention to be state hockey champions.

As we drove to Philadelphia, Grandpa Savage peppered Matt with a thousand questions. He was keenly interested in every detail of his teenage grandson's life: "Tell me about the subjects you are taking. What's your favorite? What's your least favorite? Do you have any girlfriends? How's it going in lacrosse?" Matt was on Princeton's lacrosse team, and yes, he had several girlfriends.

When we entered the Spectrum, we found seats near other parents of Lawrenceville students. There were only a few dozen spectators in that huge arena that held several thousand. There was a strange quiet, unnatural in so immense a coliseum. The empty, eerie building breathed loudly, swallowing up each sound. Its theater seats were closed tight like thousands of unopened eyes. The silence did not last long. As soon as the Lawrenceville hockey team poured out onto the ice, the voice of Bob Savage began to echo through the rafters of the giant auditorium. "There he is! Hey, Lance! Atta boy! Go! Go, team, go!" Matt bowed his head, not in prayer but mortification. He muttered, "Cool it, Grandpa" but only loud enough so I could hear. Matt was embarrassed but thoughtful and did not want to spoil Grandpa's ecstasy.

Soon the other parents got in the spirit and the little band of Lawrenceville rooters cheered their boys as the rough and tough youngsters of the Philadelphia Flyers youth team charged onto the ice. They looked ominous, like the Soviets when they played the U.S. team in the Lake Placid winter olympics. The Lawrenceville boys had heart, discipline, and enthusiasm. They fell behind, 1-0, but soon tied the game 1-1. In the second period Lance was thrown into the penalty box for two minutes and Grandpa's evangelical heart was torn. Should he congratulate Lance for his aggressiveness or judge him for committing a personal foul? It was clear he was pleased with Lance, but didn't dare admit it. For the first time in the game, Grandpa fell silent, not saying a word, while five Lawrenceville players struggled to hold off six ferocious Flyers. The gallant quintet stood their ground against the opposing monsters and when Lance's two minutes were up he leaped over the box to join his teammates. Grandpa once again took up the whooping and cheering, clapping and rooting. The tempo increased, our boys fell behind, 2-1, then caught up, 2-2. The third period began with the score still tied, the little troupe of parents nervous, hopeful, hardly willing to believe that their outmuscled boys could have any hope of winning. "Slap" went the puck, back and forth, each team sending vicious shots against the opponent's goal, all to no avail, for defense and goalies on both teams were rock solid. Then, in the last minute, "wham," a Lawrenceville player propelled the puck, screaming into the Flyer's net. Our pack of rooters went wild with cheering. Lawrenceville's defense held for the final minute and Grandpa was treated to a phenomenal win by his grandson's dauntless team.

When Lance had showered, three generations of Savages, grandfather, son, and two grandsons, went out to eat dinner together. After a rousing Bob Savage blessing for the food, we settled down to eat hearty steaks. Dad bubbled through the entire meal, raving about Lance's performance, continuing to quiz the boys about all the circumstances of their teenage lives. Then I butted in. "OK, Dad, now how about giving all three of us a complete report on your medical condition."

Dad paused, thought a minute, then said, "OK, I'll tell you. The laboratory numbers don't look good at all, but I feel fine. I get a test every few weeks called a phosphatate test. The normal count is 5. A few months ago, mine climbed to 10. The next time it was 20, then 40, then 80. Recently it reached 160."

All three of us looked grim and Dad hastened on. "Now look, you guys," he admonished, as his eyes shone with cheer, "I don't want you getting gloomy. Let's not make a big deal out of this. After all, my goal is not longevity. What's so great about living a few more years? My goal is to keep climbing while I'm alive. As soon as you catch me grumbling or complaining, then it's time for me to go home and meet my Master."

He never complained, not once.

And he kept climbing. He began a Spanish ministry at Evanston Avenue Baptist Church, reaching out to dozens of Mexican families who lived in the area. Then he initiated a

Saturday morning club for men, called "Bible Cross Fire." Few thought he would get much response at the ungodly hour of 7:30 every Saturday morning, but the men's prayer breakfast became one of the most successful programs at Evanston, well-attended, with rousing discussions every Saturday.

I was visiting one weekend and joined Dad for the prayer breakfast. It was a revolutionary meeting, for Dad had invited a Roman Catholic priest, the Reverend Louis Stasker, to speak at their meeting. The women of the church complained that they were going to be left out of this historic event, so Dad invited them to join the men that morning. The church basement was packed, every seat was full, and Dad introduced his friend to the congregation. How things had changed since the days in Colombia when Catholic priests led mobs of zealots to march against the young Protestant missionaries! Dad introduced Stasker as a brother in the Lord, saying, "We disagree on some of our theology, but I know that Louis Stasker loves the Lord. It's funny, but I agree on theology with Roman Catholics like Louis Stasker a lot more than with some of our modernistic Protestant ministers. Roman Catholics believe in the virgin birth of Christ, the historical person of Jesus, and the literal resurrection of our Lord. Ask a liberal Protestant minister what he thinks about these issues and you'll get a lot of evasion and clearing of the throat."

I was amused to note that Dad never said "Father Stasker" but simply referred to him as "Louis Stasker." As an Episcopalian, I had become used to "Father" as an appropriate title for ministers, for it was commonly used in our denomination, but a Baptist like Dad could not bring himself to say it.

Dad could enjoy good Christian fellowship with some of his Catholic brethren but there were a few bones he could still not swallow. The biggest sticking point of all was the Papacy. For Dad, as for all evangelicals, the sole authority was the Bible, not the Church, not the Pope. Unlike his early days, however, Dad could now allow that a person might be erroneous in his theology and still be saved. A Catholic like Stasker, thought Dad, was dead wrong when it came to the authority of the Pope, but his heart was right with God, he believed in Christ, and he was a redeemed man.

Stasker was very good that morning, amusing his Baptist audience by telling stories of his own youth, how he used to think that Baptists were truly evil people. He was as amazed to be standing in the basement of a Baptist church as the Baptists were to have him there.

Throughout the service, I kept one eye on Dad. He was not well. He was struggling to stand and speak, his energy low but his spirit high. By 9:00 a.m., when the service was over, he was exhausted, and I drove him home so he could lie down.

As I watched him, fast asleep on the couch, I considered the character of my father, and tried to imagine the cancer that was spreading through his body. His cheerfulness remained unabated. Although he was tired, he was not complaining. He joked about his body, saying, "This old engine could sure use a tune-up." Sometimes he would look at me wistfully and say, "Well, it sure would be nice to have a husky body again, but I'm rejoicing."

Dad's mind was still open, searching, expanding. Instead of getting narrower in his views, he thought creatively about theological issues. He said, "You know, Steve, I've been thinking a lot about the doctrine of Hell. I've preached all my life that Hell was a place of eternal torment, but I'm not sure if that's Scriptural. The Bible talks about 'eternal death.' What is death? Death is blotting out, annihilation, the end of existence."

I got excited. "Dad, that's great. I never could swallow the idea of people suffering for all eternity. Why would God want His creation to turn out like that?"

"Well, I'm not ready to preach this idea yet," said Dad, "but I think it might be biblical."

As always, his thoughts on theology were built on what he found in the Scripture. This was for him the only source of truth, and he would accept either idea—eternal torment or eternal death—if he thought it was Scriptural. My argument about "God not wanting His creation to turn out like that" was only my feeling, my opinion. For Dad, a feeling, or even a logical deduction, wasn't a valid argument if it was not supported in Scripture.

My sister Carol was part of the discussion but was not entirely convinced. She said, "But the Bible talks about everlasting punishment, the torment of the damned."

"Yes," agreed Dad, "the Bible talks about the torment of the damned. But it also talks about death. Eternal death. Death is not torment. Death is death. Therefore, I think both torment and death are Biblical. I think those who refuse Christ will go through a period of torment. But at some point, the soul, spirit and body of the unsaved will be utterly destroyed. Jesus said in Matthew 10:28, 'Fear not them which kill the body, but rather fear him who is able to destroy both soul and body in hell.' What does 'destroy' mean? It means there is not immortality for the unsaved, but the body and soul of the unsaved are snuffed out, consumed."

The whole discussion thrilled me, not only on its merits, but because Dad's mind was still so alert, so curious, so open. Still climbing.

He also was interested in outer space and pondered the idea of civilizations in other galaxies. Again, he found a Scriptural basis for the possibility when he quoted Jesus in John 10:16: "Other sheep I have that are not of this fold: them also must I bring, and they shall hear my voice; and there shall be one fold, and one shepherd."

Dad explained the classic interpretation of this verse: Jesus was telling his Jewish audience that he would also bring Gentiles into the fold. But Dad thought of another possibility: there might be lost peoples on other planets who also needed redemption, and Jesus was telling us they would ultimately be drawn together into the heavenly kingdom.

His body was getting scrawnier, his skin tinged with gray, his hair whiter and thinner, but his eyes still shone. He continually talked about the future, making plans for the church, and dreaming up ideas for other books.

One of his dreams was to write a book about modern

missionary heroes. He talked about Nate Saint, and put together a biographical outline of the missionary pilot who had been killed by Auca Indians. He was working on other missionary sketches, such as Hudson Taylor and William Carey, the two pioneer missionaries of the nineteenth century who went to China and began the modern missionary era.

Another dream was to get his popular "pocket prayer" series of books distributed in Latin America. He translated and published the Spanish version of Pocket Prayers. Tyndale, the English publisher, did not have a Spanish department, so he published the Spanish edition himself and arranged for its distribution.

He wrote down a few of his thoughts about death. "How much longer will I live on earth, enjoy my family and my ministry? The idea of simply 'prolonging my days' seems rather pointless. When usefulness and cheerfulness no longer exist in my life, I pray that God will take me home. I frequently talk this over with the Lord."

He paraphrased a prayer from Robertson McQuilkin's "Let Me Get Home Before Dark" and prayed it daily:

Lord, I'm approaching sundown. The shadows of my life stretch back into the years long spent. I do not fear death, for it will thrust me forever into LIFE—life with You, eternal, radiant, and blessed. To depart from this earth and be with You is far better.

But I do fear that I should end before I finish, or finish, but not well. Few, they tell me, finish well. LORD, LET ME GET HOME BEFORE DARK.

Spare me Lord from the darkness of a spirit grown critical and small, fruit shriveled on the vine. Let the fruit grow lush and sweet as the years roll on; stronger, fuller, brighter at the end. LORD, LET ME GET HOME BEFORE DARK.

The outer me decays. I do not fret or ask reprieve. But will I reach the gate with a body that is inept or distorted? Or will my mind become dull, incapable of wise decisions?

LORD, LET ME GET HOME BEFORE DARK—before I lose the capacity to bless other people and advance Your kingdom.

I humbly pray this in the name of Jesus and for His glory. Amen.

Since coming back to the United States as pastor, Dad had referred to God and Jesus as You instead of Thou. It was another way of growing older while adapting to the times. He felt that his ministry among young people would be more effective if he used modern language instead of archaic forms of address. He generally preferred modern translations of the Bible, and especially liked the paraphrased Living Letters by Ken Taylor, president of Tyndale House. He was old-fashioned in many ways, but as he approached his last year on this planet, he showed a resonance and flexibility rare among people half his age.

In the summer of 1986 I began a personal odyssey that I had dreamed about for years: a flight in my airplane to Alaska. The first leg of my trip was with my son Lance. We flew from New Jersey to Ottawa and spent a few days white water rafting. Lance returned to New Jersey and I began to head northwest, to the Northwest Territories of Canada and on to Alaska.

It was Father's Day as I was preparing to leave Ottawa. I called early Sunday morning to wish my dad a good day. Dad did not answer. He was in the hospital, struck down by a massive streptococcus infection. I immediately flew to Michigan. My sister and mother met me at the airport and took me to Mercy Hospital. Dad was unable to speak above a whisper and could not keep his eyes open. This man of potent energy was completely sapped of all strength. The cancer that dominated so much of his body had left him without immunity to disease; he was altogether vulnerable.

He was pleased I had broken off my Alaska trip to come and see him but insisted that I continue. "Hey, Steve, don't hang around here. Nothing to do but watch me sleep. I'll be OK. Just be back for our family reunion in July."

I wasn't sure what to do and talked to Dad's doctor. He was blunt: "Your father is a very sick man. Most people with that much cancer would be dead by now. I don't see how he can live much more than a year."

It could not be grimmer than that, but Mom had heard the report earlier and had absorbed the news. Although Dad was very sick, Mom did not think his death was imminent and encouraged me to continue on my trip. I began to look at her with renewed respect. This sensitive and gentle 66-year-old woman, face still smooth, hair still mostly brown, was holding up much better than I would have expected. She had suffered from Parkinson's disease for 15 years, been through a stroke, and now her indomitable husband was lying in bed, unable to lift his head. She was showing a streak of toughness I had not seen since I was a child. I was feeling weak and troubled. She gave me courage and calm. Often overshadowed by her powerful husband, I had come to consider her vulnerable and fragile. Now Mom was showing a deep and sure sense of herself. As Dad grew weaker she grew stronger. I saw a fine balance in her, a deep blend of steel undergirding the delicate temperament of Wilda, the artist.

Mom and Dad were right. There was nothing I could do so I left Muskegon to resume my journey to the far north.

I called each night, and was heartened to hear that Dad was gaining strength daily. He came home from the hospital, kept improving. One day Dad was praying, talking with his Savior as he always did. Suddenly, he felt a surge of strength, a sensation of cleansing, a burst of energy. He arose from prayer, stretched, looked at himself in the mirror, felt his legs and arms, then hollered to Mother who was in the kitchen, "Wilda! Come here! God has touched me. I felt it clearly. I sensed God's touch on my sick body. I am renewed. There is more work for me to do in this life. I'll be around awhile longer."

A few weeks later I returned to Muskegon, after an unbelievable flying adventure that took me up the Mackenzie River to the Arctic Ocean, down to Dawson in the Yukon, up the

Yukon River, down to Fairbanks and Anchorage, then back up to the Arctic at Prudhoe Bay and Point Barrow. I scratched Russian airspace in the middle of the Bering Strait, flew across mountains and glaciers, along the Alaska Highway, back down through Canada, and into Montana and Wyoming.

Before returning to Muskegon, I made a special pilgrimage: to La Junta, Colorado, where Grandpa Savage had grown up on the family homestead. I rented a car and drove out the highway, eastbound along the meandering Arkansas River. Seven miles out of town, I stopped and looked out at the fields where my great-grandparents Hubbard and Lucy had set down their roots. Along the river, fields were green, but both to the north and south, as far as the eye could see, there was nothing but unending grassland. Although it was a clear day, I couldn't see the majestic Rockies which erupted from the plains 100 miles to the west. Only flatness met the eye, unending, dreary flatness. I could see why Grandpa never wanted to go back.

That night, I stayed in a motel in La Junta and ordered a T-bone steak. I cut off as much meat as I could, then thought of the time when I was seven years old and had asked Grandpa if I could pick up the bone and chew the meat off. My stern and proper grandfather had said, without hesitation, "nope." That night in La Junta, when I got down to the bone, I looked around the restaurant, looked up to heaven and said, "Grandpa, I hope you're not watching," then picked up the bone and gnawed joyfully until all the meat was off and the bone completely bare.

The next day I flew to Muskegon and joined 42 members of our "Savage tribe" who had flown in from Mexico, Ecuador, California, New Jersey, Illinois, Florida, and Michigan. We had a splendid family reunion, but the greatest thrill of all was to watch Dad get up on the platform at the tabernacle to lead the audience in singing. It was only five weeks since I had seen him helpless in that hospital bed, and I was nervous as Dad got up to direct the service. Was he trying to do too much too quickly, I wondered? I looked at Mom. She was tense.

Then the tabernacle filled with his booming voice, inviting us to sing the majestic hymn "To God Be the Glory." The audience sang the first verse but I did not. My throat was choked as I watched my father waving his arms with verve and dash. Only five weeks ago I wondered whether he would live to see this family reunion. I looked at Mom again. She too was crying.

At the end of verse one Dad signaled the congregation to stop. He smiled, nodded his head, stuck his lips out in a comical look of deep contemplation, then said, "Well, that was pretty good. I'd have to give you about a B+ on that. Now this time, I don't want you to hold anything back. Take a deep breath, open your throats, turn up the volume, and let's really give God the glory. Ready? Let's sing!" Then, as organ and piano hit the beat, he stomped his cowboy boot on the old tabernacle platform, pounded his fist into his hand, thrust his arm upward and began to sing "To God Be the Glory!" Even though every one had indeed turned up the volume and all were singing with gusto, his voice was clearly heard above hundreds of voices. It was the song-leading technique he had perfected over 54 years of ministry, and it never failed to inspire a crowd. I could not believe it. He looked as vigorous as he had 20 or 30 years ago, and even though the audience was singing lustily, I could do nothing but listen, amazed, grateful.

Over the next few months, Dad was able to carry on, at a less frenetic pace than usual, but still with a full-time load. He took chemotherapy pills, but they caused him a lot of nausea.

After a few weeks, he quit taking the chemotherapy pills and instantly felt better. He said, "Why should I take these lousy pills and prolong my life a few months if it means I'll be nauseated the whole time?" Then he brightened up and declared, "Boy, I tell you what. If you're gonna have cancer, then have the kind I've got. Forget the pills. Just enjoy it."

One night I got a phone call from my brother, Jimbo, who was living in Lansing, Michigan. "I'm gonna elope!" he declared.

"Elope? Great. Does Nina want to do it?" I was enthused but

skeptical, because the prankster Jimbo was always fooling us. I was very fond of his lady, Nina Jaramillo, from Ecuador. She had a gentle disposition, long brown hair, and a beautiful and fascinating face, an intriguing combination of her Chinese grandparents on one side of the family and Ecuadorian on the other. Jimbo had been courting her for several years.

Jimbo assured me that both Nina and he were in earnest, but he didn't want to tell anyone until after it was over.

"Who will be your witnesses?" I queried.

"Witnesses?" Jimbo sounded alarmed. This might be tougher than he had bargained for.

"Yeah, you've got to have two witnesses," I said. "How about Barrie and me? We can keep it a secret."

He agreed. Barrie and I flew to Lansing. The wedding vows, although administered by a nervous and flighty young assistant Justice of the Peace, rang with the eloquence of the ages. Jimbo shuffled uneasily as the gravity of the words he was vowing to keep dawned on him. The happy-go-lucky kid was about to "settle down."

After the brief ceremony, we congratulated the newlyweds, then said, "Well, shall we call Dad?"

"Hmmmm," said Jimbo, "I'm not sure I'm quite ready to do that yet." He was already more committed to anything or anyone than he had been in his life, but until Dad knew about it, there was still some breathing room.

Nina was not reluctant. She was eager to get her new father-in-law's blessing, and wanted a religious tone set to their marriage. Raised as a Roman Catholic, she nevertheless admired Dad and enjoyed his preaching.

While Jimbo prepared himself to announce his grave step to his father, we went out for a high celebration at Lansing's finest restaurant. Jimbo enjoyed the festivities, but was still nervous about the big step he had taken, and even more nervous about telling Dad. There was something about calling Dad that made it utterly irrevocable.

Finally he was ready. Jimbo turned on the speaker phone so we could all hear. Then he called Dad and made the announcement.

"Praise the Lord!" shouted the voice over the speaker. "Hallelujah. Amen. This is great. You tell Nina I'm gonna give her a great big hug, and I'm gonna crack her ribs."

Then he paused and added, "My equilibrium isn't equal, but I'll give her a grand welcome. You can consider your Christmas gift to us a lovely new *nuera*." The word *"nuera"* means daughter-in-law in Spanish, and Dad suddenly got entranced with a bilingual double-meaning. "Yes!" he exclaimed, "We have a new *nuera* and this is the beginning of a *new era!*"

We drove to Muskegon the next day, two hours from Lansing. Jimbo had asked Dad to pronounce a blessing on their marriage. Dad had agreed. But what Jimbo asked and what Dad agreed were two different things. Jimbo thought it would be a prayer. Dad thought it would be a wedding ceremony.

We came in through the kitchen, and as soon as our hugs and kisses were over, Dad began to organize us. "Steve, you stand here, Barrie, you stand there. Wilda will be at the piano. Nina, you come down the hall, and Jimbo, you receive her right here."

Jimbo was nonplussed. He had wanted to keep it cool, low-keyed, minimum impact, and now here he was, swept right into a Baptist wedding ceremony. Bob Savage was not about to let his son get off the hook that easily.

I grinned broadly as I caught Jimbo's eye and gave him the "OK" sign. Jimbo relaxed. Nina was delighted.

But Dad could not stand up. He began to weave. I suggested, "Why don't we have the preacher sit right here in this big chair, and the newlyweds can kneel right here?"

Dad looked grateful, and his weary eyes glowed with happiness as he pronounced them man and wife.

Dad talked to Nina in Spanish: "Nina, Wilda and I have loved you for some time now, and we welcome you into the Savage family. I don't know how you're gonna put up with that crazy rascal you just married, but the Lord will give you strength." He laughed with Nina as he talked.

His four children were now all married. His family was complete.

A few months later, Dad promoted a huge Sunday School campaign, encouraging the members of Evanston Avenue Baptist Church to invite all their friends and break all attendance records on Easter Sunday. Dad had pushed it hard, and was counting on a grand day. But his body once again went weak. When that very special Sunday arrived, Dad was on his back, smitten with a jolt of energy-sapping waves that greatly weakened him. He had never missed church, not once in his life, and he was not about to start, especially on a Sunday when he had told his people, "No excuses. Come."

He was helped into church by his son-in-law Jim, and struggled to the front row, where he lay on the pew, propped up on a pillow, grinning broadly, happy to be in the place he loved best, surrounded by his flock, rejoicing in the record attendance that morning, praising the Lord. That afternoon, two of the members, Vivian and Louie Simonelli, came to visit. Dad was lying in bed. They asked him how he was feeling.

"Rejoicing!" he murmured, smiling.

Then he went on. "Vivian, if you ever come over here to visit and find me complaining, you just turn me over on your knee, give me a spanking, and set me straight."

A group of men came over to the house to sing for him. They came into the bedroom where he lay and began to sing a gospel hymn. He held up his hand and stopped them. "Hey, I can't see all of you. Let's go into the living room." He could barely walk, but they helped him into the other room, where he lay on a couch that commanded a clear view of the entire room. "That's swell," he said, "now I can get a good look at each and every one of you. Now sing!"

Shortly after that Easter service, Dad celebrated his 73rd

birthday, April 30, 1987. He had been to church for 3796 consecutive Sundays, never missing once.

Although he had surges of strength when he was able to get up and preach, Dad realized he could no longer carry on as pastor. He submitted his resignation. Some of the people protested saying, "But Pastor, 10 per cent of you is better than 100 per cent of someone else." He thanked them but insisted it was time for a young and healthy pastor to take over.

In May, 1987, Dad finally retired after 54 years in the ministry. At his retirement service, he rose to open his last service as pastor. Although his body was weak and wracked with cancer, his voice boomed out words of electric joy and praise, the way he had opened so many thousands of meetings in a lifetime of magnificent service.

A few weeks later he wrote a letter to all his family and friends and titled it "THE NINTH INNING."

What a privilege...what a joy...to be in the gospel ministry for FIFTY-FOUR years!

It began back in 1933—when our Evangel Male Quartet (four fellows from Moody Bible Institute) decided to go "full-time" in a ministry of music and evangelism.

During the "ninth inning" at Evanston Avenue Baptist Church we've had some wonderful highs. During April the church had the best attendances in over a decade ... the best offerings ... and the finest visible results (decisions for salvation, baptism, and church membership). This all took place even though I was on the sick list half the month.

During May I have felt better and we've seen some glorious things happen, but it was best that there be a definite "retirement." My last Sunday was May 31 and included a "Burn the Mortgage" ceremony meaning that as I conclude my ministry the church is completely "debt free." Amen! Praise the Lord!

Forty-nine of these fifty-four years have been with Wilda at my side. Now she is the "queen bee" of the greatest family on earth. I frequently sit in our TV room and gaze at a huge picture on the wall, with 36 of our "kith and kin." What a wonderful gang! How could any couple have such a wealth of encouragement, love, concern, and prayers from their family as Wilda and I have?

God has been SO GOOD to us and doxologies fill our hearts. April and May are the two most beautiful months of the year as we've watched a symphony of green bud and blossom all around us, mixed with tulips, forsythia, and petunias. What an amazing time to be alive and serving the Lord! It is true that in 1987 "sin is abounding" but praise his name "GRACE IS *MUCH MORE* ABOUNDING!"

To God be the glory—GREAT THINGS HE HATH DONE.

Rejoicing in Christ.

After his official retirement, Dad continued to preach whenever he could, often filling in as guest speaker when a pastor was out of town. He also assisted at Maranatha Bible Conference. But he was growing weaker. I did not realize just how weak he was until I flew in to Muskegon in August, 1987, with my youngest son, Matt. My Cessna 210 was full of Matt's duffle bags, for we were on our way to the Rocky Mountains, where he was about to enroll as a freshman at the University of Colorado, the place where his great grandfather Henry Savage had graduated in 1910.

Dad was there at the airport as usual, waving eagerly as we taxied in. Even as I was shutting down the engine, I glanced outside and noticed how thin his arm was. We emerged from the plane and Dad was singing the welcome song in Spanish: "Bienvenidos, bienvenidos." As I hugged him I noticed how bony he had become. He was not only thinner, but shorter.

Matt and I stayed overnight, then continued on, but before we left I asked Dad to pray for his grandson as he went off to college. Dad boomed out a fervent and eloquent prayer, asking the Lord to help Matt in his academic work, to guide him in his choice of friends, to keep him in good health, and to lead him on the path of goodness and righteousness. After a resounding "Amen," Matt commented, with a twinkle in his eye reminiscent of the humor of Grandpa Lawrence Johnson, "Well, there's no way I can fail after that!"

I returned to Muskegon two days later, on my way back to Vermont, and talked with Mom and Dad, quietly, just the three of us in the living room. Dad was lying on the couch, where he now spent most of his time, full of cheer, devoid of energy. I asked him, "Well, Dad, do you have any sense of how much longer you're going to live?" We had learned to be completely candid with each other in the last few years, and the question seemed natural and appropriate. He thought a minute, then said, "Well, I guess I'd be surprised if I were still on this planet two years from now. But my biggest hope is that I'll keep on being useful until the day I die."

Then I asked him another question. "Do you think your mission in life has been accomplished?"

He thought carefully, then said, with feeling, "Yes, I do."

Mom and I were sniffling. How many people could honestly say that at the end of a lifetime? Dad had been a faithful servant, a soldier of the cross, an incredibly hard worker. I gathered myself together and told him: "Dad, your achievements as missionary and pastor are legendary, and I think your greatest legacy will be the revolution in gospel hymn singing in Latin America with your discovery, composition, and publication of all those hundreds of hymns and choruses." He nodded in agreement. Then I went on. "But we, your family, feel that your greatest achievement has been the way you have lived, every day, every minute. We've all talked about it and I want you to know that your children and grandchildren all agree that we have never met anyone who so consistently and precisely practiced what he preached."

Dad was deeply moved. "Nothing makes me feel better than to know my family thinks that about me."

Then Dad went on and began to talk, matter-of-factly, about

his funeral service. "What I would love more than anything," he said, "is for my two sons, my brother, and my son-in-law to conduct the service. Jim Plueddemann, Jim Savage and Steve Savage can each speak, Jimbo Savage can play the guitar and sing."

I shook my head. "Dad, I would love to speak, but I'm afraid I can't. I know I'll be too choked up to say anything."

He looked at me, fondly but quizzically. "You know something," he said, "you're a real sentimentalist, aren't you?" It was as though he had noticed this in me for the first time. Then he went on, "Well, maybe Jimbo can get up and lead the congregation in singing 'He is Lord, He is Lord...' Ahhhh. Wouldn't that be great?"

Mom burst in: "Bob, please. We're all going to need to be comforted."

I said: "Dad, I'll talk to the three Jim's, but let's assume we all feel unable to speak. Who would you like to have for your service?"

Without hesitation he said: "Abe VanDerPuy. Abe and I worked together all those years in South America. He is one of my best friends. I would be honored if Abe would come."

"And Abe would certainly be a comfort to all the family," added Mom, clearly pleased with the idea of Abe's strong presence in our midst.

Deep inside I hoped I would be able to summon the strength to speak at his service, but did not dare promise Dad. Ever since I wrote him that letter nine years earlier, when I first heard he had cancer, the vision of Dad's triumphant and noisy arrival in heaven had been powerful and vivid in my mind. I hoped I could put that idea together and say it in public when the time came.

I feared this would be the last time I'd ever see my dad, but hoped there could be one more visit. My folks had never seen our home in Vermont, and I asked Dad if he thought he could make the trip. I hoped they could come around the first of October when the Vermont fall foliage was at its most sublime. "Let's plan on it," he agreed, "and if I can get up and walk, there's no reason I can't walk onto an airplane."

Vermont's foliage was getting more spectacular day by day, and we talked to my folks a couple of times per week by phone. Plans proceeded apace for their trip out east. Barrie and I planned to drive to Boston to meet them, to minimize any plane changes. On the morning of their trip, Dad called and said, "Shucks! This lousy good-for-nothing stomach of mine is acting up again! I'm flat on my back and can't even lift my head. We're disappointed we can't make the trip, but rejoicing in Christ."

I told Barrie, "Well, that's it. He'll never see our place." She pursed her lips together and nodded sadly.

Two days later we were surprised when Dad called and said, "Hey, I'm feeling fine. We're coming." He had a surge of strength and could now walk, although feebly. It seemed he had been living from one event to the next, and having something to look forward to had spurred him on. The trip to Vermont was something he wanted to do very much, and the very idea of seeing us gave him a renewed sense of strength.

We drove to Boston's Logan Airport, a three-hour drive from our home. We had laid a big goose-down mattress in the back of our huge Chevy Suburban, thinking Dad could sleep there while we drove back home.

As we drove, however, Dad could not keep still. He kept lifting his head to ask questions and look out the window. Each time he did, it cost him a tremendous amount of energy, and he sank back, exhausted. Finally he declared, "Aw nuts, I came here to see you guys. I want to get up in the front seat."

We pulled over, eased him out of the back, then propped him up in the front. Happy, he chattered all the way to Vermont, dozing occasionally, but always coming back for another barrage of questions.

He chirped merrily, although his voice was getting husky, "Hey, boy, I couldn't believe it when we picked up those airline tickets. We flew first class!"

"First class tickets for first class parents," I replied. The mood was chipper, but I had to struggle to keep from choking on words like those. My parents had never flown first class in their lives. Dad had flown hundreds of thousands of miles all over the Western Hemisphere, crammed into coach seats, always happy, never even considering the possibility of paying more to sit up front. After all, it was the Lord's money he was spending, and he was a good steward of those funds. I wanted his last flight to be in first class.

It was Monday, October 5, 1987 and if ever there was a clearly defined "peak" for fall foliage in New England, it was that day. In all our years of living in Vermont, we had never seen it so bright and perfect. It was as though God had specifically delayed the trip a few days just to give us this show of His creation. As we headed west across southern New Hampshire, the day was growing late and the sun was lowering in the western skies. As we came past Lake Sunapee, the colors began to blaze. The sugar maples screamed red and the aspens shrieked orange. Yellow birch leaves shimmered. All the leaves rose as the wind touched them delicately, and waved as they began to sing. They formed a heavenly chorus and sang hosannas that filled our car as we drove silently, prayerfully, awed by the resplendent perfection of color and form.

As we approached the border of Vermont, the sun began to ease down gently behind our state's lovely Green Mountains. A few clouds hovered on either side of Mount Ascutney, turning pink, orange, yellow. We passed a few lakes, glittering in the evening twilight, then crossed the Connecticut River from New Hampshire into Vermont. The river was gleaming gold, etched with light ripples of silver.

There always seems a change in the air when you enter Vermont. New Hampshire's air is sweet and rich, but Vermont's air is crystalline and rarified. We lowered the windows and I asked everyone to drink in the air. It felt like a glass of cool ice water. "Fine, fine, fine," declared Dad. "This is swell. Amen, amen,

amen." The mountain ridges became sharp and silhouetted as the sun sank behind them, but the sky was still ablaze with fantastic yellow. Mom said she had never seen anything so beautiful, not even the majestic sunsets that shone on Mount Cayambe in Ecuador.

It was a moment of beauty, a gift from God, given to all of us, but especially to the man who was gracefully dying before our eyes. How glad I was that his eyes could feast on this vision of splendor and color in the fading days of his life.

The two-day visit was a priceless time for the four of us. Dad spent most of his time lying down, but every hour or so he insisted on getting up to take in more of our beautiful home and surroundings. We had bought an 1840 Vermont farmhouse and completely restored it. Dad was fascinated with every detail. He admired our old-fashioned wallpaper with its early-nineteenth century etchings, and carefully examined the old fireplaces, imagining his own New England ancestors cooking over the open fire. He persevered from room to room, going up to the second floor, struggling up the steps, resting every few minutes, and finally slumping into the soft early American love seat in our bedroom. He snuggled into the cushions, looked up at the hand-hewn beams overhead and talked about the hard work and craftsmanship that went into making a fine old house such as this. I was amazed. Here was this man, wracked with cancer, drained of energy, still looking out beyond himself, taking in his family, showing a profound interest in each detail of our lives.

He had been living from event to event. He had now seen us in our Vermont environment and was pleased. But he wanted to live for at least five more months. Nina was pregnant and Dad wanted to welcome his grandchild into this world. He talked about it as we drove back to Boston. "I tell ya'—won't it be grand when Jimbo and Nina have their first baby? I had almost given up on good ol' Jimbo ever getting married, and now, praise God, he's about to become a papa."

When we arrived with Mom and Dad at the Boston airport, we

took them in wheelchairs right to the departure gate. Mom could walk but had asked for a wheelchair, for those long walks through airport corridors tired her. There were a few other folks in wheelchairs, and Dad immediately started chatting with them. A conversation with Bob Savage never went on very long without the inevitable question, "What church do you go to?" Then the airline announced the flight would be delayed 30 minutes. I had a meeting in downtown Boston so had to say goodbye. Because it was unexpected, it was a quick and easy goodbye. Dad was already engaged in animated conversation and Mom was sitting comfortably at his side. I was grateful it had happened so gracefully. It was not until we were driving out of the airport parking lot that I spoke to Barrie, barely able to say what we both knew so well: "That's probably the last time we'll see him."

He died seven weeks later.

It was the night of November 29, 1987. The undertakers had taken away his body. The family was sitting around the living room, subdued, talking softly, occasionally silently weeping as first one and then another took our turns at the telephone, telling our friends and relatives that Bob Savage was home with his Lord and Savior. No one was left out, for Dad had carefully made up a list of all the things to do when he died. That very night, on HCJB's weekly Sunday night broadcast, the word went forth on shortwave radio to all the world: Robert Savage had entered Glory.

Although I had missed his last few hours, my sister Carol and her family were all at his side. Dad's prayer, "Lord, let me get home before dark," had been answered. His wish that he would always be useful and cheerful was fulfilled. He died, still climbing.

I called Abe VanDerPuy who was traveling with his wife Marj in California. I had talked with Abe a few weeks earlier, asking him if he would conduct Dad's funeral service and he had agreed. Although he was conducting meetings in California, he quickly made alternate arrangements, dropped everything, and flew to

Muskegon.

Galo Viteri, one of the young Ecuadorians whom Dad had encouraged to enter the ministry, was pastor of a Spanish-speaking church in Elgin, Illinois. Carol called him and asked him to come to Muskegon and sing at the service. He agreed. Galo had a sweet, pure, high tenor voice and we wanted the service to be the type Dad had requested: lots of music, lots of praise. We asked Galo to sing two of the songs Dad had discovered, harmonized, and published.

I drove Abe to the funeral home. We were immediately surrounded by scores of people who had come to pay their respects to the man who had made them feel noble. I watched them stream by his coffin, rich and poor, athletes and handicapped, professors and farmers, doctors and plumbers, black and white, Mexicans and Anglos, adults and children. He had loved them all and now they were paying tribute to the preacher who not only told them to rejoice but showed them how.

All arrangements had been made for the funeral but one. I still wanted to fulfill Dad's wish and speak at his funeral, but was afraid to put myself on the program. For several months I had practiced my eulogy, usually as I was driving my car, where I could be alone with my thoughts. Each time, as I drove and spoke, my throat clogged with tears. It was simply too overwhelming and I didn't think I could pull it off.

I laid out the program, with short descriptions of each part of the service, eager for everyone to understand the man whose memory they would honor. The program explained Abe VanDerPuy's role with Dad in developing missionary radio and evangelizing South America. It gave a brief sketch of Galo Viteri, and explained the significance of Dad's work in developing Latin hymnology. It also highlighted the six people Dad had selected as his pallbearers—Dad's "preacher boys"—young men who had entered the ministry through his encouragement.

The hymns selected were those Dad wanted: hymns of

triumph and praise. Dad's brother Jim agreed to lead singing and the three hymns were all majestic: "Wonderful Grace of Jesus," "Crown Him with Many Crowns," and "To God Be the Glory."

At the last minute, just before the program went to press, I told the typesetter to add the spare words: "Introduction...Steve Savage, Bob's son." I figured that if, at the last minute, I was unable to speak, the service could go on just fine without me.

I left the printer and returned to my mother's home, but before going in the house I took a walk down to the shores of Lake Michigan. The waves were strong that day, much more powerful than the usual lapping that barely stroked the shore. The wind swept across the lake, all the way from Wisconsin.

As I trudged through the sand and felt the wind whip my face, I thought of this holy beach where Mom and Dad had agreed to marry, where Amy Lee Stockton had conducted thousands of campfire services, where thousands of families had enjoyed vacations in this Christian atmosphere. Then I looked up into the dunes where the Savage Prayer Tower stood serenely among the pines and thought of Grandpa and Grandma Savage and their earnest devotion to God. I continued to practice my talk, memorizing it word-for-word, shouting it into the waves, for only in this way could I say it without breaking up. The clap of the billows drowned out my words and suddenly I felt serene and confident, sure that I could indeed speak at Dad's service.

As we gathered together in the lobby of the church, I once again doubted whether I could speak. I told my daughter, Cyndi, of my fears. She was a theatre major in college and gave me good advice: "Dad, whenever we have emotional parts to play, we are told to concentrate on our lines, not our feelings. You can do it."

Cyndi's advice worked. After the opening prayer, I walked up to the platform and looked straight down the middle aisle. I did not dare look at my family. I prayed, "Dear Lord, help me through this." Then the words came out, precisely as I had memorized them:

On Sunday, November 29, 1987, at 5:15 p.m., a great and glorious roar thundered through heaven. From the gates of that fair land, all the citizens of heaven heard these words: "Fine, fine, fine. Amen! My, it's good to be here. This is G-R-E-A-T, great!"

The word quickly spread and everyone began to exclaim to one another: "I think he's here. I think Bob Savage is here!"

Soon their thoughts were confirmed as they heard more words bellowing forth: "I'm Bob Savage. Let me shake your noble hand. Let's get acquainted."

With great enthusiasm they exclaimed. "Yes, it's true. He is here. Bob Savage is home at last. Hallelujah!"

Angels, archangels, and all the company of heaven began to clap and shout and sing. They sang, louder and louder until there could be no sound any louder. But then—Bob Savage joined that heavenly chorus—and yes, it got even louder, much louder, beyond fortissimo.

Heaven, that place of perfect joy, became even more joyful, beyond ecstasy.

Quickly and exuberantly, all that heavenly throng, kings and paupers, saints and sinners, the lame, the halt, and the blind, the redeemed from all generations, gathered round Bob and escorted him to the throne of the Lamb of God, where he stood before his Master and heard the words: "Well done, oh how very well done, how magnificently well done, thou good and faithful servant."

Once again, they clapped and shouted and laughed and celebrated.

Today, Wednesday, December 2, 1987, we gather together here on this planet earth and we miss him and we cry. But we also honor his deep-felt wish, that we join in celebrating the triumphal entry of Robert Carlton Savage into the kingdom of heaven. So we rejoice.

Dad, you were one of a kind. A colossal character. Thank you for the way you lived. Thank you for the way you died.

Epilogue

> Fame is not popularity, the shout of a multitude, the idle buzz of fashion, the soothing flattery of favor or friendship.
>
> It is the spirit of a man surviving himself in the minds and thoughts of other men—undying and imperishable.
>
> —John Evans, *Pocket Quips*, p. 45

One week after we buried Dad, my son Lance and I took a trip to Ecuador. I wanted Lance to see the land where I had grown up and to observe at first hand the impact his grandfather had made in Latin America.

Lance was 20 years old, a rugged broad-shouldered athlete who played on the NCAA championship lacrosse team at Hobart College in Geneva, New York. We had planned the trip for some time, timed to coincide with his school holidays. We had agreed the trip was tentative, not knowing what Grandpa's condition would be. Lance had flown to Muskegon for the memorial service. Now that we had buried our father and grandfather, the door was open for us to fly south.

My cousin Tim Broach was a missionary with radio station HCJB and gave us a grand tour of Quito. I was jarred by the city which had sprawled relentlessly outward, covering with concrete the pastures where I had spent my boyhood. Then Tim took us north through the Ecuadorian highlands, taking us to the same Otavalo Indian market where we had taken Grandpa and Grandma Savage, back in 1945. Tim's mother, Helen, had been 18 years old at the time, and had been an ardent and enthusiastic traveler. Now, she and her husband Dick Broach had recently completed 25 years of missionary service.

As we drove across the Ecuadorian *páramo*, northbound to Otavalo, I eagerly pointed out to Lance some of the scenes of my boyhood. Mount Cayambe played elusive games with us all day, remaining most of the time behind a veil of cloud but occasionally peeping out in all her majestic snow-capped splendor. The Indian market at Otavalo was almost unchanged, a satisfying comfort in contrast to the jolt of Quito's modern sprawl.

Vicente Vieira was one of the young Ecuadorians in whom Dad had placed a great deal of hope. Vicente had spent many years with radio station HCJB and was now working with World Vision. In addition, he was starting a new church in the northern city limits of Quito. He invited Lance and me to attend.

The service was held in the living room of a family newly converted. Music was provided by Vicente's son, strumming on the guitar. As we sat there listening to the opening numbers, I whispered to Lance, "This is exactly the way Grandpa started many churches here—in someone's living room."

Lance began to leaf through the hymnal and nudged me as he began to see "Roberto Savage" listed as author, composer, or translator on hymn after hymn, page after page.

Vicente began to talk about the heritage of "Don Roberto" and pointed to himself, saying, "I am following in the footsteps of Don Roberto. This little gathering here will expand into a huge church, and I know my dear friend Roberto is rejoicing right now in heaven as he sees his work continuing on by those of us who took his place."

Vicente's wife Fani got up and said, "I want you all to know that Don Roberto was a major influence on my life, but the story is not complete unless I tell you about Doña Wilda. She was the one who led me to Christ, nurtured me in the faith, and served as my inspiration." Tears were streaming down Fani's face, and there was not a dry eye in the little *sala*.

Later, Vicente told me a startling statistic: one out of eight people in Latin America were now considered evangelical Protestants. Back in the fifties it had been about one out of 10,000. Vicente told me how big a role Dad's songs had played in this dramatic shift. One of the reasons young Latin Americans were attracted to the evangelical church was the exuberant and heartfelt singing, and those songs, born in the hearts of Latin Americans, discovered and popularized by Don Roberto Savage, had joined people all over the continent in rapturous worship.

As we ran into different people at radio station HCJB, each one told us stories of Bob Savage, about his belly laughter, joyful soul, constant encouragement, eternal optimism, and exuberant singing. One missionary said, "When Bob Savage left Ecuador it was the end of an era."

Lance and I rented a Chevy Trooper, a jeep-type vehicle, and drove east through Papallacta, over the same road Dad had covered in 1946. But now the road extended much deeper, all the way to Tena. Dad had unboarded the bus and walked to Tena, a four–day, grueling hike. Lance and I drove it in four hours. We took a canoe ride down the Napo River, then drove to Shell Mera, where jungle missionary aviation had begun. There we met missionary pilot Gene Jordan, who had grown up as a "missionary kid," son of gospel musicians Gene and Ruth Jordan. Gene was a pilot with Missionary Aviation Fellowship, carrying on the work started by Nate Saint forty years earlier.

We drove up the narrow gorge formed by the Pastaza River and the road was no better than it was back in the good old days. We had to maneuver around landslides, staring down the chasm just inches away from our wheels. Some things never change.

Back in Quito we drove past the Church of the Divine Redeemer, the church Dad and Abe had founded back in the early

1950s. It was still flourishing, but its main growth had been in the establishment of dozens of other satellite churches. Dad's dream of 1,000 members at this church had not come true, but there were many more thousands who had come to Christ through the extended ministry of the many missions founded by church members who had spun off to form new churches all over Quito and the surrounding areas. Dad would have liked that.

We drove west towards the coast, descending from the Andes down to the banana plantations and coconut groves of Ecuador's coastal region. We spent two days exploring the sprawling port city of Guayaquil and I told Lance about some of his grandfather's great crusades back in the late 40s and early 50s.

Both son and grandson were deeply moved by the incredible heritage that was ours and we returned to the United States feeling very much the presence of the man who had died only two weeks earlier. His spirit lived in his hymns and in the memories of those who had been touched by him. Everywhere we went, the one theme that everyone remembered was the phrase he used so often and lived so passionately: Rejoicing in Christ.